CW01066735

TRIALS OF AUTHORSHIP

The New Historicism: Studies in Cultural Poetics
Stephen Greenblatt, General Editor

1. *Holy Feast and Holy Fast: The Religious Significance of Food to Medieval Women*, by Caroline Walker Bynum

2. *The Gold Standard and the Logic of Naturalism: American Literature at the Turn of the Century*, by Walter Benn Michaels

3. *Nationalism and Minor Literature: James Clarence Mangan and the Emergence of Irish Cultural Nationalism*, by David Lloyd

4. *Shakespearean Negotiations: The Circulation of Social Energy in Renaissance England*, by Stephen Greenblatt

5. *The Mirror of Herodotus: The Representation of the Other in the Writing of History*, by François Hartog, translated by Janet Lloyd

6. *Puzzling Shakespeare: Local Reading and Its Discontents*, by Leah S. Marcus

7. *The Rites of Knighthood: The Literature and Politics of Elizabethan Chivalry*, by Richard C. McCoy

8. *Literary Practice and Social Change in Britain, 1380–1530*, edited by Lee Patterson

9. *Trials of Authorship: Anterior Forms and Poetic Reconstruction from Wyatt to Shakespeare*, by Jonathan Crewe

10. *Rabelais's Carnival: Text, Context, Metatext*, by Samuel Kinser

11. *Behind the Scenes: Yeats, Horniman, and the Struggle for the Abbey Theatre*, by Adrian Frazier

12. *Literature, Politics, and Culture in Postwar Britain*, by Alan Sinfield

13. *Habits of Thought in the English Renaissance: Religion, Politics, and the Dominant Culture*, by Debora Kuller Shuger

TRIALS OF AUTHORSHIP

ANTERIOR FORMS AND POETIC RECONSTRUCTION FROM WYATT TO SHAKESPEARE

Jonathan Crewe

University of California Press
Berkeley · Los Angeles · Oxford

University of California Press
Berkeley and Los Angeles, California

University of California Press, Ltd.
Oxford, England

© 1990 by
The Regents of the University of California

Library of Congress Cataloging-in-Publication Data

Crewe, Jonathan V.
    Trials of authorship : anterior forms and poetic reconstruc-
tion from Wyatt to Shakespeare / Jonathan Crewe.
        p.   cm.—(The New Historicism: studies in cultural
poetics ; 9)
    Bibliography: p.
Includes index.
ISBN 0-520-06693-6 (alk. paper)
    1. English literature—Early modern, 1500–1700—History and
criticism.   2. Literary form.
I. Title.   II. Title: Anterior forms and poetic reconstruction
from Wyatt to Shakespeare.
III. Series: New historicism ; 9.
PR421.C74   1990
820.9′003—dc20   89-32728
                                                        CIP

Printed in the United States of America
1   2   3   4   5   6   7   8   9

The paper used in this publication meets the minimum
requirements of American National Standard for Information
Sciences—Permanence of Paper for Printed Library Materials,
ANSI Z39.48-1984. ∞

Contents

Acknowledgments   vii

Introduction   1

1. Wyatt's Craft   23

2. The Suicidal Poetics of
the Earl of Surrey   48

3. Remembering Thomas More:
The *Encomium moriae* of William Roper   79

4. Remembering Cardinal Wolsey: Whose Life?
101

5. Gascoigne's Woodmanship:
Antioedipal Poetics   118

6. Shakespeare's Figure of Lucrece:
Writing Rape   140

Notes   165

Index   189

Acknowledgments

Friends who have helped by reading drafts or being hospitable, intellectually and otherwise, include John Baker, Sharon Cameron, John Coetzee, Michael Fried, Jonathan Goldberg, Alexandra Halasz, Joseph Kestner, Ruth Leys, Julia Lupton, Kenneth Reinhard, Peter Sacks, and Gordon Taylor. Eileen McWilliam's copyediting went well beyond the call of duty. My heartfelt thanks to all, and to my family for good-natured tolerance.

The author and publishers wish to thank the editors of *English Literary History* for permission to reproduce "Remembering Thomas More," a version of which appeared under the title "The '*Encomium Moriae*' of William Roper" in vol. 55 (1988): 287–306. They also wish to thank the editors of *Criticism* for permission to reproduce "Remembering Cardinal Wolsey: Whose Life?," a version of which appeared under the title "The Wolsey Paradigm?" in vol. 30 (1988): 153–70.

Introduction

This book is intended quite simply as a further contribution to an effort at representing the Renaissance that has been pursued for more than a decade now, and of which one crystallization is a recent collection of essays all of which were first published in the journal *Representations*.[1] Given the title of that volume, "Representing the English Renaissance," it would have been possible for me to entitle this introduction "Representing the English Renaissance: Otherwise." Such a title would have implied my wish to effect a critique of this representation rather than to extend it, and it would also have alluded to the general possibility of representing things "otherwise" that was for some time the staple of deconstruction, or of poststructuralism more generally.[2] Yet this title would have been misleading, since the possibility of representing the Renaissance "otherwise"—radically so—is one that this introduction largely discounts. It more confidently testifies to a continuing historical impulse to represent the Renaissance variably but still within certain parameters. Moreover, an attempted oppositional critique would have been misplaced, partly because of the dependencies and continuities linking my own work to these previous "representations," but also because this book may do little more than manifest a shift already occurring within this critical field.

In saying that this book envisages critical representation of the Renaissance as variable within certain parameters, I mean that enough presuppositions take effect as soon as a commitment is made to the Renaissance as a discursive category or object of study to preclude any representation of the Renaissance *radically* otherwise—otherwise, that is to say, than in its own prolific terms, since it is a self-naming, self-conscious, and self-problematizing historical epoch, and/or in the terms of its foundational historians and critics: Michelet, Burckhardt, Cassirer, Kristeller, Panofsky, et al. Representing the Renaissance may thus significantly entail a tacit conservation of premises, a repetition of terms, and the reprocessing of a finite although extensive body of data, as well as the production of a certain amount of new information. All this may allow the Renaissance to be represented differently from time to time, but none of it necessarily adds up to representation radically otherwise. Claims to drastic innovation or changes of ground in the representation of the Renaissance deserve to be treated with skepticism.

Inasmuch as feminism, deconstruction, or new historicism, for example, might claim radically to *re*present the English Renaissance—partly by invoking nonstandard as well as standard materials, by attacking the validity of Tillyard's World Picture, misdescribed as Elizabethan, and by examining the writing rather than "authorship" of women—questions still remain about the nature of their continuing commitment to the category and the established data. What is the point of contesting *how* the Renaissance is to be represented rather than attempting to dissolve the category in favor, for example, of the "early modern," as some social historians have done—arguably the progressive rather than the conservative move at present? What implied commitments or, more importantly, forms of specular identification, remain unalterable for as long as that category remains in force? What common property or particular investments in the Renaissance make its conservation worth pursuing in the name of feminism, deconstruction, new historicism, or any other particular critical approach? For what kinds of empowerment does recourse to the Renaissance still seem necessary in this now safely "posthumanistic" terminal phase of the twentieth century? Does this recourse still imply that the Renaissance is culturally foundational or truly monumental for us? And that its historic battles have to go on being refought, its cultural constructions reworked?

To judge by the current leading critical representations, the answers to the last two questions should probably be yes. Assuming that they are, a desire to capitalize on the most socially progressive elements in a powerful Renaissance culture and to rewrite the script advantageously would account for a good deal of work that has been done by feminist or radically inclined critics. That desire would also help to account for the peculiar sense of immediacy and engagement that has latterly characterized criticism in the Renaissance field, despite its frequently historicizing bent. Yet a certain institutional conservatism, and perhaps something more, is implied in the retention of the category and the academic field. This is also implied, I believe, in a continuing, often unacknowledged, investment in the archaic (not archetypal) forms, whether social, discursive, or representational, of Renaissance culture. It is with such forms and the continuing hold they exercise, the fascinations they exert, that I will mainly be concerned.

Indeed, this commitment to the issue of forms, meaning the forms both of Renaissance culture and of our always related representations of that culture, constitutes the major strategic decision of the book. I will not, in other words, be treating the texts I consider as primary ontic or epistemic discourse, or as instances of an undifferentiated Renaissance "textuality," but as manifestations of what I shall call "anterior forms." By these I mean constructed poetic and cultural forms, all of which may well predate the Renaissance, but all of which are, at a minimum, strongly inflected during the Renaissance. The high degree of significance attached to matters of social and poetic form during the Renaissance, at least by members of the privileged classes, is the hoariest of commonplaces, yet the implications of that commonplace are by no means fully worked out, either for the Renaissance or for the criticism that conserves that category. I do not consider this question to be a *formalist* one in the pejorative sense; indeed that pejorative sense now too often facilitates a blind denial of the ongoing constitutive and prohibitive potential of forms. The question is that of the nature, powers, and limits of discursive construction in (or of) Renaissance culture.

The conservation and development of strict yet variable forms in the English Renaissance culture I will be considering is signally attested by George Puttenham's *The Arte of English Poesie* (1589), in which so much is said about cultural, social, and poetic forms, both good and bad. In Book 2 ("Of Proportion"), however, particular lyric verse-forms are abstracted and geometrically diagrammed as if they are neoplatonically prior to, and independent of, any semantic or other charge—or as if they are arbitrary, immemorial forms of material inscription which do not (yet) signify anything in particular, if ever they can be made to do so. The indeterminacy of these forms will remain exemplary throughout my discussion, at whatever level and in whatever context "forms" are invoked.

The term "anterior" will not resolve this indeterminacy. Nor will it necessarily imply any genealogical or evolutionary scenario in my argument, as the term "ancestral" might. Nor will it claim any logical priority for these forms. Nor, finally, will it imply that these forms represent primitive (or civilized) origins. Their probable "anteriority" to the Renaissance is all that I contend for, although both their anteriority and that of Renaissance culture to our own remains a datum of my argument.

Despite my positing of a set or repertoire of forms in Renaissance culture, I also recognize what I shall call the persistent phallomorphism of Renaissance representation, a term more in keeping with the discourse of forms I propose than is the more usual term phallocentrism. If, in other words, a single ur-form is dialectically implied in or by Renaissance representation, it is that of the phallus. Yet it is the broad representational repertoire capable of being articulated in relation to, or strictly in the absence of, that monumental master-form that I shall examine. The incipient, but perhaps only incipient, heteromorphism of this representation is perhaps most clearly evident in the concluding chapter on Shakespeare's "Lucrece."[3]

Systematic consideration of Renaissance "anterior forms" will be the undertaking of the book, then, yet the corresponding question of critical form is the one I wish to take up more fully here.

This is not a question to which a great deal of attention is given at present, since methodological and theoretical premises are often given precedence. Choosing and evaluating forms is not regarded at present as particularly material to the activity of critical writing, especially since graduate-school conditioning in professional decorums may seem to settle all questions of form in advance. Yet the need to consider questions of critical form can be said to arise in principle as soon as criticism aspires to become, or finds itself condemned to be, representation. No representation—as opposed to purportedly neutral critical presentation, in which apparently no one now believes—can escape the issue of form in its own procedures.

There are of course many ways in which matters of form can be raised in connection with critical writing, yet the way in which I wish to raise it is that of critical genre or "kind." This is not necessarily the most radical way, but I would argue that it is a timely one in Renaissance studies. The power of generic constraints and determinations in historical writing, for example, was thematically addressed by Hayden White in two books written a number of years ago.[4] Given its increasing consciousness of narrativization, representation, and above all historicization, Renaissance criticism should perhaps now turn towards comparable self-reflection.

White argued that any historical discourse above the level of chronicle becomes "representation" (we might say that chronicle is long since representation) and will accordingly conform, whether its author realizes it or not, to a particular genre. In other words, there is no way of simply writing history, nor does history just write itself. Every historical narrative will, to use White's term, be emplotted, and will be so according to literary rather than historiographic specifications of genre. There is no way around this because there is no historical reality or corresponding form of historical narrative absolutely *sui generis*. Moreover, in the absence of any pure historical reality to be transcribed, reflected, or neutrally observed, historical representation will be bound to the terms of so-called literary representation. These terms need not, however, constitute anything more than an analytical formalization of the representational repertoire available in (and as) Western culture; they are therefore contingent terms, not ones dictated by prior, universal archetypes, and their "literariness" is not ipso facto honorific.

All this seems particularly clear to White in dealing with major nineteenth-century historians, some of whom emplot the same historical data—those concerning the French revolution, for example—according to different generic preferences. Thus Michelet plots the French Revolution as Romance in a narrative of eventual human apotheosis, while de Tocqueville plots it as Tragedy in a narrative of the uncompensated fall of the Ancien Régime. For White, the work of every major nineteenth-century historian (or "metahistorian") can be labeled generically in the first instance— thus again, Marx plots history as Comedy, Burckhardt plots it as Satire, Nietzsche plots it as Tragedy—and the generic choice will usually conform to a particular ideological disposition, which will in turn conform to a particular privileged trope (metaphor, metonymy, synechdoche, irony). In the nineteenth century, historiography will also have been bound to certain conventions of realism, in whatever genre it may have been written. These generic/ ideological/rhetorical considerations are not quite the only ones for White, who recognizes that historical representation is further conditioned by questions of scale, of allowable evidence, of data-integration and/or dispersal, of epistemological grounding, and of rhetorical persuasiveness; yet the issue of genre remains uppermost.

Time has now passed, and it is unlikely that many would adhere to White's closed generic set (Romance, Tragedy, Satire, Comedy), behind which stand Northrop Frye's archetypal schematizations, Kenneth Burke's rhetorical schematizations, and a fairly conventional schematization of ideological postures (Radical, Conservative, Progressive, Anarchist). Notions of pan-textuality, multiscriptedness, and generic indeterminacy have at once challenged and superseded White's stable schematizations, while the emergence of culturally repressed histories—that of women, for example—implies something in the historiographic process other than a generic choice freely made in the open market. Nonetheless, White makes a point, which I shall shortly take up.

Before doing so, however, I wish to dwell for a moment on one implication of White's argument. It is that in addition to writing history, each of these historians is projecting in the form of a chronological narrative his own more or less conscious assumption about the dominant genre of historical reality, about the genre of his own lived political experience, and about the basic trope upon which the world as representation is founded. Each particular narrative of the past is thus additionally an interpretation of the present and a prophecy of the future. No one historian is credited by White with multigeneric capacity or a countercultural perspective, so each implicitly privileges a particular genre (trope, ideology) through which he aspires to interpret authoritatively.

Without subscribing to White's assumption that the generic set is closed—for White, "satire" becomes the closed category of whatever is disorderly or threatening to the general schematization—and without assuming that generic inscription can occur in the absence of any repression or countertrend towards contestation, boundary-rupture, and dispersal, I shall nevertheless accept that totalizing generic tendencies do manifest themselves in historiography. Insofar as our own historicism(s) represent a merger of historiographic and literary-critical practices (not always a satisfactory merger), the same will apply to them. This being so, I wish to make a case for a somewhat higher degree of generic self-recognition and/or deliberation in our own critical practice, especially inasmuch as that practice has taken a historicist turn.

In making this case, I recognize that its only result may be a new formalist prescription, incapable of imposing itself and inconsequential in practice. If there is any point in proceeding, then, I suggest that it is because a great deal of current critical writing *is* generically conditioned, and not necessarily in recognized or deliberately chosen ways. Making a case will therefore mean making it for one way of doing things, or perhaps just of looking at them, rather than another. The case I will be making is for critical representation as satire rather than romance, the latter, as I take it, now being dominant, and also having difficulty recognizing itself as one form among others. This particular nonrecognition or implicit denial of form is facilitated by the almost compulsive metaformal and metadiscursive pretensions of romance, as well as by the unrestricted polymorphousness it invokes.

On the face of it, this may seem like an eccentric claim. Yet its grounds have already been implied to some degree in my initial suggestion of a continuing widespread investment in the Renaissance as a category. Among the things that can be considered romantic about that, apart from sheer nostalgia for the Renaissance as the putative origin of the modern world, is recourse to the Renaissance as a reservoir of cultural power endlessly capable of being tapped either for revolutionary social change or for more effective modes of social control.[5] "Early modern" does not quite permit that tapping, any more than it radiates the charismatic power virtually synonymous with *Renaissance* representation.

Equally romantic in my terms is the return to the Renaissance as a virtual starting point from which the broad social text, including its forms of class and gender inscription, can effectively be rewritten.[6] In this effort, Renaissance texts do more than supply positive and negative exempla; their supposedly unfixed or hitherto misrepresented energies are taken to remain available for the retroactive remaking of history—a remaking, however, that is at risk of becoming a radical denial of history and of the non-negotiable pastness of the past.[7] Romantic and also incipiently antihistorical in my terms is the widespread anthropologism of much recent Renaissance criticism. Partly facilitated by the rich, sophisticated Renaissance discourse of the Primitive and the Other, this anthropologism apparently permits recourse to a realm of imagined cultural powers, conquests, and options scarcely compromised by history but rather dominating it.[8] It is partly the recourse to such powers and putative options, especially in the name of history and radical social change, that has increasingly led to accusations of "hidden" conservatism, authoritarianism, and bad faith directed especially against the discourse of new historicism. If that particular charge is somewhat misplaced and often sanctimonious, it nevertheless implies the existence of something more to be accounted for, and something perhaps more openly to be avowed, in any continuing discourse of the Renaissance.

The persistent attraction of the Renaissance has also been apparent in a certain mimetic or identificatory desire on the part of its critics to produce large, synthesizing representations of counterontological innovation, displacement, gender-reversal, theatricality, positional mobility, power-shifting, dispersal, and cosmic remodeling.[9] The excitement and revisionary promise of these representations, often boosted by deconstruction, has been infectious, yet desire-infused representations of the Renaissance in a state close to that of free play or constitutive transgression may not only promise too much to the present, but do so at increasing risk of serious denial and misrepresentation. One way of marking this incipient lapse is to recall that a great deal of Renaissance writing invokes the figure of the Stoic. Renaissance representation is at least as conscious of Horace and Seneca as it is of Virgil and Ovid, and is thus by no means dominantly committed to translation and metamorphosis. Not only resistance to radical change and dissolution (or merely to their hallucinatory representation), but a discounting of them, accompanied by a complex problematic of relative immobility, bondage, repetition, and pain, is as characteristic of the Renaissance as its quasi-revolutionary enterprises and representations.

The satirical prescription for our representation of the Renaissance, if that term may be taken in a limited pharmaceutical sense rather than a grand legislative one, is partly for a less specular, identificatory, and perhaps narcissistic mode of representation, but also for one that resists its own extravagant synthesizing impulses, its own wish-fulfillment, its own propensity for idealization (idolization). Fortuitously or not, Hayden White's characterization of Burckhardt as the somewhat disaffected, satiric historian of the Renaissance, telling no story or only a self-consciously feeble one ("he did not really believe in his own seriousness . . . he had no respect for 'mere narration'"), can be helpful here.[10] This is the Burckhardt who produces no totalizing model, or *faute de mieux*, attempts a self-limiting one by keeping his materials *as* material as possible and fragmentarily dispersing them within a spatial field. (It is this Burckhardt who has also been read, disputably but not unrevealingly so, as the producer of a powerfully totalizing theatrical model of Renaissance culture.)[11]

Satiric representation, constituting the destructured historico-cultural field as its object rather than attempting to remodel or master it, can capitalize on the traditional etymology of satire as *satura*, a mixture of this and that: Burckhardt "apprehended the world of historical objects as a literal *satura*, stew or medley . . . figuring a host of different possible and equally valid meanings."[12] Such representation can also capitalize on the generic disposition of satire to detach its objects, whether positive or negative, from the overblown transformational narratives of romance, posing them instead as contingently and materially given.

Admittedly, there are substantial problems with any satirical conception of criticism (or of historicism). First, it can never really escape participation in the cultural discourse, which may have to be labeled as characteristically Western, of domination, totalization, and endlessly mobilized powers of appropriation. It cannot, so to speak, stand on cultural ground radically other than that of romance but only imply a change of disposition or outlook. Second, it includes the temptations of transcendent irony, of the *faux naif*, and of the banally pluralistic, for all of which, in White's account, Burckhardt will seem to have fallen headlong. Third, as a somewhat paradoxical antigenre or form of decathexis, satiric criticism risks finding itself without any form (amorphous) and with no story to tell. In practice, then, the satiric conception threatens not to facilitate a critical discourse or representation, but to degrade criticism into a disorderly mode of denial and fault-finding, of which it stands historically accused in any case. The pseudoetymological connection of satire with the figure of the satyr further suggests its possibly masculinist implication in the production of violent disorder and negation. Finally, from the political standpoint, such criticism will seem not just reactionary but that of an always-identifiable, highly privileged class having nothing further to gain, nothing new to produce, and threatened by others' narratives of mobility, change, and hope.

Without necessarily trying to defend satiric criticism on all or any of these points, I would claim that neither the threat nor the predicament of such criticism is quite so dire. A satiric disposition or critical language, however finite its grounding in class and gender, is at least not unamenable in principle to, for example, Marxist, feminist, or gay historiography; in fact, it may facilitate those practices while limiting their debilitating romanticization. Marx's characteristic intonation, as Elaine Scarry (no enemy to literary romance) has observed, is abrasive; we might further recall Marx's well-known fondness for the skeptical maxim *de omnibus dubitandum est.*[13] Hayden White's claim that Marx is a great comic historiographer (author of *The Eighteenth Brumaire of Louis Bonaparte!*) implies that there exists in his work a satirically robust disposition rather than a romantic wistfulness; it also implies the presence in his work of a dialectic of forms rather than a dream of formlessness.[14] Objections to overpromising, ultraleftist "childishness" are also practically continuous in the work of Marx and Lenin. In short, the satiric disposition is not necessarily at war with progressive or revolutionary causes and may indeed sympathize with their reconstructive aims.

Still, to point this out is not to claim that "detached" satiric criticism, always opposing itself to cultural boosterism, is saved by its availability to progressive causes, which it in turn saves from going overboard. Its characteristic posture remains discourag-

ingly aloof, punitive, conservatively attached, and "stoically" ego-
centric (this egocentricity being, as I take it, the social and moral
face of a phenomenon capable of being psychically characterized
as narcissism, but not being identical to that narcissism). Its most
conspicuous practitioners are conservatively defensive types—
structurally, losers rather than winners—namely the Juvenals, Tac-
ituses, Ben Jonsons, Tory Wits, Jane Austens, and possibly Burck-
hardts of cultural history, as well as their often genteel literary-
critical epigones. If the satiric conception promises little in the
way of polymorphy and metamorphy, that is arguably because it
has more to lose than to gain from them. Nonetheless, these limiting tendencies inhibit satiric representation from *promising* too
much; they also enable it to attempt a critical balancing act between romance idealization of authors and its antiromance inversion, namely the "filthy rites" of abuse, leaving the idol intact, into
which criticism may become transformed once it has taken an un-
restrainedly iconoclastic turn.[15]

Traditionally, the preferences of this satiric criticism are for literary forms that acknowledge (impose?) limits, namely lyric or
epistolary forms in poetry, the stoic essay-form in criticism, and
the "representative" miscellany rather than formally representational narrative, structure, or theory. Stable character (including
social, moral, or literary character) takes precedence in the satiric
tradition over fluid, fantasized, secret subjecthood. Traditionally,
too, the limitless extension and bulging to which satirical texts are
prone is construed as negative—as an index of their bondage to
inescapable excess, their own and that of others, which is also a
bondage to the infantile, the ridiculous, the dilatory, the disgrace-
ful, and the pathological.[16] (In White's account of Burckhardt, romance place-changing, power-shifting, and limitless expansion
are recharacterized with sinister felicity as metastatic rather than
metamorphic.) All the traditional satiric preferences, somewhat
tame yet almost willfully contradictory, are reflected to some degree in the chapters that follow. More importantly, perhaps, they
are also reflected in an intentional displacement of the center of

gravity in the English sixteenth century from the Elizabethan (Spenserian, Shakespearean) to the early Tudor period, and in particular to its "immobile" lyric poems and brief biographies, here treated as foundational. The sometimes unwitting yet by now widespread derivation of interpretive paradigms for the English Renaissance from Spenserian/Shakespearean writing is thus implicitly questioned as well.

~~~

Into what kind of specific project, then, do these generalities translate themselves? The following chapters loosely comprise a historico-cultural *Gestalt* (by no means a literary history) of English Renaissance authorship in the sixteenth century. The comic disclaimer C. S. Lewis appended to the title of his history of English sixteenth-century literature, "excluding drama" (that is, excluding "only" the authorship of Lyly, Kyd, Marlowe, and Shakespeare as playwrights and the sociocultural phenomenon of theater), will also be repeated here. Less comically, the further qualification "privileged male authorship" may be necessary. In English sixteenth-century writing, terms like "authorship" and "author" have, as Jacqueline Miller has shown, their own complex history and rich problematic, but they nevertheless uniformly imply invidious class and gender exclusion.[17] The repetition of that exclusiveness now, at the level of critical representation, is indefensible.

To some extent, these forms of exclusiveness belong to the English sixteenth century as they do not, for example, to the French, in which any account of successfully constructed "authorship" would inescapably include that of Louise Labé and Marguerite of Navarre. They also do not belong to medieval European culture on anything like the scale that they do to the early English Renaissance. Various studies of the English sixteenth century (notably those of Lawrence Stone) have alleged an intensification of patriarchalism, paternalism, and class-separation in it, and it may be that the effects of that historical intensification are to be seen in this representation. Yet since I have already disclaimed any possibility of representational neutrality or "pure" historicity, this book must bear whatever responsibilities it has for forms of invidious exclusion. It would, however, have seemed to me *pro forma* to include studies of such possible authorial candidates as Catherine of Aragon, Catherine Parr, Mary Sidney, or Queen Elizabeth. Moreover, it is not by belatedly manufacturing female "authors," by producing an anticanon, or by trying to give equal time that justice can be done, but rather by acknowledging both the power and the invidious exclusiveness of "authorial" construction in the English sixteenth century. It then becomes possible to take seriously the diverse forms of writing pursued by women and others (canonical authors not excluded) in this period; it also becomes possible to consider, as Margaret Ferguson has begun to do, how during this period women are made into readers but successfully prohibited from becoming authors.[18]

My recourse to the term "trials of *authorship*" does, however, carry with it a risk of invidiousness, including that of forgetting (yet again) class as well as gender exclusion. It also entails the risk of forgetting the lessons that criticism in this field has learned with such conspicuous profit from Michel Foucault's "What is an Author?" Foucault's critically enabling dissolution of the author and dispersal of authorial function(s) throughout a broad discursive field, together with his critique of the autonomous literary "work," constitutes an irrevocable critical advance. It is the move that opens the entire sociocultural "text" to reading. Yet to say that there is no author in reality does not mean that attempts to construct authorial identity and appropriate the text as an "authorial" construction did not occur in the Renaissance. Such "trials" were practically continuous throughout the period, while the terms "author" (auctor) and "authorship" were, as everyone knows, widely used and resourcefully construed in the sixteenth century. Moreover, the Foucault of "What is an Author?" elegantly and pointedly formulates *all* of this, adding that it is precisely the void and/or "functionally" dispersed character of authorship that makes authorial construction and appropriation possible in the first place. (To read Foucault as the mere harbinger of the author's "disappearance" is to succumb to a vulgarization that Foucault anticipates: "It is obviously insufficient to repeat empty slogans: the author has disappeared; God and man died a common death.")[19]

If it needs to be said, then, that every "author" named in the ensuing discussion is, ontologically speaking, an author-manqué or strictly a nonentity, let it be said; yet that does not mean that the "trials" in question are uniformly void or inconsequential, either as representations or in sociohistorical fact. Nor does that preclude our continuing attention to a problematic of authorship that is not merely historic, and that patently remains more than just a juridical fiction to those of us who put our names to texts. To dissolve authorship in theory is one thing, but to effect a full cultural divestiture of the myth of authorship is quite another. Such divestiture is hardly more thinkable at this stage than is a comparable divestiture of self-construction as such. The authorship to which I refer, then, "from Wyatt to Shakespeare," will always be on trial, subject to critical denial or self-erasure, yet that will precisely be its precarious and generally self-conscious condition.

Reverting now to the more particular and satiric aspects of this representation, the separate chapters that follow are ones in which familiar English Renaissance authors are discussed mainly in terms of their own apparent premises and undertakings, their forms of marked specificity, to which the topical chapter titles call attention. This discussion willy-nilly calls for acts of close examination of the kind now often discounted as part of a bad New Critical heritage. Yet the level at which these authors (or their historically specific forms of English) work is often virtually microscopic, as is their attention to the protocols of poetic form. Without "close reading," the texts with which I deal virtually fail to register, and in fact they are increasingly ignored or treated as minor instances of this or that larger cosmopolitan trend of the

Renaissance (for example, "courtier poetry"; the career of ambition).

There is always a risk that renewed attention to these texts can be purchased only at a high price. The price might include succumbing again to all that was myopic and naively ideological about the New Criticism; it might include reasserting the special, narrow privileges of the English language and tradition; and it might include retreating from the antiprovincial cosmopolitanism of recent critical theory and cultural studies. I have, however, staked this book on the belief that none of this necessarily follows, any more than the activity of close reading—practiced, after all, by Empson among others—necessarily coincides with the polemical caricature to which it has been reduced under the auspices of critical theory. I will suggest, on the contrary, that close reading is not only rigorously entailed in the consideration of form, but that the passage through close reading is not really avoidable even in the most expansively cosmopolitan discourse of the Renaissance. If repudiation of close reading and the dissolution of forms are widely claimed to constitute the sole authentic project of criticism at present, so be it; that is not, however, the belief to which this book testifies.

To go even further in a possibly heretical direction, this book is narrowly if fundamentally committed to the continuing interest and representative significance of three particular volumes, namely Richard Sylvester's *English Sixteenth-Century Verse: An Anthology*, *Two Early Tudor Lives*, edited by Sylvester and Davis Harding, and *Tottel's Miscellany*.[20] Not only does this positive commitment narrow the base on which this representation stands, but it reinvokes the anthology as a primary object of criticism and as a cultural index. This too constitutes a deliberate critical choice—a choice *for* criticism as well—yet it is made here subject to the limitation that the "canonicity" of the texts in question is hardly more than putative: an anthology of texts that the editor cannot bring himself to call poems ("verse"); two admired Tudor "lives" which, nonetheless, are hardly texts of major canonical stature; an entrepreneurial Renaissance miscellany. The canonical authority of these texts is neither asserted by the titles under which they are published, nor a current *donnée* of academic criticism, nor, finally, asserted here. The hovering of these texts between marginal and central status, as well as between canonical incorporation and exclusion, constitutes part of the interest I claim for them, and remains a problematic issue in the readings that follow. Among the questions the book as a whole might pose are these: what would the decisive canonical incorporation or exclusion of these texts imply about our own relation to the cultural past? What would it imply about the means and ends of our own canon-reformations?

<center>~~~</center>

Given the extent of its redescriptive aims, the book begins in a mode close to that of naive induction, its specimens being some Wyatt and Surrey poems, generally in "anterior" lyric forms. It also begins by examining some constructions, undertaken by Wyatt and Surrey, of masculine poetic subjecthood and "character." I take it that these are being analogically *and* antithetically constructed in a domain of masculine empowerment (attempted empowerment at all events) figured by the literal and symbolic ascendancy of Henry VIII. The "logical" dominance under these conditions of closed (autonomous, autotelic) lyric forms as well as their complex exploitation by Surrey and Wyatt constitutes an opening theme; so does an essayistic practice of self-writing by these authors (particularly Surrey) that somewhat anomalously or contradictorily proceeds in highly conventional, impersonal lyric forms. Indeed, the endless crossing of a never fully deconstructed life and art is a marked feature of the authorship I will be studying, and that is partly responsible for the prominence given here to two brief Tudor biographies.

Next come two chapters devoted to these prose biographies of Thomas More and Cardinal Wolsey, both figures in the reign of Henry VIII being intimately recalled, a decade after the event, under a Catholic, female sovereign. Again, the specific premises and undertakings of the authors, William Roper and George Cavendish, are given most prominence, but an underlying theme is that of the retroactive representation—and, in a sense, attempted deconstruction—of the paternal, hugely dominating figures whose names overshadow and continue to threaten the very "lives" of their biographers. The undoing and simultaneous (re)appropriation of these paternal figures, even or above all in the literary form of hagiography, comes into critical focus, while the emergence of prose as the medium of such subtle transactions begins to surface as an issue, one that becomes thematically prominent in the next chapter on Gascoigne.

Almost in spite of itself, my representation of the "minor" Gascoigne becomes pivotal in the larger design of the book. Among other things, his work figures the virtual impossibility of constructing under Elizabethan conditions of actual or symbolic feminine empowerment any centered masculine, aristocratic, poetic character of the kind cultivated by Wyatt and Surrey. This claim, I will suggest, holds good despite (or because of) Gascoigne's obsessive, symptomatic self-referentiality; what always turns out to be lacking is any self in the position of the referent, or indeed any a priori ground of individual masculine subjecthood. Gascoigne's endless recourse to the pronoun "I" and to acts of self-naming as "Gascoigne" or "George" constitutes, in other words, an unrewarded quest for the missing, stable referent in a confused welter of texts and representations. Moreover, any relatively stable positioning of the authorial self—whether in the court, the public marketplace, or elsewhere—becomes an apparently insoluble problem for Gascoigne even as multiplying contexts extend the meaning of authorship and Gascoigne's entrepreneurial capacity to pursue it.

The specifically Elizabethan culture-and-gender context figured early in the reign by Gascoigne is one that has already been rendered perspicuous in a series of outstanding modern studies by various critics, feminist and otherwise (many listed *passim* in the following chapters). My discussion of Gascoigne can add only marginally to this general perception. What I would claim for it, however, is a disclosure of some of the conditions within and against which later Elizabethan authors like Sidney, Spenser, and Shakespeare attempt to reconstruct and programmatically remaster the poetic undertaking. Sidney's stupendous transcendental idealization and masculinization of "the poet" in the *Apologie* (with Nature in the subjugated maternal-generative position); Spenser's staggering multiplication of personae, mediations, prolegomena, contexts of poetic production and reception, and poetic programs in *The Shepheardes Calender* (in which, *inter alia*, Gascoigne is footnoted); Shakespeare's "peculiar" sonnets, zero-subject plays (as Joel Fineman has called them), and controlled gender-crossing representations—all these gain intelligibility, I would suggest, when they are read after Gascoigne, and after the representational crisis to which Gascoigne's work testifies. Drastic inversions and displacements, but also attempted continuities, are apparent in masculine poetic production in and beyond Gascoigne.

My concluding discussion of Shakespeare's "Lucrece"—a notoriously copious narrative poem in which strict forms of stanzaic limitation are still maintained—picks up some issues left dormant in the discussion of Gascoigne, and constitutes the main illustration of masculine writing and gender-crossing after Gascoigne. It has been the most difficult chapter to write for a number of reasons. First, because keeping Shakespeare within the frame of this discussion is difficult in itself; second, because both "Lucrece" and the topic of "writing rape" are at present far more heavily and anxiously invested than any other texts or topics in this discussion; third, because to write about "Lucrece" at all in this context is to risk the charge of misogyny; and finally because, as a friendly reader noted, the critical circumspection now practically required of any participant in the critical discourse of rape may appear to be lacking in my discussion.[21]

Obviously, I have no wish to give offense or to produce an account of the poem that will virtually disqualify itself. Nor do I wish to sacrifice this account, which I believe to be contingent upon the preceding chapters, simply to circumspection and good form in the sense of gentility. It is not clear that all instances of the primitive have been vanquished or superseded, although they may have been repressed, at any point in the process of Renaissance cultural construction I represent. Nor is it clear that separation from the primitive has been fully effected in our own forms of cultural construction, or even in the prevailing critical discourse of the Renaissance; circumspection might therefore be misplaced. Moreover, the accusation of misogyny in this context might entail the concurrent production of a feminist legend of good women, unpossessed by any of the putatively masculine desires that lead to their victimization. The reinscription of this legend in feminism, recently exemplified, as I will suggest in due course, in criticism of Richardson's *Clarissa*, also constitutes the revival of a problematic of purity and victimization that is very much at issue in Shakespeare's "Lucrece." The Shakespearean solution or form of temporization in "Lucrece" appears, for what it is worth, to consist in the articulation of a complex system of mediations, exchanges, and shifting alignments within phallomorphic representation, not absolute self-censorship or a change of representational ground.

In dealing with the poem, then, I take up, in what I hope will be regarded as an adequately systematic, forthright, and contextually unavoidable way, the issue of "originary" masculine violence in what I have called phallomorphic representation. What lies beyond "Lucrece" chronologically and otherwise is formally outside the frame of this discussion, though it is frequently anticipated.

To conclude, then, if there is a story that this book tells it is the story of privileged masculine authorship during one phase of the English Renaissance—an authorship that I take to be pursued with relentless determination and/or culturally enforced compulsiveness through the symbolic upheavals and transformations (metamorphoses) of the Elizabethan period to the moment of symbolic "restoration" with the ascent of James I. Jonathan Goldberg has argued in *James I and the Politics of Literature* that the literary subject, implicitly masculine, is reconstructed during the Jacobean period within a huge analogical-centripetal structure centered on the figure of the ruler.[22] To this one might add that even the Jacobean production of knowledge, insofar as it is represented by Francis Bacon, remains similarly centered, and depends on conspicuous symbolic repression of the feminine and the countercultural.[23] This is not a history that necessarily has to go on repeating itself, yet the conditions of fundamental change, which would include an unambiguous desire for fundamental change, are far from having been established yet in our criticism. Failing this, and without attempting any sweeping reauthorization of the feminine and the countercultural in terms I have already criticized as those of romance, I attempt in the "Lucrece" chapter to conceive of a limited socialization of the poetic in terms supplied by the poem.

~~~

Textual and editorial problems abound in the period under consideration, and I have made no separate study of them. Problems of transcription and editorial practice are notorious in the case of Wyatt, while some very strange claims about Surrey's purported imitation of identifiable poems by Petrarch have been transcribed unchecked from one edition to another and one anthology to another. Petrarchan identifications seem also to have been complicated by editors' use of different numberings of Petrarch's poems. Sorting out this confusion is more than I have been able to attempt here; I have, however, tried to check every claimed Petrarchan identification when it has been pertinent to my argument.

State-of-the-art anthologies, but also the principal recent editions, now modernize Wyatt's poems. Whatever arguments may exist in favor of these modernizations, they are peculiarly damaging to Wyatt (for reasons that will appear); so much so that it would have been virtually impossible for me to include Wyatt, or read him as I read him, on the basis of a modernized edition. In quite a fundamental sense, to print Wyatt modernized is to censor his work. I believe that it is preferable on balance to read Surrey in an unmodernized edition as well.

I have, however, used modernized texts of the biographies by William Roper and George Cavendish. Reproducing the original spelling and typography would have been more obfuscating than useful.

Several critics, Arthur Marotti among them, have begun to explore in detail the circulation, accumulation, and social functioning of poetic and other manuscripts in the English Renaissance.[24] Since the broad social text of the English sixteenth century is not my primary concern, and since the question of forms is uppermost in my discussion, I have taken note of this work only insofar as it is pertinent to my subject.

I

Wyatt's Craft

Let us begin with an old question: that of Thomas Wyatt's craft as metrist, and as poet in conventional courtly forms. Perhaps this is *the* old question about Wyatt: almost everyone knows that the issue of Wyatt's craft, meaning his poetic artisanship, has doggedly persisted in (or amazingly preempted) critical discussion of his work. It has done so partly because the regularization of his meters when some of his poems were printed in Tottel's *Miscellany* (1557) remains a textbook case, on the one hand for the discussion of Wyatt's poetic craft (or lack of it) and on the other for the history of English metrics.[1] Yet despite its having become a textbook case, uncertainty persists about its particular bearing and implications.

The received account is that Wyatt could write metrically regular verse at least some of the time, since many of his lyrics sound to us as if they scan. There is also manuscript evidence of his having sometimes deliberately roughened his lines.[2] It is accordingly difficult to think of Wyatt's irregularities as inadvertent. Yet the question of Wyatt's deliberation or inadvertence has never been resolved in general, assuming that it could be so, and the metrical issue—the craft issue—strangely haunts at least one well-known Wyatt lyric that still indispensably grounds his claim to major-poet status: "They flee from me that sometime did me seek." Moreover, with one or two exceptions, Wyatt (unlike Sidney) has generally been credited with pedestrian rather than brilliant achievement as a Petrarchan imitator. Whether Wyatt is really up to imitating Petrarch thus also lingers as a question.

So much has Wyatt's craft, or lack of it, remained a textbook case that in the Norton *English Sixteenth-Century Verse*, for instance, some Tottel versions are printed for comparison alongside the versions derived from manuscripts.[3] It might be suspected that this is a textbook case for moderns only, since there is no evidence that Wyatt's contemporaries, especially insofar as they are represented by Surrey, Wyatt's disciple, had any doubts about Wyatt's poetic craft. On the contrary, for Surrey Wyatt is the incomparable English master. Yet Tottel did find fault, whether because of a change in historical sensibility, because of the superior marketability of polished/polite work to self-gentrifying readers, because of an advance in the sheer technique of English scansion, or for some other reason.

In taking up this persistent issue, I shall not attempt any new technical evaluation of Wyatt's craft. Nor have I any contribution to make to the history of English metrics. I would suggest, however, that the failure of the Tottel example to yield any very striking conclusions may arise from the ways in which it has been read. Many New Critical readers on the lookout for rough, hence authentic, lyric felicities found what they were looking for in Wyatt's irregular versions rather than Tottel's corrected ones, though these were kept permanently on display to highlight the moral-aesthetic authenticity of the former. It was often quickly forgotten that these rough felicities might after all be inadvertent, might be no more than historically contingent, or might retroactively have been constituted as appreciable felicities by the despised Tottel "corrections." A handful of Wyatt lyrics—a mere fraction of his total output—has generally been singled out for moral-aesthetic appreciation, while the lyrics of the Earl of Surrey, Wyatt's self-constituted heir and star of the Tottel anthology, have often been regarded as an example of the polished, the polite, and hence the trivial.

The willful exclusiveness and possible groundlessness of this aesthetic reading of Wyatt have prevented it from becoming authoritative—the particular aesthetic now also having been superseded—and the Tottel data have by and large remained data in the technical history of English metrics. Recent historicist work has somewhat expanded our sense of the contingencies involved in the Tottel anthology, and hence of the impossibility of treating metrical data as purely technical, yet certain categorical restrictions continue to limit our recognition of the Tottel data's significance.[4] In the process of reading Wyatt in this chapter I want to reexamine some of the data in the light of current critical assumptions—assumptions which, however, generally render the question of poetic craft moot. Whether there is anything to be said about the data on the basis of such assumptions thus remains to be seen, and so do the consequences of virtually excluding craft as a factor in the interpretive process.

Perhaps the crucial lesson to be learned from Tottel is that Wyatt's craft can neither be bracketed in any reading of his poems nor treated in isolation as a purely technical question. Even while silently regularizing Wyatt's metrics, Tottel characterizes Wyatt (unlike Surrey) as "depe witted."[5] Whatever Tottel may have meant when he paid Wyatt that faintly dubious compliment, it is an appreciation of Wyatt seemingly at odds with, but also related to, Tottel's metrical fault-finding. Conceivably it implies recognition by Tottel that the irregularities he is correcting are not necessarily inadvertent or merely old-fashioned but in some sense threatening to good order. It certainly allows for contrasting "surface" and "depth" evaluations of Wyatt's poems, or for contrasting but still related evaluations of their technical and intellectual achievement. It may even imply a perceived continuity between surface faultiness and a deeper fault, possibly that of underlying deviousness or something worse. Finally, the logic of the situation is such that we may have to regard the deep-wittedness and faultiness perceived by Tottel as structurally related: how is depth to be perceived except through surface faults or fissures? The Tottel who simultaneously regularizes Wyatt's lines *and* appreciates his deep-wittedness is arguably in the grip of what I shall call Wyatt's craft. And, wittingly or not, Tottel becomes in an exact sense Wyatt's exemplary critic, meaning fault-finder and appreciator, the two functions being exercised in an apparently necessary structural relation to one another.

~~~

In taking up the issue of the troublesome Wyatt over whose craft we keep stumbling, it is important to recognize that we may only be picking up where Wyatt leaves off:

> What vaileth trouth? or, by it, to take payn?
> To stryve by stedfastnes for to attayne?*
>   To be iuste and true, and fle from dowblenes?
> Sythens all alike, where rueleth craftines,
> Rewarded is boeth fals, and plain.
> Sonest he spedeth, that moost can fain;
> True meanyng hert is had in disdayn.
>   Against deceipte and dowbleness,
>   What vaileth trouth?[6]
> *Variant: "to be tayne"

In this excerpt from a Wyatt rondo we encounter not just a material instance of Wyatt's lyric craft (to some features of which we will return in due course) but an apparently negative, conventional thematization of "craftines" as bad rule—as a disavowed form of calculating despotism. Conflating a technical notion of "craft" with this "craftines" may seem premature or illegitimate or to beg the question, yet it is arguable, partly in the light of Tottel's remark, that any limitation of the term to the purely technical realm would beg the question in Wyatt's case. In the poem "ruleth" may refer to the rule(s) of craft as well as to political despotism. A semantic and etymological connection also exists in Wyatt's language between "craft" and "craftiness": in its derivation from Old English *craeft* (Old High German *chraft*) as well as in sixteenth-century usage, "craft" indeterminately denotes "strength," "skill," "cunning," "deceit," "art," and "structure" (*OED*). (It denotes "boat" or "ship" as well, of course, on which some later poets seem figuratively to pick up in constructing their various ships of death, and which even Wyatt may exploit in his Petrarchan imitation that begins: "My galy [galley] charged with forgetfulnes / Thorough sharpe sees in wynter nyghtes doeth pas"). In Wyatt's poem, this term can apparently circulate (inimically or otherwise) in the same field as terms we might consider more properly hermeneutic: "truth," "meaning," "falsity," "feigning," "veiling." Historically, then, it would seem that "craft" is not necessarily a term apart; it does not necessarily designate technical skill alone, or any particular set of technical skills.

To go even further, Wyatt's "craft" in its broader and perhaps more threatening sense has, in an apparent return of the repressed, come back to haunt modern interpretation. Stephen Greenblatt has claimed that Wyatt's poems articulate harsh views of the Henrician regime, despite censorship and the threat of reprisal, through "deniable" innuendo.[7] Wyatt is thus discovered to be (rediscovered as) a *crafty* poet—crafty enough, it would seem, to go one on one with Henry VIII as putative strongman and dictator of political truth in his time.

This Wyatt, whose craft can be construed as a form of strength rather than faultiness, may be thought to dissimulate that strength, though of course not entirely so, in typical, recurrent performances of clumsiness, weakness, martyred innocence, passivity, marginality, and masochistic abjection. The strong Wyatt may also be thought to inhabit, though not quite to fit, weak or alien courtly forms, to enact mock Petrarchan courtships, and cunningly to fabricate his maimed or frustrated poetic personae (in which case, we may begin to see what "vaileth" truth).

To think of Wyatt in this way is admittedly to risk projecting an anachronistic image of the strongman on the screen of his poems, all the more so since appreciation of Wyatt's "manliness," initiated by Surrey, can readily take this preposterous turn. It is to risk renewed indulgence in the dream of the poet as an autonomous, masterful presence, invulnerably withdrawn from his own representations, and it is correspondingly to be tempted by the idea of the poet as an integral being signified by his own name (that is, as one who is not, after all, a conflicted, discontinuous, textualized subject alone). Yet this way of thinking about Wyatt may have to be risked (partly because Wyatt tempts us to renew the wager on these unforeclosed possibilities), and the negative consequences I have listed may either not follow at all or may follow only in a curiously displaced form.

First, the symbolic order to which the poet as culture hero belongs is one in which craft is typically effaced, a fact to which practically every currently favored mode of interpretation testifies in bypassing the issue of poetic craft. This effacement (and his own) is what Wyatt repeatedly forestalls; in a sense he thus fails to accede to "the perfecte paterne of the poete," though in doing so he intrudes the possibility that accession might constitute a disempowering transfiguration or uncompensated loss of "craft"-identity. Second, the identity of the craftsman is not equivalent to full poetic subjecthood (that is, to phallic empowerment within a universal symbolic order) but remains a quasi-anonymous guild-identity, not even exclusively masculine in practice.[8] While the gentry name of Sir Thomas Wyatt may be appended to various poems, it stands in highly problematic relation to their anonymous craft. Third, the crafty (strong, cunning, skillful) poet is apparently bound by conditions that at once confer and limit his access to full power. His craft is destined to remain unrecognized or unrecognizable except through periodic "accidents" that bring it into question or reveal its somewhat paranoid excess—or else through forms of humiliating dissimulation.

Indeed, the figure of the crafty strongman (almost a contradiction in terms) need be no more than the effect of a sophism whereby any palpably crafted/crafty simulation of weakness, emasculation, or abjection must "logically" imply its opposite. (Similarly, any crafted/crafty admission of faultiness will imply that nothing damagingly true of the self is being confessed; indeed, a self is being constituted through this dissimulation.) It is through this sophism that the constant presence and integral selfhood of the strongman, neither fashioned nor fashionable within a narcissistic order of image-making, can be implied, and so regularly is it implied in Wyatt's poems that it can virtually be called a distinctive Wyatt-effect. Yet it can only be implied, not revealed, and the necessary deniability of the implication cuts both ways. If deniability allows the threateningly crafty poet to assert his own innocence or virtual nonexistence in the face of suspicion, no less does it allow the presence of any strongman to be denied by others. Nothing is more dubious than the dissimulation of the strongman except perhaps his narcissistic simulation, and "craft"-identity is accordingly maintained and threatened by deniability as a knife that cuts both ways. Let us for the moment leave it cutting both ways.

~~~

If it can now be granted that Wyatt materially and thematically intrudes the question of craft upon us, virtually as a return of the repressed, we still need to consider more fully Wyatt's staging of that intrusion. Reverting momentarily to the cited lyric, I would suggest that under the aspect of craft, the conventional, plaintive rhetorical questions of the courtly Petrarchan speaker begin to sound less like rhetorical questions and more like politico-material ones put to rather than just within Petrarchan representation: what vaileth truth? or by it to take pain? How, by the same token, is "crafty" doubleness to be avoided in a language of which doubleness is one physical property, at the metrical level if no other, and in which terms that denote states of ideal fidelity (for example "stedfastnes") are connected by so-called feminine half-rhymes to bad doubles like "craftines"? In which a common "singleness" may characterize the words or syllables that supposedly differentiate between "false" and "plain," and in which "plain" itself, doubling as the nonornate and the plaintive, is connected by a so-called masculine rhyme to "fain?" In which even "trouth" hovers between the property of being true (truth) and the act of devotion (troth)? In which, finally, the compulsion to "flee" from doubleness in the poem leads straight *to* "doubleness"?

These are features of language that deconstruction has taught us to regard as the (potentially liberating) despair of Truth, yet that is not necessarily how Wyatt teaches us to regard them. Under Wyatt's prompting, we may recognize them as "wild" or "natural" features of language, or of any particular language such as English, that it is the prerogative of poetic craft to take seriously, and to identify and regulate systematically, however arbitrarily—or, *faute de mieux*, to regulate arbitrarily before anything else, as the precondition of any possible meaning or truth in language (hence as the precondition of any deconstruction or critique of meaning and truth as well). Inasmuch as this "craft" is bound to seem reified, constraining, or simply falsifying, it sets up the poetic craftsman to be a victimizer (tyrant) but also to be a conflicted self-victimizer, guises in which Wyatt frequently appears.

To what, then, does this craft conduce in Wyatt's lyric? It may seem as if the arbitrary rule of "craftines" remains simply at odds with an unregulated Truth that it always defeats:

> Against deceipte and dowblenes,
> What vaileth trouth?

Ostensibly, the bad rule of craft is one under which the platitude that truth *avails* is categorically inverted: it does not. It may seem, moreover, as if the speaker in the poem suffers the rule of craft, instantiated by the skillful doubling, repetition, and endless recursiveness of the poem's lyric form, either as a steadfast martyr (witness) to an impossible truth or imaginably as the covertly masochistic subject of the poem's endless round (rondo) of pain-as-pleasure. Yet if the final line does recursively repeat the first, it does so with a difference.

"Taking pain" has dropped out of explicit consideration, possibly by virtue of having been assimilated to the "painstaking" craft of the poem, in which case a certain economizing of pain reduces both its visibility and its questionable or dysfunctional excess. But that is not all. If the poem's conclusion does invert the platitude that truth avails, it also effects an interchange between truth and the "deceipte and dowblenes" that conventionally oppose and nullify it. Finally, truth is made into the homophonously *veiled* ["vaileth"] agent of the poem rather than the plain one, hence it, rather than obvious deceit and doubleness, emerges as the figure of craft. The presence of this craft—as the poem's prime figure and as a material fact—does not so much deconstruct the poem's constitutive oppositions as simultaneously resist their deconstruction and realign them in such a way as to bring truth into possibly *availing* relation to craftiness—or vice versa.

Truth and craft are accordingly conserved in the field of the poem, but not just in conventionally opposed (or antithetically gendered) terms. One possible result of this act of conservation is manifested in and as the New Critical appreciation of Wyatt's powerful, craft-related "authenticity"; another result, more interestingly committed to Wyatt's truth, can be seen in Surrey's recurrent characterizations of Wyatt. For Surrey, Wyatt is the plain speaker of the word itself:

> Salomon sayd, the wronged shall recure:
> But Wiat said true, the skarre doth aye endure.[9]

This soothsaying Wyatt is also, for Surrey, virtually the martyred Christ of the age:

> But to the heavens that symple soule is fleed:
> Which left with such, as covet Christ to knowe
> Witnes of faith that never shalbe deade;
> Sent for our welth, but not received so.
> Thus, for our gylt, this jewell have we lost;
> The earth his bones, the heavens possesse his goost.
>
> (210)

These characterizations, it should be emphasized, are never simplistic, since Surrey has a highly developed sense of the generic, rhetorical, and literary-historical determinants of Wyatt's poetic career, as well as of his own vexed discipleship. Yet his commitment to Wyatt's truth—his own "troth" to it—evidently remains uncompromised, even when he must recognize that Wyatt's truth is either not plainspoken or not recognized at all. Indeed, it almost becomes Surrey's paradoxical vocation to restate more plainly

Wyatt's veiled or unperceived truth, as when he explains what Wyatt meant in his *Penitential Psalms*. Becoming more recklessly explicit than the crafty Wyatt, Surrey brings their message closer home to the presumably intended receiver, Henry VIII:

> [Here] rulers may see in a myrrour clere,
> The bitter fruyte of false concupiscence.
> How Jurye bowght Uryas death full deere.
> In princes hartes godes scourge yprinted deepe
> Mowght them awake out of their synfull sleepe.
>
> (187)

Such "clarifications" may partly account for Surrey's having been executed by Henry VIII on dubious charges of treason, while Wyatt's nontreasonable activities—or dissimulated treasons—enabled him to avoid this fate, despite some exceedingly close calls.[10]

Ironically, it is the romantic disciple rather than the master who appears most fully to have assumed the burden of truth and martyrdom in this case (but to what avail?). Wyatt's truth seems, in contrast, to be constituted merely in hinted opposition to that of the ruler—and thus by indirection—and to be a truth of which one verifying criterion, and possibly the only one, is its censorship in the public arena. By virtue of what may only be another impenetrable sophism, that which is allowed or may safely be said cannot be true. Truth, necessarily veiled or masked unless it is to be exposed in an act of literal suicide (martyrdom), remains constitutively bound to conditions of doubleness, indirection, public censorship, and imaginable private articulation. Even the higher witnessing of the martyr, insofar as it occurs on the public stage of the world, may be contaminated, as will be suggested in the next chapter, by a hysterical narcissism. "I cannot speke and loke lyke a saynct" (185), writes Wyatt in his first satire, a rather deep-witted utterance that conserves truth by not staging or playing it, that reclaims sanctity for what does not look like sainthood, and that relieves Wyatt of the tiresome obligation to bear suicidal public witness.

Refraining from any further conclusions at this stage, especially since drawing them now might still mean repeating Tottel, Surrey, the New Critics, or Wyatt himself, I shall turn to another rondo (quoted in full) in which the craft issue almost programmatically emerges:

> Goo burnyng sighes vnto the frosen hert!
> Goo breke the Ise whiche pites paynfull dert
>   Myght never perse, and if mortall prayer
>   In hevyn may be herd, at lest I desire
> That deth or mercy be ende of my smert.
> Take with the payn whereof I have my part,
> And eke the flame from which I cannot stert,
>   And leve me then in rest, I you require.
>   Goo, burning sighes!
> I must goo worke, I se, by craft and art
> For trueth and faith in her is laide apart,
>   Alas, I cannot therefor assaill her
>   With pitefull plaint and scalding fyer
> That oute of my brest doeth straynably stert.
>   Goo, burning sighes!
>   (17)

Here, Wyatt becomes more obviously Petrarchan and conceited than in the previous lyric, yet in both lyrics he cultivates a weighty sententiousness and deliberation, possibly alien to the light courtly lyric and presumably inimical to the achievement of *sprezzatura*. In each poem, the divisions of the rondo are spanned by a somewhat ponderous periodic syntax, one way in which Wyatt characteristically produces an effect of graceless severity and weightiness (another Tottel characterization) in "light" forms. In this poem, however, the repetitions of the form acquire an emphatic relentlessness that characterizes many Wyatt lyrics, including the admired "My lute awake." The graceless "abuses" of the form are accompanied by an intensified repetition of courtly love conceits ("Goo burnyng sighes . . . breke . . . perse . . . take with the payn . . . and leve me then in rest") that infects the poem with an openly sadomasochistic brutality not uncommonly regarded as Wyatt's special contribution to Petrarchanism. (A text of bondage may even be incipient in the poem, with pain becoming the man's "part" [l. 6] in relation to that of the silent/silenced Petrarchan woman as disciplinary mistress.) Coincidentally or not, "craft" is thematically and perhaps disconcertingly intruded, not just into an implicitly aristocratic courtly love representation, but into a field that might otherwise be considered exclusively that of gracious "art"—*ars poetica*, *ars amatoria*, or whatever other art might be taken to apply. We are thus called on to recognize the existence of craft differentially doubled with art. Perhaps we have already stumbled upon some effects of this doubling in the heavy movement and repetition of the lyric, and in its intensifed violence; to what, however, does this craft conduce?

The announced entry of craft and art into the poem, along with an ungenteel profession of the need to go (to) work, occurs after the apparent failure of "burning sighs" to penetrate the breast of the other or effect the speaker's deliverance. What may be presumed to intervene between lines nine and ten, triggering the new resolve of the speaker and bridging an otherwise rather unaccountable gap, is the ipso facto pitiless silence of all or any to whom the appeal has been conveyed. (This silence will be akin to the more obviously tormenting one of the poem that begins "Madame, withouten many wordes" [25].) Yet whether we assume this negative intervention or not, the resolve to go to work by craft and art, putatively justified by the woman's having laid truth and faith apart, apparently makes no difference in the end, since this movement in the poem culminates in an anticlimactic repetition of "Goo, burning sighes." This repetition also takes us back to where we started.

Tempting as it may be to psychologize the poem or to invent a naive persona for it, incapable of recognizing that the language of his passion has been that of craft and art all along ("strainably" is a term applied in Wyatt's time to effective *rhetorical* delivery [*OED*]), we need to pause over the situation represented in the poem. The courtly, Petrarchan speaker, who begins in a mode of thoroughly conventional hyperbole, with its implied conventional courtly setting, becomes in increasingly literal terms one of the damned. He has his part in the pain of a restless and deathless hell; he is fixed in a flame from which he cannot "stert"; he repetitively dispatches the same infernal emissary ("Goo, burning sighes"), charged with contradictory instructions, to a silent, even imaginary, respondent; he remains seemingly locked into an endless round of pained resentment and renewed violence. In this situation, "mortall prayer" paradoxically becomes the prayer for death or, indeterminately, a wish for the death of the other as a means of self-deliverance.

If the almost crudely attempted change of ground midway through the poem, from putatively innocent plea to calculated craft and art, changes nothing in the end, that is partly because both craft and art are unavailingly present if unacknowledged from the beginning; craft is the ground of the poem as well as a device in its action. Moreover, no narrative of deliverance can be produced in the recursive form of the poem. (The scenario of the speaker's aggressively working or scheming his way out of hell is no more plausible than that of his passionately pleading his way out, and his suddenly seeing the need to work can hardly be regarded as anything but an ironized insight of infernal blindness.) The surfacing of craft, and its supplementary doubling with art, appear to belong to a single, infernal condition of desired but insufficient power. A simultaneous displacement of courtly grace and a reflexive, stoic ironization of the "craft" program accordingly seems to be occurring as the scene of the poem shifts to the underworld. The repeatedly dispatched "burning sighes" apparently have nowhere to go at the end of the poem (where they also, however, "stert") except back to the beginning, and if any transaction is capable of being effected in or by the poem, it evidently remains an intrapsychic rather than an intersubjective one.

It is possible, no doubt, to regard the predicament enacted in this poem as testimony to the peculiarities of Wyatt's historical situation as well as to broader sociocultural impasses. The failure of mediations, causally or symptomatically identified with the withdrawal of the maternal-intercessive figure of the woman (virgin mother) and her replacement by an imagined cold, disciplinary mistress, can be regarded as a crisis precipitated by the Protestant-masculinist rigors of the Henrician period to which, in some other respects, Wyatt's *Penitential Psalms* bear extended witness. At the same time, the fantasy of the infernal emissary, charged with bearing pain out of the closed system and preferably transferring it to another, constitutes one projection of Wyatt's political and cultural role as diplomatic emissary, at once acting for a master no doubt similarly placed and experiencing the provisional release of self-removal from the system. The repeated production of emissary devices in and *as* Wyatt lyrics is, however, accompanied by their repeated failure. The repeated introjection of pain into the self-constitution of the poetic subject (as well as a recurrent summoning of the disciplinary mistress) thus becomes virtually unavoidable.[11]

Similar contradictions within the subject, or rather within its desire, become perspicuous in many Wyatt lyrics as well as this one, while the endless recursiveness of courtly forms constitutes Wyatt's craft as a narrative-thwarting problematic of perverse repetition. Wyatt's "perverse" stoic in-turning makes it possible, however, to regard him as an analytically consistent, hence singularly "honest," practitioner of closed, recursive forms. Wyatt's agnostic disengagement of the lyric subject from so-called salvific narrative or so-called vision contributes to this effect of honesty.

To say this is not, however, to assign any stable value to this effect; Shakespeare's having given honesty a bad name stands in the way of any such ascription, and one need hardly recall Iago to see in Wyatt's honesty an unplumbed capacity for dissimulation, for limitless pursuit of negative mastery in the guise of stoic limitation, and for a willfully invidious shortsightedness in respect, for example, of the visionary Petrarch or even the beatific Dante. All that can be claimed is the irrepressible and endlessly disturbing datum of Wyatt's "honesty," at once threatening to and capable of being reinscribed in more complex forms than that of the rondo. This possibility is one I will now explore in a sonnet that not only rehearses a number of the craft issues I have considered but remains a crux for contemporary interpretation of Renaissance literature.

> Who so list to hount, I knowe where is an hynde,
> But as for me, helas, I may no more:
> The vayne travaill hath weried me so sore.
> I ame of theim that farthest commeth behinde;
> Yet may I by no meanes my weried mynde
> Drawe from the Diere: but as she fleeth afore,
> Faynting I folowe. I leve of therefore,
> Sins in nett I seke to hold the wynde.
> Who list her hount, I put him owte of dowbte,
> As well as I may spend his tyme in vain:
> And, graven with Diamonds, in letters plain
> There is written, her faier neck rounde abowte:
> *Noli me tangere*, for Caesars I ame;
> And wylde for to hold, though I seme tame.
>
>   (7)

Discussion of this poem has concerned itself not just with a certain literary history in which Wyatt gets credit for introducing the sonnet form into English poetry, but with the poem's peculiarities as an imitation of Petrarch's sonnet "Una candida cerva sopra l'herba." Contexts of religious, political, and aesthetic culture have been adduced to explain Wyatt's apparent refiguration of the visionary Petrarchan poem as a secular one in which the political and the erotic are ferociously entangled; the poem's fabled allusion to Henry VIII and Anne Boleyn has also allowed it to become an exemplary poem for new historicism as such, putatively restoring the historical referent lost or suppressed in certain forms of theoretical criticism. Recently, moreover, the poem has become a test case for the gendered and/or "progressive" reading of Renaissance texts: at issue are a wide range of questions regarding our critical investment in the forms of power, gender, ownership, and subjecthood supposedly represented in the poem. (Conversely, questions are asked about the critically invoked "we" who read.)[12] What is often missing from these discussions, however, is any sustained consideration of the poem's craft. Does this matter, and if so how?

Few readers would be likely to dispute that an allegorical hunt is being staged in the poem. Indeed, the taken-for-granted allegory, or, in Puttenham's terms, extended metaphor, is what generally gets literalized in—or as—discussion of the poem. This allegory, we are variously led to believe, is one of predatory masculine courtship in which competition, indistinguishably for political power and sexual ownership, is pursued. The allegorically masked yet revealed scene of this pursuit is the court of Henry VIII, either as such or as an instance of the Renaissance princely court. In this setting, Caesar/Henry claims exclusive ownership of the hind/Anne, perhaps to the exclusion of her rumored erstwhile lover, I/Thomas Wyatt. (Caesar's choosing to place his mark of bondage/ownership on the hind's "faier neck" may thus seem chillingly prophetic.) The speaker in the poem, apparently represented (or dissimulating himself) as the envious loser, may nevertheless participate in a masculine, absolutist production of power and subjecthood, fashioning his own identity in complicitous opposition to the "Caesar" of the poem. An element of craft is already implied in this summary insofar as allegory is a crafty form and the possible dissimulation of the speaker is recognized. Yet is that recognition enough? Such is the question this quintessential Wyatt poem—a poem written by/writing Wyatt—poses to our reading of it, and of the English Renaissance, insofar as it has been made exemplary in recent criticism.

Let us recall that, as an imitation of Petrarch, the poem is recognizable but hardly faithful.[13] The Italian form of the sonnet is anglicized, and the visionary narrative of Petrarch's sonnet, although arguably undercut there, is simply written out of Wyatt's poem. Its being so evidently lets another story be told in, and perhaps finally about, the hollowed-out sonnet. The new story seems to be of a mysterious deer hunt in progress, not a deer epiphany, from which the speaker's repeated unsuccessful attempt to withdraw threatens to become a story in itself—possibly a psychological one of obsessional fixation and/or compulsive repetition mimed by the repetitions of Wyatt's three identical quatrains. Another possibility, however, is that the form of the sonnet compels repetition, in which case its subject (the "I") can be regarded as one simultaneously constituted and victimized by its own internal repetitions. Moreover, this sonnet does not extend itself positively by adhering to a narrative line, but negatively by virtue of its (or its speaker's) inability to stop doing the same thing. (Similar negative extension occurs in the lyrical quatrains of "My lute awake," in which the poem not only keeps on repeating its own wish to end, but in which the desire to end is paradoxically what causes the poem to start in the first place.) The sonnet may thus be turning in upon itself, and upon its own repetitions, and as it does so, the allegorical distance between tenor and vehicle diminishes towards a point of absolute identity, as does the space between author and persona, language and referent. This closing-in increasingly preempts the glamorous stories capable of being told in, by, or about the sonnet, the self-identical craft of which may seem to have become Wyatt's sole pursuit, as it is in the lyric forms previously considered.

This sonnet appears to be doubling back in other ways as well. The hind that is being pursued, apparently to be captured and possessed rather than killed, is subject to various allegorical constructions, yet it is still (also) Petrarch's hind or deer (dear). No doubt it is being pursued with a good deal of "vayne travaill" (conceit, labor, travel, repetition) by others as well as by Wyatt, of whose belatedness the poem may speak. Yet this particular hunt is a curious one, since what begins as the apparently material object of the quest for possession turns into immaterial "wynde"— a voice, a breath?—uncapturable, it must be assumed, in the net of the sonnet, perhaps even by Petrarch.

Against these apparent negative or reductive trends in the sonnet, including the prophecy of failure, capture and possession are nonetheless asserted at the end of the poem. An extraordinary transcendence of the speaker's limitations and even those of "ordinary" lyric form is projected in the final couplet. The claim to material possession of the hind is cleverly staked in a language other than that of the poem: not just in tight Latin rather than porous English, but with a maximum of lapidary concision, brilliance, memorability, and clarity. It is staked, moreover, in the final couplet, which is to say in a place ostensibly apart from that of the poem's repetitive speaker. The epigrammatically (or epigraphically) sublated relation of the end couplet to the rest of the sonnet can be called upon to effect the desired triumph. In the couplet, unlike the previous quatrains, the diamond-writing of prohibitive power, truth, and eternal duration is articulated as "another" language, now engraved on the very flesh to which it lays claim, and in claiming constitutes. (The word is virtually made flesh, the implied collar notwithstanding.) Not only is the speaker's prophecy of failure in the sonnet apparently defeated, but the "empty" repetitions of the first twelve lines apparently yield to a language of plenary authority.

How this shift in the poem is read depends partly on the assumptions made about what the quotation "Noli me tangere" ("touch me not," "render unto Caesar," etc.) imports into this context.[14] Yet whatever might be concluded about the proper context, legitimate speaker, and hence proper reading of so enormously resonant a quotation, Petrarch is one potential claimant of the Caesar position—not for nothing did he get himself crowned in Rome as king of the wits—and he is strangely recalled in the sonnet. The "nessun me tocchi" spoken by his deer (dear) has apparently been misappropriated—or is it reappropriated and revalorized?—in Wyatt's imitation to become the imperious *noli me tangere* of an invulnerable male owner. At the same time the phrase has been restored to its "original" form, Petrarch's phrase thus being reduced to imitative secondariness and vulgar eloquence. In fact, the English close of Wyatt's sonnet enables it to reach more imperiously than Petrarch's towards an enviable, presumably masculine, language of eternal power, duration, alterity, and exclusiveness. Similarly, the language in which Petrarch's deer asserts *her* eternal freedom is here rewritten around her neck (or on the implied collar) as the language of her eternal bondage. Inasmuch as Wyatt is repeating Petrarch, he appears at once to invert Petrarch's priorities, to recapture the deer that has escaped (or been set free) in Petrarch's sonnet, to disqualify Petrarch from occupying the Caesar position either in relation to the deer or to the tradition of the sonnet, and possibly to effect his own translocation from the position of the one who comes behind to that of the one who comes first. Crafty imitation in the Wyatt vein of aggressive *réssentiment* thus characterizes the poem, the invented final couplet no doubt embodying (or betraying) the unregulated "hidden " desire of stoic Wyatt to change places in the poem as well as in the tradition of the sonnet. This program will include the reconstitution of masculine identity, not in a mode of empty, belated repetition but as the intangible sovereign alterity of the one who, turning the tables yet again, subjects the feminine to his absolute proprietary bondage.

Turning the tables in this way is in character for Wyatt, who indeed acquires strong literary "character" through certain forms of consistency and predictability. Yet this regularity of character is at once subverted and regenerated by a dialectic of subjecthood that lends the poem its peculiar fascination. (Equally and relatedly fascinating is the poem's double nature as imitation and translation.) In the poem, the Latin language of absolute power, transparency, and difference has, after all, no definitive speaker, and has none in the broad cultural tradition invoked by the quotation of *noli me tangere*. It accordingly becomes—always and already is?— the imagined, overinvested language of an originary absolute subject. The Latin phrase is thus the linguistic marker of a position incapable of being successfully occupied by anyone—or to which anyone may lay claim, Latin being "universal." Moreover, as the imaginary language of pure masculine domination, it is reappropriated by the hind and barbarously made to miscegenate in an English sentence ("*noli me tangere*, for Caesars I ame") in which its gendered purity and difference are at once exploited and impeached. Appropriating the unspeakable, nonvernacular language of the absolute as her warrant, the hind not only becomes the untouchable one, but constitutes herself in the rigorously subject-forming relation of bondage, claiming to be the sole authentic subject of the poem: "I ame." Thus constituted, this single subject renders itself doubly invulnerable to possession by withdrawing into the endless self-division of being and seeming, wildness and tameness. Its identity is thus secured as a form of nonidentity, or more precisely of non-self-identity.

We might now say that the couplet paradoxically makes the discovery, or repeats Petrarch's discovery, that the true or successful subject of the sonnet as a form is the feminine subject, not constituted by the author but self-constituting in relation to the always imaginary absolute subject as masculine, and self-defensive in relation to any further penetration or appropriation. The deer (dear) woman alone thus seems to emerge as the one rigorously authentic occupier of the subject position, displacing rather than sublating the negative "I" who occupies that position in the first twelve lines. As a putatively masculine form seeking its own and its author's *Aufhebung*, the sonnet instead becomes a misogynistically ironic form in which the *logical* belatedness, inauthenticity, and failure of the masculine "I" stands cruelly exposed. Incapable of being in the imaginary position of the absolute subject, the masculine speaker, whether Petrarch or Wyatt, cannot occupy the strong subject position in the sonnet either, and his place in the order of precedence will always be that of the one who comes behind the hind.

In this misogynistic or strictly satiric rather than romance schema, it is not too surprising that Wyatt's feminized hind (female subject) emerges as a crafty rather than an idyllic figure. She is at once bound and free, single and double, truthful and dissem-

bling. This misogynistic projection of the feminine is wholly conventional—as well as being subject to mimetic reappropriation by
the masculine poet-speaker. What is, however, less routine in this
sonnet is that crafty doubleness, projected as the quality of the
feminine "other," seemingly allows Wyatt to effect a decisive
translatio of the Petrarchan sonnet into English. It is the hind
who finally becomes the exemplary English (mis)translator in the
poem rather than the imagined material object of capture; she
also becomes the metamorphic figure working for the stoic subject of the poem. Such is the distinctive Wyatt-effect of this sonnet, and such, perhaps, is the displaced form of bondage to which
Wyatt's craft of the sonnet most aspires.

At the risk, now, of collapsing these dialectical structures, it remains for me to add that they at once presuppose and partially
rationalize certain underlying instances of complicity or non-
difference. Despite the positional and functional interchanges of
the poem, its gendered oppositions are not, and cannot be, wholly
self-identical *or* wholly different. The "Diere," for example, is not
identical to the "hynde," though it may be capable of substituting
for it in the poem's allegory or extended metaphor, which is always a rhetorical figure of sameness and difference. "Hynde" is
also a term in English for the boor or rustic swain, perhaps the
one who comes be-hind in the hunt. There are thus two hinds that
are also one. Crossing occurs homophonously between the
poem's constructed subjects in this and other ways; perhaps more
disconcertingly, both hinds may partake of the Diere through
which they cross.

Not only is this "Diere" not identical to the "hynde" of the
poem, its nonidentity with anything, including itself, becomes increasingly striking. Its possible morphological indeterminacy as a
singular or plural form calls to mind that it, as well as the modern
English "deer," is singular and plural at once. Yet although it slides
towards identification with the gentle English "deer," it also remains an archaic (non)signifier that in modern Germanic lan-

guages can shift towards the naming of predatory creatures. It is not, however, identical to "deer" even in English, since it also punningly invokes "dear" ("dear hart, how like you this?"). Perhaps Diere just is/are Diere, yet to say this may be to say nothing—or to name the unthinkable instance of nonidentity that precedes and limits any form of positive identification, including that of differentially gendered human subjects or even different cultures.

Admittedly, this Diere's archaic reek of the primitive and the predatory may suggest why the regularly censored Wyatt is the seemingly atavistic one who ravages categorical distinctions between animal and human, sex and gender, nature and culture, allowing so many of his poems to play out in a strange no-man's-land populated by imperfectly identified Diere momentarily resembling courtly people. Yet the question is not necessarily one of primitive atavism, but of that virtually unthinkable state of non-difference that grounds and ungrounds the struggle for identification.

Partaking of the Diere, no self-constituted or differential identity in the poem appears complete, although a virtually specular twinning, despite posited gender-difference, is the ironic result of the "I ame" that both speakers pronounce. The competing, gendered subjects are both imperfect or partial ones who exist in no doubt asymmetrical relation to the imaginary absolute subject as guarantor of identity and difference—yet who may in turn be doubly construed though not definitively identified as Christ or Caesar. On the plane of the poem's action, however, which is also that of its language and form, these imperfect persons not only cross over but through the mysterious Diere.

Whether Wyatt's craft finally consists in a struggle for or against identification, for or against appropriation, it emphatically constitutes doubleness—or, rather, the nonidentity of any identity—as the peculiar condition and undoing of all attempts at identification. Such, I would suggest, is the condition of any Renaissance self, or of the Renaissance itself, as instantiated by Wyatt. Partial and indeed partisan Wyatt's craft may be, yet it challenges the greater partiality, which is also to say the premature closure, of standard readings of his poems.

~~~

Wyatt does not of course practice only tight lyric forms, and treating him as if he does might be regarded as a motivated misreading left over from the New Criticism. Yet as the poet of the satires, epigrams, and *Penitential Psalms*, Wyatt does not cease to be crafty in all the senses described above. Indeed, it is in the *Penitential Psalms* that both his political craftiness and peculiar confessional *impenitence* are perceived by Greenblatt. The first satire is also exemplary. It is an arguably self-ironizing Horatian poem in which the pious (also self-constituting) withdrawal of the speaker from scenes of courtly corruption and abuse turns out to have been "caused" (l. 2) as much by his inability to compete in that arena ("My wit is nought—I cannot lerne the waye" [l. 57]), or by his banishment from court, as by a stoic decision to withdraw.[15] His noble disclaimers of courtly vice and dissimulation ("I am not," "I cannot," etc.) are thus indeterminately related to his sense of being unqualified, to his having been prohibited from participating (perhaps for unruly "naughtiness"), and to his stoic integrity; three causes are at least two too many. The poem is also negatively extended by the withdrawal of a speaker who seemingly remains fixated on that from which he is withdrawing. Whether the desire or place of the speaker is accordingly to be located in those disavowed forms of courtly dissimulation and excess, or in the stoic self finally produced in the moment of simulated Horatian self-possession ("Here I am"), remains in doubt: we don't know who or where the speaker is. Again, however, a certain complicity and manipulated exchange between these twin selves, the one who is not and the one who is, must be suspected ("I am not what I am"; "nothing is but what is not," to recall here the language of two of Shakespeare's represented masculine subjects).

Inasmuch as the poem seems frankly to appeal beyond itself to the judgment of a candid [*candida?*] and authentic other—the John Poyntz to whom it is addressed as an epistle—it also turns in on itself when that John Poyntz is first incorporated by name in the poem ("Mine own John Poyntz") and then possibly subverted as the candid "other" when we hear that "None of these points [*sic*] would ever frame in me" (l. 56).

Perhaps it is now safe to claim that Wyatt's craft constitutes his exemplary poetic weakness and/or strength in his own period. This craft is undoubtedly subject to various contextualizations; in addition to the specific historical ones constructed, for example, by Wyatt's successive editors or by Greenblatt, one could cite the context of Tudor censorship discussed by Annabel Patterson among others; of an emergent English-humanist poetics of dissimulation memorably crystallized in chapter 7 of Puttenham's *The Arte of English Poesie* [*"qui nescit dissimulare, nescit regnare"*]; of a highly sophisticated, traditional, stoic aesthetic; of an Anglo-Chaucerian poetic in which *ars longa vita brevis* is capable of being Germanically translated, as it is in *The Parliament of Fowls*—"the lyf so shorte, the crafte so longe to lerne"; and no doubt others.[16] From the standpoint of my own interpretive concerns, however, Wyatt's foregrounding of craft is not without heuristic power and positive significance. Apart from centering the question of doubleness—the nonidentity of identity—as *the* constitutive phenomenon of Wyatt's world, it also relates craft, that of the lyric above all, to a "painstaking" albeit problematic stoicism. This attitude and this practice remain conservatively opposed to, even as they remain implicated in, certain sweeping romance discourses of power, truth, and desire, the unregulated, wish-fulfilling emptiness of which they suspect. Furthermore, "craft" is a term under which an always faulty *agency* as well as repertoire of skills can be imputed to the poet.

Finally, Wyatt's craft strongly resists the bracketing, effacement, or even repression of the craft issue in practically all contemporary interpretation, whether canonical or anticanonical (a disappearance facilitated by the transfer, with stultifying consequences all round, of the entire craft issue to schools of creative writing, and the relegation of close reading either to the bad history of New Criticism or, as trivial, to the undergraduate classroom). To speak even of a craft "element" in the production of cultural forms, including poetic ones, is to speak at a minimum of that which always inflects those forms, and at a maximum of that which constitutes their "bad" cultural origin and nonnegotiable ongoing condition: always arbitrary, always limited, always preemptively constructed, always powerful only by assertion and default. The suppression of the craft element accordingly facilitates an account of poetic and cultural forms that may refuse to acknowledge the only ground on which they (and it) can hope to stand. The difficult, crafty, stoic Wyatt, no doubt a figure more forbidding than appealing ("They flee from me that sometime did me seek"), may thus seem principally to contest or sabotage rather than confirm our own most fashionable interpretive discourses. Yet it is also this Wyatt who lays claim to the truth of the matter.

2

The Suicidal Poetics of the Earl of Surrey

The Earl of Surrey may be more intimately known to present-day readers through Thomas Nashe's fictionalized portrayal in *The Unfortunate Traveller* than through his own writings. Or, to put it somewhat differently, it may be Nashe's Elizabethan (mis)reading rather than any supposedly unmediated close reading that has rendered the Earl of Surrey imaginatively present, to the extent that he is so, to modern readers. This situation will surprise no one, since, whatever incidental factors may have helped to produce it, intertextual reading and powerfully mediated access to historic authors constitutes the virtual norm of our reading. Yet Nashe's reading of Surrey, while in one respect confirming our normal expectations, may conflict with them in another. *The Unfortunate Traveller* represents Surrey as original—indeed, as one of the great originals of the period of Henry VIII, others being the king and Sir Thomas More. An anxiety, not so much of influence, but regarding origin and preemptive originality thus manifests itself in Nashe's representation of Surrey, which is intensely proprietary and agonistic at once. In being so, it becomes paradigmatic for post-Henrician recall of the Henrician.

Nashe is not alone during the Elizabethan period in regarding the period of Henry VIII and its leading figures as powerfully and/or threateningly original, as my next chapters, with the possible exception of the one on "Lucrece," will imply. It is arguable that our own reading of Elizabethan authors, including Spenser, underestimates both the frequency and motivated intensity with which that period is recalled by Elizabethans. The hellraising "laureate" Skelton, originator of the Colin Clout persona, is especially important in Spenser's *Shepheardes Calendar*, for example, in which Henry VIII also figures as the historical "Pan" of the April eclogue. Shakespeare too reviews this "primal scene" in *Henry VIII*.

If this period is predictably recalled as one of awesome masculine rule, it is often done so parodically or problematically, partly because of Henry VIII's virtual inability, registered in Spenser's April eclogue and elsewhere, to produce male "issue." Its recall is also ironic thanks to the deconstructive pun on "remembering."[1] What this joke suggests is a restoration of the potent "member" to a symbolic figure whose lack of it in the first place is to be suspected, or from whom one will have wanted to take it away. What the pun thus implies, and what is often apparent in the Elizabethan recall of the Henrician, is a cultural and even individual dialectic of disempowering (forgetting) and reempowering (remembering). The retroactivity of this dialectic in the sphere of cultural construction and interpretation is partly what facilitates ironic recognition of its manipulative opportunism, yet the association of phallic empowerment and disempowerment with the vagaries of memory also implies whe possibility of its occurring involuntarily, perhaps as a phenomenon of repression and return, of denial and acknowledgment. In the latter case, manipulative mastery of an *ars memoria* will be threatened by the irresistible return of forgotten or "alien" forms of power. Both irony and anxiety of this order are apparent in *The Unfortunate Traveller*, for reasons that a reading of Surrey may partly suggest.

~~~

Let us begin this consideration of Surrey's suicidal poetics simply by recalling how Nashe fictionalizes the literary-historical figure of Surrey. Embedding parodic but still beautifully forged versions of Surrey's amorous sonnets, Nashe incorporates the Earl into an anti-Petrarchan *prose* fiction. This fiction constitutes a typically Elizabethan treatment of the Henrician poet. Nashe's story is one in which the servant, a "page," successfully impersonates his master. Not only does the servant-page, Jack Wilton, successfully pass for Surrey, while Surrey passes for a servant (one of the roles in which the Petrarchan lover conventionally casts himself), but Jack plays the part to brilliant excess. In doing so, noble Surrey ceases to be the pining lover-from-afar of the idealized Geraldine and becomes the possessor of a more readily available flawed diamond (Diamante/*di-amante*). Telling this story of the Earl of Surrey, Nashe plays out a now rather familiar Elizabethan game of socio-cultural imitation and one-upmanship, aggressively virilizing himself as he does elsewhere in *The Unfortunate Traveller*. At the same time, he exploits his print-conferred ability to forge any poetic title to gentility, and to play the master or the servant with equal facility.

It is normally, and no doubt correctly, assumed that Nashe seizes on the Earl of Surrey as the one who most "authentically" represents English sonneteering gentility. Not only are Surrey's poems littered with highly exclusive class markers, but the Howard family is "real" aristocracy as distinct from Tudor/Elizabethan upstart nobility.[2] However, in seizing the Earl's "goods," including his title, and converting them to his own purposes, Nashe apparently repeats an action already performed in 1558 by Tottel. It is now commonplace that in Tottel's *Miscellany*, the ostensibly private literary goods of the Earl are already appropriated for profitable distribution to a by no means exclusive reading public, and for future use by literary upstarts. Although Tottel's *Miscellany* is just that, and although it includes poems by Wyatt, Surrey's acknowledged master, Surrey is given the most prominent billing. Moreover, a romantic story of the Earl of Surrey as a type is being editorially constructed by Tottel. In supplying running titles for untitled lyrics, Tottel begins (or helps) to construct the sequential romance narrative of the wistful, distinguished, eternally pining Surrey-type: "The lover for shamefastnesse hideth his desire within his faithfull hart," "The lover sheweth how he is forsaken of such as he sometime enjoyed," and so forth.[3] Tottel, it would seem, tends to assimilate all courtly lyrics and their makers to the Surrey *imago*.

In addition to soliciting the attention of self-gentrifying readers, Tottel is, I suggest, playing safe by studiously withdrawing attention from the more dismal or threatening features of the Surrey and Wyatt stories: Surrey, with some claim to the English throne, is executed at age thirty by Henry VIII on dubious charges of treason; Wyatt, tried for treason himself under Henry VIII, is the father of a son (a friend of Surrey's) executed for treason as a result of having participated in the Lady Jane Grey rebellion. Quite another story could be written in the light of those events. Perhaps Tottel knows this too, since he at once recognizes "the weightinesse of the depe-witted Sir Thomas Wyatt" and masks it behind the Surrey front. Whatever the case may be with Tottel, who seems to have been no fool, it is the "dark" story of courtly poetics that recent criticism has been writing: the story of politically ambitious sonneteers, of coded love-poems, of power and subversion, of class mobility and class defense.[4]

If the mediated reading and even marketing of Surrey is evident in all this, what also begins to emerge in a reading of Surrey's poems is the possible extent of his "dictation" of these stories, and not only these, to his successors. The narrative construction of "the Earl of Surrey" begins in Surrey's poems, many of which are openly and *selectively* autobiographical. When Nashe transcribes this story, or text of Surrey's life, he distorts it, but he also continues it in preset Surrey terms. The fictional biography Nashe writes is, in short, preceded by Surrey's poetic autobiography, which is not of course a continuous narrative but comprises a number of essays in lyric form. The story Surrey tells of himself includes both the amorous and the political ingredients we have already noted, but it is a rather different story from any of the ones identified so far.[5]

It is a story, I will suggest, of suicide, in which a "poetics of suicide" is elaborated, and it is therefore irreducibly a story of willfully embraced failure or defeat. What complicates the situation, however, is that this suicide is never a simple fact or an end in itself. Its pursuit is inseparable from a process of aggressive-defensive self-construction in a matrix of power-infused social relations, and in pursuing it Surrey yokes neoclassical poetics to a seemingly perverse teleology. The Surrey suicide-plot is typically double: in it, *Selbstmord* has *Brudermord* for its counterpart, and these two elements may fuse in a *Liebestod*.

The propriety of introducing these Germanic terms in connection with Surrey's poems remains very much to be proved; I imply no more than the possible existence of certain cultural plots and masculine "values" of Teutonic *Bruderschaft* as structural elements in Surrey's poetic discourse. Or, to put it differently, these terms supply us with a conceptual currency for dealing with otherwise elusive aspects of Surrey's performance.

At least partly conscious manipulation of such plots and "values" by Surrey is not unthinkable, yet they can also be identified by us as "alien" to the neoclassical repertoire Surrey has so large a role in translating into Renaissance English. Moreover, the suicidal Surrey may make visible a certain unconquerable darkness— a repressed—within the very Latinity that he assiduously promotes.

In short, "the Germanic" here need constitute little more than a critical intuition or rhetorical figure of our own for something "other" that makes the case of the Earl of Surrey more complex and interesting than it is normally assumed to be: more interesting, that is to say, than the case of Surrey as a gifted minor courtier-poet (Wyatt's shadow, in the modern evaluation that reverses Tottel's); as gentleman-amateur; as one who translates two books of the *Aeneid* into English and simultaneously founds the English blank-verse pentameter as an equivalent for the Latin hexameter; as a "silver poet of the sixteenth century"; as a figure in a Norton anthology of English sixteenth-century "verse"; and as a rather violent aristocratic booby in an incipient Monty Python tradition.[6]

~~~

It is certainly recognized that Surrey brings considerable social prestige as well as talent to his undertakings as an early Petrarchan imitator, a stabilizer of the English sonnet form, and a translator of Virgilian epic. Less fully recognized is his wide-ranging imitation of Latin lyric and elegy. If read alongside Wyatt, Surrey will seem not just neoclassical through and through, but neoclassical predominantly in a pastoral-elegiac vein.

This undeniable and crucial Latinizing by Surrey may be on the side of neoclassical enlightenment and cultural success, but it also means that he renders that Latinity somewhat alien to itself. It means that he unavoidably cuts across its grain in an "uncouth" (barbarous *and* unknown) semi-Germanic language. And it means that he brings such Latin authorities as Petrarch and Virgil into conflict with the paternal English figure of Chaucer. The "easy" Chaucer of *Troilus and Criseyde* is an obvious presence in Surrey, since his courtly lover Troilus, already having a Petrarchan *canzone* put into his mouth, is a recognized prototype for Surrey and other Renaissance sonneteers; but there is also the more forbidding Chaucer of *The Knight's Tale*.

The plot of that poem is one in which rival "brothers" struggle for—or through—the same woman under the "fatherly" eye of Theseus. Love and death are both awarded at the end of the struggle, and it is not clear whether these awards are fundamentally different; "death" in the erotic pun of premodern English is the goal of "love" in any case, as Surrey reminds us in the concluding line of one of his Petrarchan imitations: "Sweet is the death that taketh end by love."[7] In *The Knight's Tale*, it is finally not clear which of the two young men wins, which one has the more "romantic" end, or whether Arcite, in receiving death, receives what he does not wish. By the same token, Palamon's being awarded Emily as bride may confer upon him only a lesser version of Arcite's satisfaction (*la petite mort*) while deferring his true and truly desired satisfaction, which is also the dark goal of all romance. In any event, something other than Athenian enlightenment may propel this Athenian plot and cast of performers, whose terminus is a theater of love and death.

Let us now consider a Surrey poem in which suicide is directly invoked. I will suggest that in this poem the rudiments of a Surrey poetics of suicide are discernible, as are its peculiar contradictions—not to say impossibilities:

Thassyryans king, in peas with fowle desyre
And filthye lustes that stayned his regall harte,
In warr that should sett pryncelye hertes a fyre
Vaynquyshd dyd yelde for want of marcyall arte.
The dent of swordes from kysses semed straunge,
And harder then hys ladyes syde his targe;
From glotton feastes to sowldyers fare a chaunge,
His helmet, far above a garlandes charge.
Who scace the name of manhode dyd retayne,
Drenched in slouthe and womanishe delight;
Feble of sprete, unpacyent of payne,
When he hadd lost his honour and hys right—
Prowde tyme of welthe, in stormes appawled with drede—
Murdred hymself to show some manfull dede.

(188)

This poem is identified by Sylvester as an imitation of Petrarch's *Rime* 145, and it must be said that if it is an imitation of that poem it renders it unrecognizable. One would assume that this identification was a simple mistake (or misprint) if similar attributions were not made in other cases, in which Sylvester is presumably relying mainly on the authority of previous Surrey editors.[8] The case is interesting, since either the identifications are simply mistaken, or the imitations utterly transform their originals, or Surrey is enabling editors to "see" something odd in Petrarch. All these possibilities are compatible with my argument.

The Surrey poem in question presents an image of the Assyrian king Sardanapalus without naming him. Sylvester notes that Sardanapalus was "often viewed as the type of royal degeneration," which will also mean of royal unnaturalness, in which the king departs from his *genus* or "kind." A note adds that "it is tempting, but not necessary, to see this poem as a covert allusion to Henry VIII" (188 n. 1). Inasmuch as Surrey can be thought to imitate Petrarch here, he will be Latinizing, but he will also be eliciting an other in Petrarch—or another Petrarch—here figured as the "Assyrian" Sardanapalus. He will also be drawing attention to the representation of radical cultural alterity in Petrarch.

This otherness, of which there are unmistakably "Persian," "Babylonian," or "Carthaginian" counterparts in Petrarch, implies intense but feared or stringently prohibited self-identification. Such alterity can seldom emerge in the form of an alter ego, however, since it generally represents only the utter undoing of the culturally determined and ideal-ridden ego. (Conversely, the stabilization of a self—or "portrait of the artist"—depends on the endless conquest and subsuming of these "others.") Such alterity is strongly marked, for example, in the seminal "Ascent of Mont Ventoux," in which Petrarch's buried or subtextual identifications are with the Carthaginian Hannibal who assails Rome and the would-be parricidal sons of Philip of Macedon, also making war on Rome, rather than with the ego-idealized St. Augustine or the "dear" father-confessor to whom he writes his letter.[9]

Even the Germanic form of alterity is registered in Petrarch's *Rime* 128. The poem, which begins: "Italia mia, ben che 'l parlar sia indarno / a le piaghe mortali / che nel bel corpo tuo sì spessi veggio," goes on to admit that although "ben provide Natura al nostro stato / quando de l'Alpi schermo / pose fra noi et la tedesca rabbia / ma 'l desir cieco, encontra 'l suo ben fermo, / s'è poi tanto ingegnato / ch'al corpo sano à procurato scabbia" ["My Italy, although speech does not aid those mortal wounds of which in your lovely body I see so many . . . Nature provided well for our safety when she put the shield of the Alps between us and the Teutonic rage . . . but our blind desire, strong against our own good, has contrived to make this healthy body sick"].[10] A bad Italian politics that facilitates the entry of German mercenaries into Italy apparently coincides with the undoing, by sick desire, of Nature's plan for a Latin *mens sana in corpore sano* shielded against mad Teutonic passions and illnesses.

If alterity is apparent in Petrarch, it is equally so in Surrey's imitations, though in the Sardanapalus poem with an additional twist: inasmuch as Surrey's imitation leaves a blank to be filled in with the name of Sardanapalus, a.k.a. Henry VIII, it also allows the name of Surrey to be written in that blank in place of either of those names. Surrey's being executed, apparently as a potential claimant to the English throne, implies Henry's ability to see Surrey in *his* place, an ability shared by Surrey himself in a number of poems including this one. Indeed, as we shall see, Surrey recurrently and perhaps suicidally flaunts in his poems his superior entitlement to the place occupied by Henry VIII. The Surrey who purportedly imitates Petrarch here is thus one who can put himself in the place of the other—other poet, other king—the death of whom he simultaneously dictates. But in projecting himself into the desired and hated place of the other, he also dictates his own fitting end. Already, *Selbstmord* and *Brudermord* move towards their fateful conjunction.

Despite this development, it may still seem as if there is nothing in Surrey that is not fully anticipated *and recuperated*, not just by Petrarch but by Latin culture. Inasmuch as both poets are subject to a "death wish" that coincides with a wish to occupy the position of the unrivaled oriental tyrant as degenerate, Petrarch preempts Surrey, and the alterity represented by Sardanapalus seems always to be recaptured and annulled by Latin *virtus*. It may seem, for example, that royal degeneration in this poem—still a kingly and not a common phenomenon—conclusively manifests itself in the cowardly or perverse act of suicide, the consistent and least "manfull" conclusion to a life of dissipation and failure. Indeed, this suicide is "manfull" only in "show," no different from other failed acts of virility. Yet this failing act is also madly embraced as the sole possible annulment of all the failed poses, roles, and attempts through which royal degeneration has passed. Only through the terminal degeneracy of suicide, which is also a flight from the emasculating power of women (a power to which Petrarch, the too much married Henry VIII, and the married and Petrarchan Earl of Surrey are subject), can there be hope of recovering masculine identity. This will be the manhood in "dede" that is tantamount to authentic sovereignty, and that is monstrously "shown" in the act of suicide. The punning conclusion to the poem (manful deed/man full dead) implies the notion of a sovereign male identity capable of being realized, meaning fully recovered and made manifest, only in the act of self-annihilation.

This "sick," "Assyrian" ending is, however, the very one that Latin stoic suicide comprehends and definitively reclaims as an extreme but still recognizable version of Roman *virtus*.[11] Indeed, this reclamation is undertaken most energetically during the reign of Rome's very own Sardanapalus, the poet-actor-matricide-emperor Nero, through and against whom "the degenerate" is incorporated into the Latin repertoire of *mens sana in corpore sano*. Death, at least, is to be saved from corruption through the anti-degenerate suicides of Seneca, Petronius, and other Tacitean worthies; it is to be saved even by the mad act of *ecpyrosis* or universal conflagration, to which Nero seemingly aspires and in which Sardanapalus succeeds: he "committed suicide by throwing himself into a fire in which he had burned up all his treasure" (188 n. 14). Against this background, known to Petrarch and Surrey alike, no gesture that Surrey ever makes towards establishing an openly death-*wishing*, perverse, or Teutonic Petrarchanism is thus ever likely to succeed—Surrey's Petrarchanism remains in this respect an aesthetic of willfully embraced failure as well—or enable him successfully to compete with Petrarch. Furthermore, his only chance against Petrarch paradoxically seems to be that of becoming more Latin than Petrarch himself.

In this poem, for example, Surrey can be said to intensify Petrarch's suggestion that the one decent recourse for the Petrarchan poet, including Petrarch, is to terminate the poem and his own lush, "courtly" existence as soon as the fourteen-line sonnet permits. (In interesting contrast to Wyatt's sonnet-figures, the Sardanapalus of this sonnet is explicitly impatient of pain, hence also of the "painstaking" discipline and regulation of the sonnet as a form.) Every emasculated, self-indulgent, moody, "gentle" gesture that betrays the desire of the Petrarchan is also royally degenerative, calling for cancellation; likewise every Petrarchan sonnet calls, more urgently than anything else, for its own ending, which is also to say its abrupt cancellation. If its writing cannot escape the loathsome sweetness of the decadent, its ending can at least be accomplished with a certain brisk *éclat* that may save the poem from further degenerate ranting. Indeed, the English sonnet form, to the institutionalization of which Surrey importantly contributes, seems more naturally than the Italian to seek its own termination in the strong close of a rhyming couplet. Here Surrey tries for a good English ending, not just rhyming the final couplet but punning "terminally," as only a Germanic language allows him to do, on deed/dead. All these gestures, however, remain captive to the iron form of the sonnet, to a Latinate witty *éclat* that is Petrarchan whether or not it tries to be otherwise, and above all to a Latin stoic epigrammatism. (When Surrey, for example, concludes his imitation of *Rime* 140 with "Sweet is the death that taketh end by love," the epigrammatic aspires to an epitaphic lapidariness that is almost more Latin than Latin itself, while *Liebestod* acquires a stolid Latin rectitude.)[12]

One can predict (and invariably find) difficulties of this order not just whenever Surrey imitates Petrarch, but whenever he engages in any neoclassical imitation. Not even his English or Chaucerian difference will necessarily escape the preemptive reach of Latinity. English is as much a Latin romance language by Surrey's time as it is a Germanic one, and it is the former that has conquered and colonized the latter, superimposing its "values" and prohibitions. English Chaucer is no less assiduous a Latinizer than any of his Renaissance successors, including Surrey, and wherever difference appears, it almost immediately disappears into universal Latin sameness. Yet Surrey persists, and in his perverse persistence we can track his poetics of suicide.

Before moving on to the next poems, I shall briefly emphasize the extent to which the Surrey story is being told between the lines of this sonnet. The poem's subject (anticipating the poem's termination) is definitively "in peas" with foul desire rather than at war on the battlefield. Insofar as he has tried to do battle, all he has revealed is his unfitness for it, an accusation that has freely been made about the military exploits of Surrey (and Henry VIII).[13] In no sense, however, does his art appear to be "marcyall," meaning that it is the art neither of the successful real-life warrior nor of the poet as martial artist (Virgil, Chaucer). Whether this military, hence masculine, ineptness is the effect or cause of his choosing to live in a "sick" peace with "foul desire" is not clear. Nor is it finally clear whether the subject of the poem turns from the hard masculine to the soft feminine or vice versa, or which of the two he really finds harder or more painful, more alien to his royal nature. Perhaps both equally, or perhaps it does not matter in the end, since the poem seems to trace the avoidance of both in a generally passive, impotent degeneracy accompanied by mounting hysteria. Something therefore remains to be pursued here, perhaps especially under the rubric "Drenched in slouthe and womanish delight."

~~~

The next two poems I shall consider, the second only briefly, are Petrarchan sonnets without clear Petrarchan originals. These are genealogical poems of a kind that Surrey writes/that write Surrey and that distinguish him from Wyatt. They are poems in which the Surrey/Howard story of noble descent and dynastic intermarriage is invidiously writ large:

> From Tuscan cam my ladies worthi race,
> Faire Florence was sometime her auncient seate;
> The westorne Ile (whose pleasaunt shore doth face
> Wylde Chambares cliffes) did geve her lyvely heate.
> Fostred she was with mylke of Irishe brest,
> Her Syer an erle, her dame of princes bloud;
> From tender yeres in Britaine she doth rest
> With a kinges child, where she tastes gostly foode.
> Honsdon did furst present her to myn eyen,
> Bryght ys her hew and Geraldine she hight;
> Hampton me tawght to wish her furst for myne,
> And Wind'sor, alas! doth chace me from her sight.
> Bewty of kind, her vertues from above,
> Happy ys he that may obtain her love.
>
> (183)

Since this is a well-known and much-analyzed poem as well as one of a kind that modern historicist criticism, here explicitly including Stephen Foley's, has effectively taught us to read, I shall venture some preliminary comments under the heading of the summary and uncontentious. The poem establishes Geraldine's double line of unimpeachably noble descent. First, as real-life Elizabeth Fitzgerald, she purportedly descends from the Italian

Giraldis to the Irish Fitzgeralds (183 n.). Second, as Petrarchan Geraldine, she descends from her high Florentine original, Petrarch's Laura, in an already distinguished line of poetic succession. On both counts, Surrey seems destined to "own" Geraldine, just as he seems destined to possess the highest English political and poetic eminence.

It inevitably happens that the line of the Fitzgeralds, like that of the Howards, keeps intersecting with the current English royal line: Elizabeth Fitzgerald's mother, Elizabeth Grey, was a first cousin of Henry VIII (183 n. 6). (Henry VIII, let us additionally recall, had Catherine Howard as one of his wives, and Surrey's sister was married to the Duke of Richmond, illegitimate son of Henry VIII, all in a presumably normal process of dynastic weaving and unraveling.) Given her antecedents, it is understandable that Elizabeth Fitzgerald should in childhood "rest / With a kinges child," identified by Sylvester as "either Princess Mary or Princess Elizabeth, Henry VIII's children" (183 n. 8). Whether she would have tasted "gostly foode" in the company of these apparently disowned and neglected children, later rescued and educated by Catherine Parr, is more questionable, and it is not clear why only one, although unnamed, should be singled out.[14] Obviously, other candidates for the role of prince ("kinges child") exist, and her continuing in the present to "taste gostly foode" narrows down the range of candidates, probably to one.

Exploiting the distinction between the real-life Elizabeth Fitzgerald and the fictional Geraldine as well as his own double identity as Surrey and Howard, the author wins throughout this sonnet, and does so in a way that must be regarded as prophetic of Astrophil/Sidney and Stella/Lady Rich. He wins even when he seems to lose, as when "Wind'sor" chases Geraldine from his "sight." This may mean that "Geraldine" has been betrothed by Henry VIII for political reasons, including ones inimical to the Howard interest, to the Sir Anthony Browne she marries in 1542 (183 n.). If so, the poem's concluding "Happy ys he that may obtaine her love" carries at least two strong implications favorable to the author: first, that whoever marries Elizabeth Fitzgerald, her love inalienably belongs to the royal quasi-sibling of her childhood; happy is he who may obtain her love, but that happiness is probably not reserved for her husband, any more than it is for Lord Rich, "Stella's" husband. Second, whatever comes between Henry Howard and Elizabeth Fitzgerald simply makes no difference, since Surrey's possession of Geraldine's "love" is his indefeasible possession of Laura's Anglo-Irish heir and of the Muse's special regard. This is a possession that Welsh Tudor "Wind'sor" cannot expropriate, an especially gratifying fact inasmuch as Windsor himself has competing poetic-humanistic pretensions.

The possibility that the Petrarchan Geraldine is the only one about whom Surrey really cares is implied in his distinction between the worthy Tuscan "race" of his mistress and her taking "lyvely heate" only in Ireland. The Geraldine who is *born* in Ireland is not necessarily the same one who originates in Tuscany, a possibility to which the dubiousness of any line connecting Irish Fitzgeralds to Italian Giraldis strongly contributes. The preferred Geraldine may well be the "dead" image rather than the one who possesses "lyvely heat."

So far, the poem conforms in practically every currently recognized way to the "gentle" sonneteering of the sixteenth century. It allusively flaunts invidious distinctions of family and poetic giftedness, apparently in such a way as to close out the unworthy, but at least equally to seduce self-gentrifying readers into a network, at once poetic and dynastic, in which Surrey is the principal. It promotes Howard interests by subverting those of "Wind'sor," and it establishes the style of the Earl of Surrey as the exemplary gentle one of the period. In all these respects, as well as that of obviously stellar brilliance, Surrey dictates a compelling script for his successors. Perhaps it is because they recognize this that Nashe represents Surrey as original in *The Unfortunate Traveller* and Tottel promotes the Surrey name in his *Miscellany*. Indeed, Tottel's dissemination of the Surrey poems becomes a logical extension of Surrey's own cultural program, the nature of which is as deviously seductive as it is willfully exclusive. Dynastic Surrey, part of whose story is being told in this poem, can aspire to found a poetic line, as autistic Wyatt apparently cannot.

This Petrarchan Surrey is aligned not just with projects of Latinization and cultural success, however, but, less admirably, with everything that is puerile, narcissistic, flashy, self-promoting, pseudomagisterial, and pretentiously cosmopolitan in Tudor humanist culture. If Surrey establishes a stellar precedent for Sidney, for instance, that precedent may include the frustrated political disaffection of the overweening narcissist, resulting in quarrelsomeness, bogus radicalism, failure, and virtual suicide, all of which Sidney appears to repeat in his own noncareer.[15] Or it may be that the stellar precedent is one of such profound inauthenticity that it calls for the self-cancellation of a stoic close, with which again Sidney, declaiming in the end against vanity, is notably credited. Or yet again, it may be the performance of one who is always in love with death and/or a ghostly line of female figures only. This possibility becomes inescapable in Surrey's extraordinarily haunting (and totally recognizable) imitation of Petrarch's *Rime* II ("I never saw youe madam laye aparte / Youre cornet black, in colde nor yet in heate"). Here the figure is implicitly Geraldine, but also Chaucer's Criseyde, prophetically Astrophil's black-eyed Stella, the ever-recurring *belle dame sans merci* of Petrarchanism, and the seductive figure of death "herself." Wishing and fearing, pursuit and avoidance, aspiring and being driven all tend in the same direction for Surrey, while the disclosure of death as the single terminus undoes oppositions that might otherwise be regarded as structural or constitutive in his work.

This self-undoing peculiarity is no less evident in the Tuscan sonnet we have been considering than in any other Surrey poem. Indeed, this poem can continue to serve as a prime example. Personified place-names make their appearance here, and they become one of the Surrey signatures. Apart from the right names, the right places evidently constitute the action, and are not merely the passive scenes of it. Correspondingly, the actors are functions of the places in which they originate and the places they hold, and this seems to be the one indefeasible fact of Surrey's "life" (as it will later become that of the fictional Unfortunate Traveller). Tuscany, Florence, Britain, Hunsdon, Windsor, connected to each other by complicated, intersecting lines, including poetic ones, constitute the grid of Surrey's being, and if they do so in such a way as to close out the unworthy (all those without real names or places), they also threaten to close out Surrey himself in the end. The impersonal fatefulness of these names, subject only to limited manipulation, gives Surrey his privileged entitlement, but his ability to possess any real name or occupy any real place is finally questionable. This is clear as regards Hunsdon and Hampton Court ("Wind'sor"), places to which he has had privileged access as a child, but to which he does not belong as an adult, except, perhaps, as a prisoner or envious onlooker. ("Wind'sor" has the power to chase even Geraldine from his "sight.") The irony of Surrey's predicament consists in his inability to acquire a name—the Tuscan, the British, the Irish, the Petrarchan, even the Howard or the Norfolk—even while he cultivates the Surrey style. Indeed, his cultivation of that style becomes increasingly inimical, it would seem, to any such possession, and thus becomes the cultivation of his own undoing. The brilliant, energetic *prosopopoeia* that animates Surrey's "places" seems capable of contributing in the end only to a poetics horrifically bent on self-destruction—and one in which the Surrey mask will not save Henry Howard from his real fate.

One of the differences, in fact, between Wyatt and Surrey is that if Wyatt's attacks on Henry VIII in his satires and *Penitential Psalms* are "deniable," as Stephen Greenblatt has said, Surrey's flaunted rivalry with the king, as well as disdainful assaults on his character and powers, is not.[16] The poetic veil becomes practically transparent, and just in case anyone should have missed the point of what Wyatt had been saying, Surrey clarifies that as well:

> What holie grave, what worthye sepulture,
> To Wyates Psalmes should Christians than purchace?
> ·
> Where rulers may see in a myrrour clere,

> The bytter frute of false concupicence
> How Jurye bowght Uryas death full deere.
> In princes hartes godes scourge yrpinted deepe
> Mowght them awake out of their synfull sleepe.
>
> (186–87)

In the production of power, status, image, virtue, and so forth, Surrey not only has to keep asking for what he might have received from Henry even without asking, but is seemingly willing to make his poems the authentic "grave" and "sepulture"—paradoxically the doom-inviting *open* renderings—of Wyatt's always encrypted or introverted truth.[17]

A poem of fateful naming, akin to the previous one, is the superb elegiac sonnet in which Surrey's squire, Thomas Clere, is remembered:

> Norfolk sprang thee, Lambeth holds thee dead,
> Clere of the County of Cleremont though hight.
> Within the womb of Ormondes race thou bread,
> And sawest thy cosin crowned in thy sight.
> Shelton for love, Surrey for Lord, thou chase:
> Aye me! while life did last that league was tender.
> Tracing whose steps thou sawest Kelsall blaze,
> Laundersey burnt, and battered Bullen render.
> At Muttrell gates, hopeles of all recure,
> Thine Earle halfe dead, gave in thy hand his will;
> Which cause did thee this pining death procure,
> Ere summers four times seven thou couldest fulfill.
> Ah Clere! if love had booted, care, or cost,
> Heaven had not wonn, nor earth so timely lost.
>
> (191–92)

We need to recall that the possibly displacing or treacherous cousin (the cozening cousin) whom Clere has seen crowned in his "sight" is Anne Boleyn, also of the Ormond family; that "Shelton" is Mary Shelton, a cousin of Anne Boleyn's; and that Surrey's little essay in "marcyall arte" records his apparently inept participation in somewhat botched Henrician campaigns in Scotland (1542) as well as France and Belgium (1544).

If, as Sylvester notes, "Surrey, throughout the poem, makes every effort to draw Clere into the Howard family" (191 n. 2), he

also repeats the exclusionary/inclusionary dialectic of the previous sonnet, though what becomes even more patent here is that
the price of inclusion may be having to share Surrey's melancholy
fate. In the Tuscan sonnet, it may precisely be Surrey's interest in
Geraldine that gets her chased from his sight and possibly married
off to avert a threat. In this poem, the Earl nearly dies on the battlefield, and "causes" the lingering death of Clere. Increasingly in
Surrey's poems, it seems as if the Earl's touch is mortal; as if Surrey inhabits a world of loss, death, and perpetual elegization; and
as if the play of names ever more relentlessly becomes a play of
violent doom: doom to the cities insofar as they defy the name of
the English king; doom to those who besiege the cities in clumsy,
protracted campaigns.

In this poem, the fatality of names at once masks and collab-
orates with another form of fatality, the presence of which I have
already intimated, and which constitutes a significant element in
the Surrey story. S. P. Zitner has excellently shown the indebted-
ness of this poem to a stoic and elegiac Virgilianism, thus incon-
testably establishing its Latinity and revealing "another" Virgil
whom Surrey covertly imitates rather than overtly translates. This
other Virgil is one rendered *sympathique* by his poetics of mourning and his assimilation of the lapidary ethos of Greek memorial
inscriptions. All that remains to be stated is what this other Virgil
imports into Latin poetics even if he finally Latinizes what is
"strange" about it—and what this Virgil enables Surrey to import
into English poetics.

In a word, it appears to me that what is doubly imported here
is homosexual love, eventually unmasked in Shakespeare's sonnet
sequence as the hidden topic of all hitherto known Petrarchan
sonneteering.[18] This is the love that may exist in the aristocratic
knight-squire relationship and in the comradeship between men
on the battlefield; it is even the love in the image of which male-
female relationships may be reconstructed. All this can be admitted up to a point in neoclassical culture, since Greek love is "classical" if not fully Latin. Moreover, the "league" between Shelton,

Clere, and Surrey is open: it looks right and maintains the proper Renaissance distinctions of rank and gender; it also distinguishes between male service and heterosexual married love.

As a right triangle of this kind, it may also seem—may indeed be—fraught with possibilities for jealousy and invidiousness; for homosocial rivalry and cynical inclusion/exclusion of the woman.[19] Yet the triangle is additionally readable as an open/secret league of those who like each other and are all alike; in it, "Shelton" is known only by her surname, as if she were one of the boys. It is a "tender" league, meaning private as opposed to public, open to injury, but nevertheless intimate and loving. (If this league is broken by Clere's death in the poem, it seems nevertheless to have continued in the real-life devotion of Mary Shelton to Surrey through his trial and up to his execution.)

What we see on the battlefield—and perhaps this is what "marcyall arte" really means—is the moment of homosexual consummation, for which perhaps Shelton has to be temporarily absent. Admittedly there is a "fateful" story of some kind about Surrey's giving Clere his will (last testament) on the battlefield, as a result of which Clere dies; the mortal touch of the Earl is infallible, here as elsewhere, though the precise relation between deadly cause and effect remains opaque in this instance. But there is also a literal, erotic, and even "touching" meaning to the Earl's placing his will in the hand of his servant, and this meaning would hardly have been obscure to any author of Greek epitaphs. There is that other tradition in which the salutation of a dead friend and comrade is the salutation of a dead lover, though perhaps that is the tradition that gets buried under the stoic weight of the Latin "*Vale!*"

It is with reference to this tradition that we can elicit the doubleness of the story Surrey tells about his own condition and that of Clere, both on the battlefield and afterwards. It is a story of "dying for love" in which all literal and figurative senses combine, and it is a story of love capable of being fulfilled only with death as its beginning (its imminence forces the consummation), its middle (death is experienced *in* love), and its end (it inflicts a lingering mortal wound). To love in this way is at once to court sweet death and to inflict it, indeterminately on oneself and another; for Surrey, it is homicidal and suicidal at once. Perhaps it is also "poetic," since the death of the self and/or other is the cause of elegiac writing.

~~~

Departing from sonnets of strange fatality—but not departing very far, as it will turn out—I shall now consider one of Surrey's happiest and most frequently anthologized efforts (a *revealingly* happy one) as a pastoralist in a tradition that can probably be called universal, or which thinks of itself as universal when it places itself under the aegis of Pan:

> The soote season, that bud and blome furth bringes,
> With grene hath clad the hill and eke the vale:
> The nightingale with fethers new she singes:
> The turtle to her make hath tolde her tale;
> Somer is come, for every spray nowe springes;
> The hart hath hong his olde hed on the pale:
> The buck in brake his winter cote he flings:
> The fishes flote with new repaired scale:
> The adder all her sloughe awaye she slinges:
> The swift swallow pursueth the flyes smale:
> The busy bee her honye now she minges:
> Winter is worne that was the flowers bale:
> And thus I see among these pleasant thinges
> Eche care decays, and yet my sorow springes.
>
> (190)

If this poem can be regarded as part of Surrey's classical translation project, that is because one can discern in it a shadowy Theocritan-Virgilian heritage (perhaps, too, an almost obligatory postclassical recall of the Song of Solomon) capable of being matched with English language and landscape. Despite the apparent happiness of the match, however, Surrey strongly foregrounds an English native tradition through which classical pastoral is already mediated, and which may indeed have its own claims to originality. Surrey effects this foregrounding by allusively invoking Chaucerian pastoral of the "soote season," a phenomenon not just of the *General Prologue*, but of the Knight's and Squire's tales, *The Parliament of Fowls*, and much else besides. The Langland of the visionary "May morwenyng" on the Malvern hills may also be recalled, especially since Surrey stages an alliterative/assonantal *tour de force* in the "Latin" form and metrics of this sonnet. What may then be at stake here is something more than matching or coupling (a conspicuously rare occurrence in this spring poem, acknowledged only in a single past-tense reference to the turtle and his "make"). Almost by definition Renaissance practices of imitation and translation put more than copying at stake: reorigination, appropriation, and above all renovation of an existing heritage are energetically pursued.

For Surrey, at all events, the pastoral project is not simply one of applying Latin forms to an English landscape or of finding English words for Latin thoughts. In addition to such English predecessors as Chaucer and Langland, Surrey recalls and incorporates an English native lyric tradition, virtually composing this sonnet from its first lines and stock phrases: "Fowles in the frith, fisshes in the flud," "Sumer is icumen in," "Nou sprinkes the sprai" (of which the unquoted second line is "Al for love ich am so seke"). If a pastoral palimpsest is being produced here, its English thickness begins to obliterate universal, Latin, or even Petrarchan origins. (*Rime* 210, claimed as the Petrarchan original for this sonnet [190 n.], is practically unrecognizable in it.)

Granting at least the possibility that Surrey's Anglicization displaces Latin pastoral—or renders it deeply alien to itself—it remains to be asked what kind of pastoral results. Clearly, a pastoral of almost raw, energetic renewal and "repair," strongly antimelancholic in that its landscape is one in which not life but "care" decays, and in which various old coverings, impediments, and griefs are easily sloughed. The uniformity of the scene of renewal is emphasized by the simple catalogue-form of the sonnet, comprising mainly end-stopped lines rhymed *abab* throughout, which results in a suppression of octave-sestet and other internal divisions. All that deviates from the pattern and yet seemingly confirms it, allowing the poem to end on a rhyming upbeat, is the mysterious first-person speaker who is disclosed at the end.

This contradictory figure, in which the Black Knight (Man in Black) of Chaucer's *Book of the Duchess* may well be recalled, is one of "sorrowing" now rendered absolutely perverse, inexplicable, intransigent, and paradoxically *uncaring*, in the last respect being at one with its landscape. The figure is now ostensibly one of pure melancholy, without any justifying or expiatory narrative and without any apparent recourse to a compensatory or therapeutic poetics. Insofar as this sonnet is elegiac, it is a poem both of mourning and apparent self-mourning by one who is apparently possessed of sorrow, hence inferentially desiring death, and nothing else. Yet that is his property. Moreover, the recuperative turns, compensatory fictions, and codified ceremonials of Theocritan pastoral elegy are abruptly cut off by the obligatory close of the sonnet, the form of which seems almost to be exploited for this sole purpose.[20] This perverse figure of grieving, inconsolable or denying all powers of consolation, represents himself as the sad exception to a generally happy nature that he nevertheless "sees," and thus constitutes, in opposition to and in conformity with himself. The constant figure of death accordingly becomes the source of renewed life in this sonnet.

The primary narcissism of the pastoral subject who sees all nature as a mirror of his own condition has here been abrogated, but then perversely, contradictorily, summarily reclaimed in full force. It is now the sorrower's unchanging *difference* that definitively instantiates and even constitutes the irrepressible "springing" of pastoral, here having little to do with Helicon or the fountain of Arethusa. The exception to nature emerges as the exceptional, distinguished nature, unforgetfully sorrowing, and making sorrow not so much the anomaly in a landscape of renewal, which is also markedly one of pastoral artifice, as its deep cause and rule. And insofar as that landscape does differ from the grieving subject who inhabits it, it differs mainly in the direction of energetic superficiality; of "spring" as a shallow forgetting and change of costume rather than a profound "springing" from un-identified wells of grief. The art of this poem, then, is not one that mirrors nature so much as one that makes nature the shallow, in-verted image, both same and other, of the sick and unnatural. Per-haps this is pastoral with a difference, of a melancholic type alien to the Latin tradition or alienating that tradition from itself. What it also threatens is the place of pastoral in the Latin repertoire of *mens sana in corpore sano.*

In the next poem, regrettably too long to quote in full, but fairly well known in any case, pastoral alienation may become even more drastic. This is the highly autobiographical poem in which Surrey speaks from within a cell at Windsor, where he was im-prisoned in 1537 for striking Sir Edward Seymour at court (an in-cident that prefigures Sidney's notorious public quarrel with the Earl of Oxford). Recalling his own childhood experiences at Windsor, Surrey inhabits the double perspective of childhood in-nocence and adult experience, of an idyllic before and a melan-choly after:

> So crewell prison, howe could betyde, alas,
> As prowde Wyndsour, where I in lust and joye
> With a kinges soon my childishe yeres did passe,
> In greater feast then Priams sonnes of Troye;
> Where ech swete place retourns a tast full sowre.
> The large grene courtes, where we wer wont to hove,
> With eyes cast upp unto the maydens towre,
> And easye sighes, such as folke drawe in love.
>
> (195)

Here the "kinges soon" can be identified as the Earl of Richmond, Henry Fitzroy, the illegitimate son of Henry VIII who married Surrey's sister in 1533 (195 n. 3). But Surrey registers his own princely claim again by making himself as well as Henry Fitzroy into one of Priam's sons. Moreover, this Henry Fitzroy is another interchangeable Henry, now with a name actually meaning "king's son" and thus identical to Surrey's secret name for himself. Brothers-in-law; brother-outlaws; the two noble kinsmen are close to being identical twins.

The resemblance of the two youths to Priam's sons seems in

the light of innocence to confer upon them an extraordinarily privileged identity, yet in the darkness of knowledge it has seemingly doomed them: to death; to disinheritance; possibly to heroic suicide; specifically even to the melancholy fate of Troilus. Surrey's companion and alter ego in the poem is also typically the true but disinherited son of the king, the eternal prince doomed to die young and never reign. Yet the likeness to Priam's sons also allows a difference at least in Surrey's case; not literally being one of Priam's sons, he is potentially exempt from their determined fate, and is free to become the Aeneas rather than the Troilus of the poem, and possibly a Virgilian rather than a Homeric imitator.

Another figure intervenes, however, or has already done so by the time Surrey writes, and that is the Chaucer of *The Knight's Tale*. This intervention deflects the poem in a pastoral direction, marked not only by the neoclassical *topoi* of idyllic friendship in an ideal landscape but by many specifically Chaucerian locutions: "On fomynge horse, with swordes and frendlye hertes" (l. 18); "With sylver dropps the meades yet spredd for rewthe" (l. 21); "The clothed holtes with grene" (l. 29); "The teares berayne my chekes of dedlye hewe" (l. 42); and so on. The games (or matches) between the two friends, including that of pastoral singing as poetic initiation (ll. 25–29), are like anticipatory rehearsals of the adult struggle that will murderously explode between Palamon and Arcite in *The Knight's Tale*, particularly since the situation in Surrey's poem is triangulated almost from the start: "With eyes cast upp unto the maydens towre, / And easye sighes, such as folke drawe in love."

The maiden in the tower, unlike the Shelton of the earlier poem, is emphatically not one of the boys. Whether or not she might want to be one, she is the distanced, imprisoned, putative spectator and putative object of rivalry. The anonymous maiden (singular or plural makes no difference here) is at once the judge and the prize in the contest, safely removed, along with her sexuality, from it, but also, in her tower position, empowered and curiously virilized as the boys are not.

Again, the triangle can be read out in more than one way. As an incipiently Petrarchan woman, the maiden is also the mother—the always virgin mother—of filial incestuous fantasy, who adjudicates between the rival sons and, in the apparent absence of a prohibitive father, is the prize for which they struggle. Since, however, the father is not really absent—is present in and as the empowered woman—the prize includes, or finally is, death. A "death-wishing" Petrarchanism is thus anticipated from the start. There is also no getting away from the preemptive paternal figure of Chaucer in this scenario, least of all when an ostensibly exotic Petrarchanism becomes the game in which various talented sons feel driven to compete.

If, on the other hand, we regard this as a poem of homosocial bonding, it is possible to read the maiden's confinement to the tower as the act of distancing and invidious spectatorial exclusion—of reduction to purely nominal adjudication and prize-winning—under which homoerotic passion can flourish. This possibility is almost overwhelmingly strong in the poem:

> The palme playe,* where, dispoyled for the game,
> With dased eyes oft we by gleames of love
> Have mist the ball and got sight of our dame
> To bayte her eyes which kept the leddes above.
>
> (ll. 13–16)
>
> *=handball

Ostensibly, the "dased" lovers have their minds on the "dame" in the tower, whose attention they solicit; but this dazing follows the description of male stripping for the game, and the "bayting" of the woman's eyes can also imply their deception. Is the game of handball, like all other tournaments and competitions to which the poem refers, the pretext and deception under which homoerotic passion flourishes?

If anything, the homoerotic idyll of the poem intensifies as it goes along, becoming increasingly explicit:

> The secret thoughtes imparted with such trust,
> The wanton talke, the dyvers chaung of playe,

The friendshipp sworne, eche promyse kept so just,
Wherwith we past the winter nightes awaye.

(ll. 37–40)

The problem, of course, with this love, which possibly includes the "chaung of playe" entailed in homosexual role-reversals, is its "adolescence" according to a neolatin teleology of psychosexual development to which Surrey apparently subscribes: it is doubly doomed, meaning fated to happen and fated to end. The autobiographical Surrey becomes a collaborator in this fate.

The external circumstances that separated Surrey from his boyhood friend, including the death of that friend in 1536, should by now have assumed their proper "fatefulness" in my discussion, as should the circumstances that made Surrey a prisoner in Windsor in 1537. There is however another fatality in the poem, namely the incipient, "Chaucerian" murderousness of the rivalry between the two young friends. This is the aspect of Greek love that Latinity will not tolerate within its repertoire of *mens sana in corpore sano*. When we hear, for example, that each "did plead the others right" (l. 10), we are hearing of a process in which one learns to take the enviable place of the other. Similarly, when we hear that the youths speak "With wordes and looks that Tygers could but rewe" (l. 11), we need to recognize that these heart-melting lambs may already be exchanging veiled words and looks that tigers might envy rather than pity.

The idyll, which is also the poem's rather labored, prolonged, and retroactive representation of innocence (staving off a knowledge already possessed), ends when Surrey remembers the nights, shocking to recall, spent with his noble "fere" (companion; one to be feared): "And with this thought the blood forsakes my face" (l. 41). What then comes back is the present in which the friend is dead and the imprisoned Surrey is left to mourn inconsolably: "thus I my playnt renewe" (l. 44). Windsor, too, becomes the "place of blys! renewer of my woos!" (l. 45), and it is now called to account for the death of the friend.

If there is clearly something suspect about this nostalgic grieving and fault-finding, perhaps that is because we have learned to regard Surrey's touch as mortal and thus always in some sense the cause of disaster to all who love him. We will also recall the totally arbitrary, willful, all-renewing happy sorrower in the English spring landscape. Perhaps it is he who here again "renews" his plaint—having made plaint his own lethal genre—in a rather willful and synthetic act of mourning. This sorrower is not one who taps a bottomless well of grief so much as one who engulfs everything, including the friendly rival whose death has become necessary, in the abyss of his own self-love. If Surrey's brotherly love is tantamount to an effective death wish on behalf of the beloved, however, it is so on his own behalf as well; he is not just his own inadequate love-object, but a "weak" subject who cannot even begin to occupy the void of his own desire.

Surrey concludes here with the relatively familiar *topos* of a free childhood landscape turned adult prison (as does Wyatt on occasion), but with that *topos* rather unusually and explicitly hollowed out:

> Each wall, alas, that dothe my sorowe rewe,
> Retournes therto a hollowe sound of playnt.
> Thus I, alone, where all my fredome grewe,
> In pryson pyne with bondage and restraynt.
>
> (ll. 49–52)

The plaints of Surrey imprisoned in Windsor are "hollowed" in the sense that they come back to him as the endless, amplified rebounding of his own self-admired lyric voice. It is thus the wanted response—he has found the audience of his own desire in the resonant vault—although it is a stony response, mocking any appeal for sympathy from one who has so thoroughly alienated it. The plaints are also hollow, however, in that they mourn a defeated rival, whose death has been wished on him, and whose death is also necessary as a cause of renewed plaint. They are hollow, finally, since Surrey has put himself in the place of which he complains: the prison suicidally pursued through public indiscretion; the place of the king; the place of the sole poetic inheritor, possessed of the one (solo) voice that constantly regenerates itself, at whatever cost to its possessor or to others. Surrey's pastoral freedom is never more relentlessly pursued than when its other face as pastoral imprisonment has been disclosed, and when its no longer innocent conditions include *Brudermord* and effective *Selbstmord*.

The poems in which Surrey's murderous/suicidal/amatory poetics (a.k.a. politics) most markedly reveal themselves are ones that mourn Wyatt, an undertaking to which Surrey systematically dedicates himself, narcissistically hoping, no doubt, in the manner of "Lycidas," that some brother will do the like for him.[21] The poems in question are too numerous and complex to consider in any detail here, but perhaps enough has been said already to establish some terms for their reading.

> Dyvers thy death doo dyverslye bemone.
> Some that in presence of that livelye hedd
> Lurked, whose brestes envye with hate had sowne,
> Yeld Cesars teres uppon Pompeius hedd.
> Some, that watched with the murdrers knyfe,
> With egre thurst to drynke thy guyltles blood,
> Whose practyse brake by happye end of lyfe,
> Weape envyous teres to here thy fame so good.
> But I that knewe what harbourd in that hedd,
> What vertues rare were tempred in that brest,
> Honour the place that such a jewell bredd,
> And kysse the ground where as thy coorse doth rest
> With vaporde eyes; from whence suche streames avayle
> As Pyramus did on Thisbes brest bewayle.
>
>   (189)

Surrey's almost hysterically melodramatic disavowal of "dyvers" bad ways of mourning Wyatt—though there seem only to be two, the hypocritical and the envious, which are finally the same—again almost undeniably fingers Henry VIII as the troubler of Wyatt's final days. As usual, this fingering incriminates the one who points, just as the disavowals incriminate their speaker. On this solemn occasion, however, Surrey exploits the elegant octave-sestet division of the sonnet and the pivoting disjunction of the "but" it allows. Through this self-differentiating turn, Surrey breathtakingly appropriates authentic mourning of Wyatt—as distinct from others' vampirism—and hence possession of the true Wyatt heritage. (This presumption, too, we have encountered before in Surrey, and it is that of the poet-as-best-critic.)

In a sense, the rites of inheritance that Surrey is staging here are wholly normal, and look more like the rites of oedipal accession than of brotherly grieving. Yet typically Surrey goes the extra yard. Claiming to have known what was in Wyatt's mind is claiming to have been in his place—to have been him, in effect—and thus to have died with or even, weirdly, before him. The "live" Surrey is now also a posthumous one, surviving his own extinction in, with, and as the beloved Thomas Wyatt. This peculiar scenario, in which times of death, causes and effects, and gender roles seem notably confused, is what we are left with in the Pyramus and Thisbe story with which the poem ends. About this conclusion it may be enough to say with the editor: "Thisbe slew herself, thinking her lover Pyramus was dead. He then committed suicide" (189 n. 14).

~~~

To conclude, then, what does Surrey "dictate," not so much from a position of absolute originality but from a powerfully mediating one, to his English successors? His are admittedly the peculiar poetics of a minor poet, self-consciously a loser, and the Germanic enormities promised at the beginning of my discussion tend on closer inspection to shrink, leaving a commanding but commonplace Latinity in possession. The phenomena of *Selbstmord*, *Brudermord*, and *Liebestod*, however peculiarly inflected by Surrey, apparently remain phenomena that Latinity has effectively decreed to be those of *puerility* or *adolescence* on the one hand, or of *degeneracy* and *unnaturalness* on the other. They are not forms of a virility or virtue that magisterially controls them and exists only in the act of controlling them. Yet, as I have already suggested, Surrey's perverse dictation is a fairly conspicuous phenomenon through the Elizabethan period. And although it would be absurd to claim that he dictates *Hamlet*, he nevertheless prefigures the Hamlet who, apart from everything else, dictates at the end of the play that his story continue to be told in perpetuity.

It is not just that the melancholic Surrey is the type of Hamlet; there are similar types in the culture before Surrey or Hamlet, and perhaps Chaucer's Black Knight is the English original. Rather, the Germanic narrative of Saxo-Grammaticus, which for Shakespeare (or Hamlet) is openly a counterclassical, anti-Virgilian one, seemingly imports an unconquerable death wish/drive into the overlaid, competing oedipal and homosocial scenarios of the play (the former, of course, having been identified by Freud at the expense of the latter, with such momentous consequences).[22]

It is the endless scandal of *Hamlet* that it has a hero who apparently wants to do nothing but die (or to own death); who is and is not mad; is and is not a loser; is and is not supremely distinguished; and whose cruelly manic-melancholic willfulness seemingly provokes and defeats all healthy constructions. A hero who distinguishes himself, in the phrase of Wilson Knight, as the ambassador of death, but who must also acknowledge that the pursuit of death is the ridiculous pursuit of what is absolutely "common," not quite the distinguished thing at last. A hero who, knowingly walking into a death trap, finally effects *Selbstmord*, *Brudermord*, and *Liebestod* in the same sublime moment with a rival (Laertes). In short, what Shakespeare imports in and through *Hamlet*, Freud may finally intuit to be the Death Wish, a scandalous, unspeakable, and perhaps Germanic absurdity or repressed origin in any normal scheme of neoclassical self-construction and cultural advancement, however harsh.[23]

And what Surrey's poetic *oeuvre* speaks of is not just "narcissism." This is the condition that Latinity has already gendered masculine and decreed to be puerile (a question of images); has retroactively determined to be infantile as well ("his majesty the baby"); and regards as incipiently delusional but subject to abrogation and complex cultural reconstruction. Rather, what it speaks of is something prior to narcissistic *determination*, which, remaining in the Germanic register, I shall try calling *Selbstsucht*: that which is at once selfish, self-seeking, and self-wishing. This "original" *Selbstsucht*, of which the "born" aristocrat is a figure, can be conceived as that which at once knows a self and knows it only as the object of a perpetual, insatiable wishing and seeking ("Sucht" is also "quest") to which the only feared and desired end is the paradoxical one of annihilation. This premoral *Selbstsucht* can then be regarded as the constant, inadmissible origin, interior, and undoing of all constructions and putative embodiments that it subsequently inhabits; it can also be regarded, on account of its undoing of itself and everything else, as the paradoxical origin of any possible originality. This *Selbstsucht*, which knows no self except a defective one, wants all selves except mediocre ones, and can be satisfied by none. It may play itself out most successfully in drama, but for its revelation we may find it convenient to turn to the lyric poems of Surrey.

3

Remembering Thomas More: The
Encomium moriae of William Roper

My subtitle refers to *The Life of Sir Thomas More*, written by More's son-in-law, William Roper, and circulated, for obvious reasons, only after the English Catholic restoration in 1553.[1] This subtitle also announces that I will read that text as Roper's *encomium moriae*—as praise of folly, with the well-known pun on More's family name—despite its guise as sober biography and powerful hagiography. My purpose is to see what reading this text as one in the peculiar Renaissance antiform (also metaform) of *encomium moriae* can elicit from it or reveal about the much-studied life it represents. It is also to establish, in the light of the foregoing discussion, just what is generic—or singular, or oddly both at once—about More's historical presence and textual representation in the English Renaissance.

Erasmus implies a condition of generic singularity in writing his *Encomium moriae*. The parodied form of the classical encomium becomes the form proper not merely to fools as a class, but to a singular, punningly named individual (More) who thus acquires, so to speak, his definitive personal form as well. Or, to put it differently, praiseworthy fools as a class will forever be eponymously represented by the individual More. The form of absolute identity, then, which consists in "owning" a particular form but also thereby representing a large (or universal) class of others, seems to be achieved on More's behalf in the *Encomium moriae*.

This achievement, however, is also one that ironizes the aspiration. Erasmus "achieves" a form that comes close to being a Renaissance invention, but only as a form of pure self-contradiction;

a loose, parodic antiform, of which the singular Thomas More is the absent, nominal, or coded subject. This state of affairs constitutes the *reductio ad absurdum* of, as well as the logical conclusion to, certain trends in the discourse of form that we have been pursuing. It also constitutes an extreme and indeed universal instance of identity as nonidentity, in which the nonidentity of Erasmus as author of "his" *Encomium moriae* is also implicated.

Roper's version of *encomium moriae* is less radical than Erasmus's—certainly less humorous—yet it may also be informed by a certain realization, whether conscious or not, of what is implied in Erasmus. My reading of Roper's text can most conveniently proceed through successive steps corresponding to various senses of the world "folly" (*folie*), and it will come to the point at the end rather than at the beginning.

～～～

With the help of the Yale edition, Roper's *Life* of More has now safely entered academic circulation, so a certain primary assimilation of it can be taken for granted.[2] Roper's *Life* has also supplied some leverage in modern criticism insofar as Stephen Greenblatt has used its opening anecdote, in which the young Thomas More shows his prowess as spontaneous theatrical performer in the revels of his patron, Cardinal Morton, to establish a theatrical (folly) version both of More's life and of the Renaissance political world.[3] In Greenblatt's work, we find More as primordial self-fashioner on the threshold of the English Renaissance.

This use of the Roper anecdote is legitimate, and the argument I will be making extends Greenblatt's rather than being at odds with it. I want to suspend the question of theatricality for a moment, however, returning to it only at the end of the chapter. Here I will simply remark that a theatrical Thomas More is the antithesis of the one that Roper apparently wants to present, who is a figure of saintly constancy.[4] This is the view taken by the Yale editors, who consider Roper to be portraying More as a fundamentally

un- or antiprotean figure, stoically opposed to the theatrical metamorphoses that he is so prodigiously equipped to perform. The
editorial premise, which is that Roper's *Life* stably and straight-
forwardly instantiates the genre of stoic hagiography, is the base-
line from which my own argument will progressively deviate.

If there is one slightly discordant note in the editors' appreciation, it is sounded when they draw attention to a general feature
of the book, namely that William Roper is present in it in at least
two guises. He is the middle-aged author recalling a Thomas
More who has died twenty years earlier, and he is also the young
William Roper, first a member of More's household and then his
son-in-law by virtue of marriage to More's eldest daughter, Margaret. Generally, the younger Roper is shown as a participant in
pithy dialogues with More, in which More typically has the last
word. About this self-representation by Roper the editors ob-
serve: "The fictional Roper is simple, direct, unsophisticated—
Lemuel Gulliver in sixteenth century dress" (xv). The suggestion
here is that the gentle and possibly unwitting humor of Roper's
self-portrayal operates wholly at his own expense as worldling,
which is also to say, to the greater glory of Thomas More. Nevertheless, the unsettling possibility already surfaces that sanctity exists only in the eye of the naive beholder.

Before I discuss the split identity of Roper, I want briefly to
retrace with the editors the straightforward hagiographic reading
of this text, bearing in mind that medieval and Renaissance hagiography often perspicuously incorporates elements of classical
biography and eulogy. Roper begins by announcing a strict hagiographic intention, namely that of recording the life of a Christian man of "singular virtue and of a clear, unspotted conscience
. . . more pure and white than the whitest snow" (197). In principle, the canonization of More is fully anticipated here. More
broadly, Roper reveals a hagiographic intention in the sense that
he proposes no authorial criticism of More. Under whatever guise
More will appear in the book, whether as Christian or humanist
wit or lawyer or chancellor—and More's well-known accomplish-

ments are mentioned early on—nothing will compromise the presentation of the saintly figure.

This intention is supported throughout the book by Roper's making More a figure of exemplary constancy in an unstable world, and beyond that by showing More repeatedly calming those, particularly in his extended family, who are afflicted by the terrors of the moment. More as father, as father-surrogate, and as authoritative teacher will typically recall the anxious to a religious conviction of the transitory unimportance and certain misery of worldly affairs, directing them always to consider final rather than immediate concerns. His response to his wife near the end of his life repeats and summarizes many such responses earlier on: when she chides him about the stubbornness that has landed him in a prison cell under threat of execution, he says: "Is not this house as nigh heaven as my own?" (243).

Roper's moving hagiographic presentation is strengthened by a recurrent emphasis on More's piety and devotion, on his regular withdrawal to his own private building for meditation and religious exercises, by the sober-mindedness and independence that lead him slowly to withdraw from the privileged roles of house humanist and "merry" entertainer to the young, light-minded Henry VIII.[5] This sobriety is compatible, in Roper's portrayal, with More's primary sense of obligation to his family, not the court. It also implies the capacity for self-detachment that will enable More to become, as he quintessentially is for Roper, a hero of conscience, first in relinquishing the chancellorship and then in the act of martyrdom. The More who is eventually martyred in Roper's account is not, however, the passive victim of Henry VIII's scandalous will, nor just a conscientious objector to it, but one who has long since made destiny his choice. Or, to appropriate a phrase of T. S. Eliot's, he is the one who has foreseen and foresuffered all, in which case his relation to many events in the course of the narrative can only be ironic. Even the phase of the narrative that ends with More's execution is preempted by More, and is presumably redundant except for its heuristic value to the reader.

Altogether conventionally in Roper's account, More is presented from the start as one marked out by destiny. The prodigious display in Cardinal Morton's house, to which I have already referred, leads the Cardinal to prophesy that "this child here waiting at the table, whosoever shall live to see it, will prove a marvellous man" (198). In the revels context in which the prophecy is made—and it is not the only prophecy of which More is the subject—it would seem as if a great secular career is being predicted for the protean *Wunderkind*. This prophecy is of course fulfilled in More's chancellorship, then in a sense negated when More ceases to be chancellor, but finally and authentically fulfilled on the scaffold, where the "marvellous" approaches the level of the miraculous. By the time this authentic fulfillment occurs, however, More has also become the book's one truly prophetic speaker, and thus preemptively the author of himself and everything else around him. What he prophesies in the long term is the displacement of the Catholic Church in England, and in the short term he foresees that as a result of the king's marriage to Anne Boleyn an oath will be administered that he will be unable to swear. He thus implicitly prophesies his own martyrdom for the true faith, even though, to avoid the mortal sin of suicide, he does attempt by legal fencing to stave off this outcome. So fully does he become the book's prophesying speaker, and thus the real author of his own and Roper's *Life*, that a certain dread begins to attend his pronouncements. On one occasion Roper records that: "I, at that time seeing no likelihood thereof, yet fearing lest for his forespeaking it would the sooner come to pass, waxed therefore for his so saying much offended with him" (229).

One could go on listing hagiographic components, such as More's lifelong wearing of a hairshirt under his secular dress, thus making himself a secular performer on the outside only, and enabling him to carry the monastic vocation with him into the world. One could also remark with the editors that More's appearing increasingly alien and unintelligible to those around him implies his belonging to an order radically other than that of "the world." But instead of listing forever, I want to remark on one rather important feature of Roper's hagiographic representation. It is that the "angelical wit" of Thomas More, alluded to in the first paragraph of the book, remains a constant even though it passes through successive phases. It is what first makes him acceptable as a boon companion to the young king, but More repudiates that role and that meaning of wit. His wit then more soberly and didactically manifests itself in the sharp conclusions to the dialogues in which he participates, and in his legalistic fencing at his own trial. Finally, however, the witty jester—still the *Wunderkind* of the Cardinal Morton festivities—reappears in and as the figure of the martyr on the scaffold; it is there that More once again becomes a joker, uttering such witticisms as "I pray you Master Lieutenant, see me safe up and, for my coming down, let me shift for myself" (254). Not only does the full meaning of Roper's phrase "angelical wit" get disclosed right at the end, but the scaffold, in its double or now indifferent sense as stage and execution platform, becomes the appointed end to the line of wit, both in this text and in the life of its subject. Already we have uncovered one sense in which Roper's *Life* is *encomium moriae*, a praise of the witty reveler, and none the less so for its being a representation of saintly constancy.

To read Roper's *Life* as a praise of folly in this sense is to read it compatibly, I would suggest, with Erasmus's *Encomium moriae*, which not only appreciates More but makes Christian piety virtually unthinkable except as saving (not merely suicidal) folly. Roper names Erasmus in the first paragraph of his text as More's principal character witness, and perhaps his understanding of that testimony is a little more profound than it has received credit for being. Even this saintly "deviation" into folly, however, threatens the pious hagiographic concord, not just in the book but between it and the reader. The possibility that surfaces together with that of saintly folly is obsessional "humor"—that is, pathology—of which More has quite widely been suspected by critics and biographers. And once the hagiographical concord has been disturbed by any *satirical* discord, the damage will be hard to limit. We will also have to begin talking about representation rather than immediate presentation.

If this occurs to the editors when they introduce the Gulliver comparison, they give no indication of it. They make the comparison in passing only, without consequence. Yet if it is taken seriously, a reversal of perspective must also be anticipated, in which the naive observer becomes a device of exposure. This threatening possibility—threatening in the end to any reader of the text as well as to those represented in it—is not recognized by the editors, who further appear to believe that Roper, unlike the major historical figures with whom More interacts, is merely a neutral witness to the drama of More's life.

Whichever way the Roper persona works, and it will not have to do so consistently in any single way, the fiction of the book (or at least of the editors) is that neutral observation can be separated from interpretation. We are to believe that while young Roper discharges the observer function in the book, the authorial Roper, now empowered by age, experience, and hindsight, discharges the interpreter function. If we accept this fiction, we will see what young Roper sees in the immediacy of his present tense, and will also be able to compare this with the interpretation presented by the author. For certain purposes, this fiction will do; it even helps to elicit the full range of "folly" in the text. Adhering, then, for the moment to the distinction between seeing and interpreting—to which in this context we can add eyewitnessing and bearing deliberate witness—let us consider what young Roper sees. Equally, let us consider what young Roper hears, supposedly without any power to interpret it.

To avoid redundancy, I shall briefly summarize young Roper's testimony under two headings, first, that which concerns More as political figure and second that which concerns More's family life.

These two classes of testimony are not unrelated, since throughout the narrative public and family life apparently stand towards one another in a relation of simultaneous difference and sameness: difference inasmuch as the family becomes a retreat from public life and a locus of Christian-stoic value opposed to the passionate valuelessness of public life; sameness inasmuch as the family becomes a small commonwealth presided over by More. Difference again in that the almost theocratic family commonwealth is the good one opposed to the bad one outside; sameness again insofar as the figure of More who presides over that commonwealth is, in his own way, as absolute a monarch as Henry VIII— if not "more" so, in a pun that will insist on being heard as my argument continues.

For authorial Roper, More is a hero of conscience, but what we see from the perspective of his son-in-law is catastrophic political failure. This perception is confirmed to some degree by modern interpretation of the Henrician political scene.[6] In the narrative, More is formidably equipped to succeed, first by being naturally gifted, second by being uniquely well qualified as a lawyer, and third by virtue of a certain nerve, which he displays as a very young parliamentarian opposing a tax demanded by Henry VII. If, from the hagiographic point of view, More is already acting on principle by opposing Henry at the risk of his entire future and perhaps his life, from a political point of view he is taking the necessary gamble for which the prize is recognition. The same applies to a second incident, when he opposes Henry VIII's will as articulated by the hugely domineering Cardinal Wolsey. In this instance again, carefully calculated resistance, eventually dissipated in charming flattery of Wolsey, does More no long-term damage; indeed it is one event in a train that leads first of all to his becoming the king's favorite and then to his becoming Wolsey's successor as chancellor. The rule of *post hoc, non ergo propter hoc* certainly applies here, but the oppositional Thomas More is as certainly the one who becomes the coopted, successful Thomas

More—and perhaps the one who has betrayed his commitments as parliamentarian and citizen to become a royal favorite.

More's advance in political power and social status is accompanied, however, by behavior that, while undoubtedly fitting the hagiographic interpretation, also looks self-thwarting and perverse. Having made a place for himself in the royal household, he calculatedly withdraws from it in order, as Roper tells us, to return to family life. Later, when he is nevertheless made Lord Chancellor, he opposes Henry VIII's desire to divorce Catherine of Aragon and marry Anne Boleyn. Foreseeing a complete impasse, he relinquishes the chancellorship after a term lasting less than two years. The great promise is thus defeated, and More's political career ends. All this we can "see," with the help of young Roper as neutral witness.

But we can see more than this. Roper, for example, reports two significant exchanges between More and the Duke of Norfolk, in which the Duke unavailingly tries to act as a political mentor to More. In the first of these exchanges, the Duke objects to More's behavior when More, as Lord Chancellor, joins the choir at a service in the parish church of Chelsea. The Duke says: "God body, God body, my Lord Chancellor, a parish clerk! You dishonor the king and his office" (225). For the Duke, who is exasperated rather than awed by this show of pious humility, More has violated a decorum proper to the political world as such. The Duke also confidently opposes royal to holy office, blasphemously underlining his own allegiances.

Ironically, if we recall *Utopia*, it is More who is now placed in the Hythlodaeus position while the Duke occupies the More position; in that text, Hythlodaeus is criticized by More for affecting singularity in the name of conscience, and is also accused of failing to recognize the political world as theater, in which the violation of decorum is simply inadmissible.[7] And in *Utopia* the issue of conscience is not all on one side either. The point made by the More figure is that nothing can be achieved in the political world, which is in effect everywhere while utopia is nowhere, unless the game is played according to the given rules and conventions, and with the given performers already onstage. To enter the play and then repudiate it, or indecorously to flout its generic require-ments, is to unfit oneself for any constructive part in it. The Duke of Norfolk, in other words, is no praiser of More's folly, but a sharp critic of it. Of course, More has the last word:

> "Nay," quoth Sir Thomas More, smiling upon the Duke: "Your grace may not think that the King, your master and mine, will with me for serving of God, his master, be offended or thereby count his office dishonored." (225)

Here More as pious didact corrects the Duke *de haut en bas*, but on this occasion at least his political prophecy is so wide of the mark that the Duke is retroactively vindicated. Even if we hear irony in More's reply, as young Roper apparently does not, it is of the kind that merely replaces naive with sophisticated complacency.

In the second exchange of this type, the well-meaning Duke again sounds the note of exasperation with one who, despite being Lord Chancellor and presumably acquainted with the king's character, continues to behave like a political idiot:

> "By the Mass, Master More, it is perilous striving with princes. And therefore I would wish you somewhat to incline to the king's pleasure. For, by God body, Master More, *Indignatio principis mors est*." (237)

The Duke enunciates the time-tested *doxa* of political realism, here wittily sharpened by the More/*mors* pun that makes More's behavior into *suicidal* folly. From the hagiographic standpoint this is indeed a profane wisdom, here articulated by a relentlessly pro-fane speaker, yet again its witty truth is borne out in the event. And the Latin term that links the king's rage to his humiliation—*indignatio*—also links the Duke's criticism in this instance to his previous one, with the implication that insofar as the action of conscience threatens the appearance of royal power, the dignity of royal office, it only exacerbates the violence of political life instead of rendering that life morally answerable.

So what we see with young Roper and hear through his report is the history of More's incorrigible, perverse, and impenetrable folly, as when More replies again to the Duke: "Is that all, my Lord? Then in good faith there is no more difference between your grace and me, but that I shall die today and you tomorrow" (237). From this perspective, *encomium moriae* fully takes on the character of satirical praise, becoming in effect an *act* of praise through which complacent foolishness is steadily exposed. And the revelation of More's idiocy is in the most profound sense political rather than spiritual revelation, inasmuch as idiocy in its root sense, along with its cognate idiosyncracy, implies a condition not of organic brain damage but of individual separation from the *polis*, that is, from the language, conventions, and personages that constitute the political world as the only world.

Even if it were granted at this stage that young Roper's eyewitnessing and eavesdropping facilitate a disenchanted political critique of More, perhaps above all by allowing a witty voice other than More's to be heard, it may still seem premature to refer to the political world as the only world. Both that characterization and the contingent critique of More as a political figure will lack force if there is indeed a world elsewhere to which More can turn. Such, it might seem, is the little kingdom of the family, which More values more highly, and in which, as family man, he is at home. It is there that More seeks refuge; it is there that he seemingly imagines he will be left alone once he has relinquished high office, as if his personal kingdom were a place apart from the other one, in which a king has been humiliated.[8] And it is into the family domain that Roper penetrates as eyewitness, enabled to do so by being "family."

Here we must recall that the man we have been calling "young Roper" is called "son Roper" by More throughout the narrative; that is to say, son-in-law, but also virtually adoptive son. However dispassionate we may imagine the young Roper's spectatorship to be in the large public world, in the world of the family he and all those around him are dependents. More's political recklessness accordingly becomes a danger to all, including "son Roper," and it is in the face of this recklessness that son Roper inwardly steps out of his part as passive observer. The time is that in which More is threatened by the Act of Supremacy, and Roper waits for him to come home from London with news of whether he will be subject to the bill or not. More returns looking "merry," to repeat the term that is so often applied to him in the book, and Roper naturally assumes that the political danger has passed. It turns out, on the contrary, that More has practically sealed his own fate. More explains his merriment as follows: "In good faith, I rejoiced, son, that I had given the devil a foul fall; and that with these lords I had gone so far as, without great shame, I could never go back again" (236). It is then that Roper admits an inner difference: "At which words waxed I very sad; for though himself liked it well, yet liked it me but a little" (236). As son, Roper must experience More's triumph in a hallucinatory wrestling match with the devil as a direct threat to himself as well as to More: the impersonal dative construction of "yet liked it me but a little" implies Roper's sense of being vulnerable to an alien, exterior force bent on *his* destruction. What we see as well is the utterly self-regarding and self-applauding nature of More's triumph.

Son Roper admits more than this inner difference on another occasion. In the act of praying that it will not come to pass, More foresees that the marriage of Henry to Anne Boleyn will, as he says, "be confirmed with oaths," in which case he will not be able to swear. Threatened by this possibility, but even more so by the prophetic More's apparent ability to make his words come true, Roper says: "I, at that time seeing no likelihood thereof, yet fearing lest for his forespeaking it would the sooner come to pass, waxed therefore with his saying much offended with him" (229). The dread of son Roper is that More is virtually a malignant wizard, empowered to speak the future into existence though not to revoke his spells with pious disclaimers. For the son, this father is all-powerful for evil rather than for good, and as it turns out, he is also a father who cannot look after his own.

By relinquishing the chancellorship, More drastically reduces his income, and the family is threatened with impoverishment and eventual dispersal. When More returns home with this news, he facetiously explains how a progressive reduction in diet may be enough to keep the family together. But if that should not suffice, says More, they can always take to the roads: "then may we yet, with bags and wallets, go a-begging together, and hoping that for pity some good folk will give us their charity, at every man's door to sing *Salve Regina* [which queen?], and so still keep company and be merry together" (227). This archaic medieval fantasy of utopian beggary—or loser's dream of populist incitement— comes strangely from the author of *Utopia*, whose unforgettable account of the real conditions of Tudor vagabondage found a prominent place in Marx's *Capital*. What we are able to see through the eyes of son Roper is a father now grown foolishly irresponsible to the point of lunacy. The narrative records no laughter in the family at More's pleasant sallies.

More's inability to take care of his own becomes apparent after his death, when his estate is confiscated. He has admittedly made a will providing for his family, but by then his legalistic defense of himself has already failed despite its brilliance, simply because it defies the king's will. He must or should know that every legal device will similarly fail under the same circumstances, and so it proves—or almost does, since there is an interesting minor exception to which we will come in a moment. In principle, however, More cannot expect to avoid the king's anger even posthumously through any legal maneuver, and the book confirms his inability to protect his "subjects" in his life or after it.

The book also, finally, records a moment of outright rebellion in this ill-governed "kingdom." Towards the end, More has his own last dialogue with his wife, which is also the only dialogue with her that the book records. The wife, Dame Alice, apparently belongs to the world of vulgar comedy rather than saintly seriousness, and she has certainly been taught to regard herself as a fool. Her whole impassioned appeal to More expresses flat incomprehension at his stubborn choice of a prison cell over his congenial house and gardens and the company of his devoted family. His singularity in this respect is all the more provoking to her as "the bishops and best learned of this realm" (243) have all fallen into line. Again, as in the case of the Duke of Norfolk, the note of blank exasperation is sounded: "I muse what, a God's name, you mean here still thus fondly to tarry" (243). More responds to this accusation precisely of *folly* ("thus fondly") with syllogistic precision, and typically concludes by saying: "Is not this house as nigh heaven as my own?"

This is where the exchange should end, as it does when More says virtually the same thing to the profane Duke of Norfolk. Yet Dame Alice replies: "Tille-valle; tille-valle" and "*Bone deus, bone deus*, man, will this gear never be left?" Provoked by this vulgar resistance, More goes beyond his normal script:

> I see no great cause why I should much joy either of my gay house or of anything belonging there unto, when, if I should but seven years lie buried under the ground and then arise and come thither again, I should not fail to find some therein that would bid me get out of doors and tell me it were none of mine. What cause have I then to like such an house as would so soon forget his master?

What is betrayed in a flash here is the paranoid nature of his own absolute and self-regarding domestic kingship and his sense of beleaguered isolation even in the family. He has heard his wife's appeal virtually as manifestation of her greedy attachment to his property. His unexpected punitive resentment makes the subsequent failure of his will to hold up look like a horrible *success* foreseen by the brilliant lawyer he is. The family will be stripped of the property that it covets, and that it would deny him. What we see, moreover, is a More already dead in his own imagination: a Martin Guerre rejected at his own return or a resurrected Christ repudiated by those to whom he returns. Anticipating his own betrayal, More betrays himself, and the enormity of the revelation is not diminished by Roper's deadpan reporting. The text as *encomium moriae* becomes at this moment the exposure of More as a diabolically melancholic wit, on reflection a specialist in wicked gallows humor throughout the book, who can well afford to jest on the scaffold in anticipation of the coming revenge on his faithless subjects.

What I have suggested so far is that Roper's *Life* of More can be read as an *encomium moriae* in the positive, evangelical sense we rightly or wrongly associate with Erasmus and also, after the initial editorial prompting, in various negative or satirical senses. In the latter case, the "exposure" of More implies a filial loathing so virulent, an iconoclasm so ferocious, a desire to commit biographical murder so irresistible, as to call for practically unconscious expression, or for the deep self-censorship of hagiographic decorum.

To draw attention to this doubleness in the text is, however, to reinforce certain other oppositions, such as that between epideictic praise and blame, between seeing and interpreting, between the sacred and the profane, between the spiritual and the political. This two-sided reading, facilitated by the split identity of Roper in the text, tends thus to be a prematurely restabilizing one: the opposed terms are not only fixed traditional ones—all a bit tired, at that—but mutually confirming. Yet the *encomium moriae* as a Renaissance genre does not readily shake down in this way or produce balanced equations. The endless circulatory play of folly in the text, a circulation we can track to some degree through the semantic transformations of "merry" and its derivatives, doesn't come to rest along the simply polarized lines that I have drawn so far.

Nor does the witnessing of folly. This is the function we have so far assigned to young Roper, but really the act of witnessing is widely dispersed through the text: Thomas More as martyr witnesses or bears witness to something; so does the Erasmus who testifies paradoxically to More's upright character; so does the Richard Rich who informs against More; so does the text itself; so does the reader of the text. I will end, then, by identifying one final version of folly to which this text bears complicated witness. I would identify it as the superform of folly in the text, meaning either the one that subsumes the entire play of folly considered thus far and redetermines its content, or the one that emerges as a hallucinatory transcendence of that endless, debilitating play.

One detail on which son Roper dwells is the hairshirt that More, a sometime Carthusian, wears throughout his life under his secular costume. Whether we regard this as impressive, or silly, or masochistic, it implies More's desire to prolong the monastic vocation even under the circumstances of public life. We can readily say that the text problematizes the value of political sainthood both in general terms and in the specific, postmedieval context of Henry VIII's reign. This is, however, to take the hairshirt as having, and having only, a rather narrow and conventional range of significations. In the text, it is no such simple or stable signifier, as the following passage with its interplay of singularity and doubleness will begin to suggest. Of More, Roper says that:

> [to avoid] singularity would he appear none otherwise than other men in his apparel and other behavior. And albeit outwardly he appeared honorable like one of his calling, yet inwardly he, no such vanities esteeming, secretly next his body wore a shirt of hair. Which my sister More, a young gentlewoman, in the summer as he sat at supper singly in his doublet and hose, wearing thereupon a plain shirt without ruff or collar, chancing to spy began to laugh at it. My wife, not ignorant of his manner, perceiving the same, privily told him of it. And he, being sorry that she saw it, presently amended it. (223–24)

Through this accident, the hairshirt becomes an open secret in the family and perhaps beyond. Whatever one makes of this—and we are dealing, after all, with Thomas More, whose almost sinister command of literary *sprezzatura Utopia* exemplifies—it is an artless disclosure that makes known More's "private" self-mortification; it also incipiently makes More not a figure with an inside and an outside, but an empty or inaccessible one wearing costumes within costumes.[9] But it turns out that even before this accidental disclosure, the secret of More's hairshirt was already open, since in the same paragraph I have quoted, we learn that More's secret habit was already known to his other daughter Margaret, Roper's wife, and probably to Roper as well. Did it become the *famous* hairshirt only after Roper had published his work, or was it famous during More's lifetime? And if it was, is the wearing of the hairshirt an act of monstrous vanity—of folly in that sense? This is a question about More, but it raises questions about son Roper's being privy to the secret of the hairshirt, and finally publicizing it.

In fact, the amount of emphasis Roper gives to the hairshirt in his narrative implies that it becomes *his* hairshirt as much as it is More's. We learn that the hairshirt is officially a secret, so to speak, between More and his daughter Margaret. If it is a secret between More and his own wife, we are not told so. Margaret is not just in on the secret, which thereby becomes open, but has the unique privilege of washing the shirt periodically, apparently not objecting to this intimate and somewhat distasteful requirement of her father's. The hairshirt accordingly constitutes an open/secret bond of considerable intimacy between More and his married daughter. Son Roper not only records the facts, but remains a constant enforced witness to them in a triangular relationship that he impossibly inhabits as son, brother, husband, and voyeur. Hardly a condition of neutral spectatorship.

Through the agency of what we might now call Roper's *interested* spectatorship, we are enabled to see that the hairshirt functions as an incestuous bond and continuing line of enforced division; as a mark of endless symbolic transgression and self-punishment; and as the emblem of a carnal soiling that is repeatedly washed away by the only one who has the power of ablution/absolution, namely the daughter who is the object of More's passion. I must emphasize the term "incestuousness": *incest* between More and his daughter can neither be assumed nor ruled out, and we will presumably never know; *incestuousness*, on the other hand, allows for both these possibilities, to which attention is drawn in the text by the behavior of *all* parties involved. It more importantly implies, moreover, that incestuous desire is not inwardly consumed in any individual or in the nuclear family; either it is cut off in the family and displaced outward into the world, or at least a sufficient residue remains for "outward" politicization.[10]

These incestuous suppositions are reinforced when, towards the end of the book, Margaret waits for More as he is led to the Tower. Or, as Roper tells it, "his daughter—my wife—[was] desirous to see her father" (251). She wishes to see her father for the last time and receive his blessing (etymologically benediction and wounding), says Roper, and so urgent is this wish that:

> without consideration or care of herself, pressing in among the midst of the throng and company of the guard, that with halberds and bills went round about him, hastily ran to him and there openly, in the sight of them all, embraced him, took him about the neck, and kissed him. Who, well liking her most natural and dear daughterly affection towards him, gave her his fatherly blessing and many goodly words of comfort besides. From whom after she was departed she, not satisfied with the former sight of him and like one that had forgotten herself, being all-ravished with the entire love of her dear father, having respect neither to herself nor to the press of people . . . suddenly turned back again, ran to him as before, took him about the neck, and divers times together most lovingly kissed him. (251–52)

Among the things More is then quoted as saying to her is this:

> I never liked your manner towards me better than when you kissed me last. For I like when daughterly love and dear charity hath no leisure to look to worldly courtesy. (252)

At the last moment, the ravished Margaret passionately declares herself, against all odds including the threat of death. Stoic, self-punishing More simultaneously acknowledges both the motive and the fact of gratification—of supreme *pleasure*—in the moment of sanctified incestuousness in which "daughterly love and dear charity" display themselves without regard to worldly courtesy. The law of nature finally prevails within and against the law

of nations that More has professed and in his own way subverted;
it prevails within and against the entire order of Renaissance
"courtesy"; it seemingly prevails even within and against the discourse of Christian charity.

More can perhaps afford to joke on the scaffold, the imminence
of which alone could have forced this consummation, cutting off
all dilatory "leisure" and leaving nothing to be desired. *This* is the
great scene of the text, precipitated when Margaret makes a scene;
the one on the scaffold can only be a tragicomic postlude to it.
And the significance of this scene appears to be confirmed by the
fact that Margaret and son Roper alone escape the ruin that engulfs the rest of the family: More has transferred property to them
before his death, in an apparently successful effort to protect his
favorite. (On the other hand, that the device is both sensible and
successful leaves us to suspect that it may be Roper's. He is a lawyer, and it may be that he works through More's witnessed passion
for his daughter to save what he can from the wreck.)

By including this moving scene, Roper's *Life* becomes the *encomium moriae* that enshrines the grand folly of two passionate
natures even as it exposes the nature of that passion. Or perhaps
it can be a praise only of Margaret's folly in that romantic sense—
if even of hers—since for More what is at stake seems to be something more like power than love. At last, he rather than she becomes the object of tabooed passion, and the witnessing of her
passion by the world is the witnessing of his utterly exclusive and
unassailable power over her, over his son-in-law, over "worldly
courtesy," and finally over the king who cannot touch him in this
one place of utter singularity. More is *solus rex*, while Henry with
his flighty Anne Boleyn is on the way to becoming a public
cuckold.

If this praise of folly has to be paradoxical indeed, considering
what is praised and by whom, some of its vertiginousness comes
from Roper's impossible situation as spectator/participant. As
son, he is at once given and denied the sister/daughter his father
covets; as husband, he must become at once a spectator to his own

displacement and a vicarious participant in his father's forbidden conquest; as theatrical onlooker he cannot but be moved by the great final spectacle at the Tower gate; and as putative author he is the privileged witness to something like the primal scene. Well may he write in the paragraph in which he introduces himself: "I, William Roper . . . knowing—at this day—no one man living that of him and his doings understood so much as myself . . ." (197). What this syntax implies, however, is that not even Roper is *"one man living"*—one man whole and all-knowing—and that to know More *well* is not to know him impartially or from any single standpoint, but always in a number of interesting (and interested) aspects and positions that don't wholly add up.

The question now is what, critically, is to be made of all this. I would not want to make Roper's *Life* the text in which incest becomes the dirty secret poisoning the atmosphere and giving the reader something like a blackmailer's grip on the "character" of Thomas More. I would also not want to make the discovery of this secret into a form of pious, antihagiographic exposure, partly because the secret *is* open, and its being so seems to be the point of it for More; partly because the form of hagiography is a fascinatingly problematic one throughout the Renaissance.

In the thematic context of this book, however, I should like to suggest two things. First, that this text embodies a strong paradigm in establishing the daughterly seduction and absolution scenario as one central to the patriarchal construction of power, a definitively triangular construction requiring the presence of the father, the willing and consenting daughter, and the displaced, spectatorial son.[11] If the aspect of daughterly absolution and ultimate reciprocation must be emphasized, it is because without it there is no patriarchy but only tyrannical male abuse. By the same token, however, the role-reversal entailed in this reciprocation paradoxically transforms the daughter from the victim into the legitimating conservator of patriarchy. She either naturalizes it by becoming the figure in whom nature will out, or else legitimizes it as abused/political woman who appropriates the father's "abused" power and position as her own. In neither case, of course, does this construction of power cease to be patriarchal. Moreover, it is Margaret who not only makes the scene but immediately repeats it, thus making herself responsible for the repetition of daughterly seduction. Without willing daughters, whether biological or constructed, there may be abusive fathers—there may, for that matter, be aging, melancholic clowns, running through increasingly threadbare routines—but there will be no patriarchs.[12]

It is to this triangular structure that Roper's text strongly draws attention, and Roper's More is one who finally inhabits its structure of simultaneous total masculine empowerment and implied dependence, of familial enclosure beyond both power and law, even—or above all—when it is seen. I would suggest that not only Roper's *Life* but such works as *Lear*, *Pericles*, and *The Tempest* eventually bear witness to the ascendancy of this scenario, whether we take it to belong exclusively to masculine fantasy or to the order of political reality.[13]

Inasmuch as this scenario prevails, I would also suggest that it implies successful resistance on the part of the father to oedipal displacement. Such is the dream of the patriarch—of patriarchy per se—and the frustrated presence of the "understanding" oedipal son, "son Roper," constitutes the best testimony to the patriarch's indefeasible ascendancy. Roper's act of biographical murder comes too late, and its paradoxical condition is that of prolonging the life of Thomas More. The incipient oedipal scenario in Roper's *Life* of More is forestalled; More remains forever in possession as father, forever possessed of the only "life" in the book. Two things enable him to do so, one being the generational cross-coupling effected with and finally by his daughter, and the other being the complicity, voluntary or otherwise, of the "son" who looks on—and whose "rightful" role has been usurped. I believe that this scenario, in which oedipal resolution is at once denied and forever deferred, calls for attention in the most "patriarchal" Renaissance texts, partly because of what I take to be its prevalence and partly by way of accounting for the relative failure of straightforward oedipal readings to engage fully with the data of these texts, as Greenblatt has recently argued in somewhat different terms.[14]

My second point is that the peculiar charge of this book's great scene comes from the public violation of taboo that occurs in it, a violation that includes the role-reversal in which the daughter becomes the pursuer of the father. The invulnerable public enactment of what is "secret" or forbidden—the *staging* of violation—becomes the supreme pleasure of this text, and perhaps quite broadly of the world in which it comes into being; even Henry VIII's pleasure seems to be of this order. Yet this staging of pleasure is indeterminately, and not contradictorily, the staging of power.

To say that this particular charged moment, which can be induced by the violation of any recognized taboo and not only by that against incest, constitutes the aesthetic moment of many Renaissance texts is not thereby to reduce the discussion of Renaissance literature to the celebration of illicit thrills and ineffable moments. It is rather to recognize in yet another way the continuity between the aesthetic and the political in those texts.

4

Remembering Cardinal Wolsey:
Whose Life?

This chapter follows in various ways from the previous one. In it, questions of "remembering," of hagiographic form, and of spectatorship rather than spectacle in the field of power are pursued, yet a certain deviant discontinuity also makes its way into the picture, both formally and thematically. While my general discussion largely assumes the inflected continuity of "anterior forms" through the Renaissance, the previous chapter has at least noted that the *encomium moriae* constitutes so marked a Renaissance distortion of the classical encomium—and even of the paradoxical encomium, which is still a classical form—that it becomes virtually an invented form as definitive of the period as it is of Erasmus or More. In this chapter, I wish to take up a bit more fully the issue of deviant discontinuity, but also of the Renaissance "paradigm" as an instance of historical discontinuity, one that still, for us, implies a break with the Middle Ages. To invoke the Renaissance at all is still to assume a moment of oppositional discontinuity between it and whatever is conceived as anterior to it, and this oppositional moment has to be continually envisaged as long as the category remains in force. Cavendish's *The Life and Death of Cardinal Wolsey* lends itself peculiarly well to this enterprise, since it can be read as the most "paradigmatic" Renaissance text of all those I consider.

Admittedly, there is reason to be wary of the Renaissance's own ways of constituting itself in its paradigmatic difference from, and implied or explicit opposition to, what preceded it. As C. S. Lewis pointed out long ago, the self-distinguishing hubris of the Renaissance in relation to the Dark Ages, the Gothic, scholasticism, medieval latinity, monasticism, and so on is at least as constitutive of its barbarism as it is of its civilization, a thought that must repeatedly strike any reader of Burckhardt.[1] It goes almost without saying now that modern attempts to privilege the Renaissance as the good origin of humanism, as the source of a liberating "Renaissance philosophy of man," or even as a period of "epochal" innovation have largely been discredited, partly because of their suspect reinvestment in certain historic forms of Renaissance *méconnaissance*,[2] and partly because recent criticism and historical representation have found it increasingly unrewarding to attempt a discourse of *fundamental* historical difference and discontinuity. For this reason among others, it is not unthinkable that we are now close to the end of a discourse of the Renaissance, yet the moment of oppositional discontinuity must no doubt continue being envisaged until the end. Or, perhaps its final unthinkability will constitute the end.

I will claim, then, that part of what is interesting about Cavendish's *Life* is precisely that it registers the emergence of a new paradigm as such. I do not claim that a concept akin to any modern one of the paradigm is available to Cavendish.[3] My suggestion is rather that we can usefully relate some features of the text to the apparent stresses of a paradigm shift—or, to put it differently, that the text behaves as if a paradigm shift were occurring.

〜〜〜

As in the case of Roper's *Life*, I shall initially approach this text from a standpoint antithetical to my own—that of Judith Anderson in *Biographical Truth: The Representation of Historical Persons in Tudor-Stuart Writing*.[4] Her discussion adopts certain notions of continuity and deviant discontinuity between the texts I am considering, and her argument is a strong one that my own discussion at once parallels and opposes.

Anderson treats Cavendish's *Life* not so much as a contingent *representation* of Cardinal Wolsey as a deficient and/or ironized portrayal of him in a tradition that begins and ends in the truth of hagiography. For her, Cavendish's text belongs to, but almost perversely deviates from, straightforward, naive-looking hagiography of the kind exemplified by Bede's *The Life of St. Cuthbert*. In Anderson's reading, the main effects of Cavendish's text are those of a confused or merely incipient artfulness and a curious, alienating distortion of the topics and patterns of the saint's life as a genre.

Having established this relation of deviant continuity between Bede's as it were naive *Life of St. Cuthbert* and Cavendish's incipiently sophisticated *Life and Death of Cardinal Wolsey*, Anderson aligns and contrasts Cavendish's text with Roper's *Life of Sir Thomas More*. In this coupling, Cavendish's text becomes the deficient, anticipatory version of a biographical kind perfected by Roper, namely the artful rather than naive hagiographic representation of a hero of conscience. More's life, according to Anderson, assumes the integrity or wholeness proper to it in Roper's complex, sophisticated, but *true* portrayal.

Anderson objects, accordingly, to the discordant and fragmentary sense of any life, including More's, that emerges from Greenblatt's discussions of self-fashioning. For her, it is as if the notion of self-fashioning can testify only to a simultaneous failure of art, life, and truth, the perfectibility of which are, however, indistinguishably manifested in a text like Roper's, a life like More's. The ipso facto privileged genre of biography—of the life—resists assimilation to the model of *self*-fashioning, and can, in a uniquely exemplary way, restore life, art, and truth to a unified wholeness. In good biography, which inseparably manifests good life, all difference (*différance*) vanishes and unity prevails.

It would be possible though no doubt unavailing to say that Anderson's conception is vulnerable to criticism—that all its categories, hierarchies, and progressions are questionable, and that problems of mimesis are elided rather than eliminated in her reading. It is probably just as unavailing to say that Roper's biography of More can be read otherwise. Anderson's reading of More/Roper constitutes an act of faith—of Christian and perhaps inescapably of Catholic witnessing—presumably unreachable by such objections. One cannot even call it a weakness of her argument that it presupposes the ideal integrity of a life prior to, and independent of, any biographical representation. Such, for her, *is* Thomas More's life, and Roper gets it right while Nicholas Harpsfield, another near-contemporary biographer, gets it wrong.

For Anderson, this integral autonomy of the life, identically reproduced in a biographical art beyond art, is not just the result of the individual's biological or cultural continuity in time. Rather, it is the manifestation of an immanent power of being. What the individual life thus instantiates is something that used to be called life itself, and for Anderson the source and guarantor of that self-identical life is Christ. His is the one Life that every saint and every good biographer must faithfully imitate, whether with naive or artful success—or failure. Even "failed" hagiography, like the failed life to which it bears witness, exists as a deficient or self-ironizing image within this preemptive order of Christian imitation.

I have rehearsed Anderson's claim at some length, and will continue to do so, partly to establish the paradigmatic reading of Cavendish not just as a reading, but as an alternative reading that can incorporate Anderson's data and arguments in terms somewhat different from her own. Before considering what is at stake in developing such a reading, however, it is necessary to say that Anderson's argument can be taken up not as an act of Christian witnessing, but for its implied view of the nature and appeal of biography as a genre. In biography, the particular image of the good life may differ according to the particular ideological frame of reference—that of Plutarch's *Lives* will obviously differ from the one in which Christian hagiography is produced—but the genre of the "life" will be one in which art and life can aspire to unite, identically manifesting the form of the *good* life. When Anderson's argument is taken up in this way, however, its force as a generic argument about biography also acknowledged, it is Cavendish's "distorted" text rather than Roper's arbitrarily designated ideal one that emerges as the interesting text.

For Anderson, Cavendish's text does not escape the rule of biographical identity: its imperfect art and life are as seamlessly fused as their perfect counterparts. Nevertheless, it is the text that as it were ironically alienates and renders defective a naive tradition of sanctity. It is the text that disturbs hagiographic representation and threateningly distorts Christian imitation before both are set to rights again by Roper. It is a text the "imperfect" quality of which implies its being unfinished; not "whole" in spite of the death of its subject and its own attempt to end. It is the text that, according to Anderson, embodies Cavendish's extremely belated recall of Wolsey (a "recall" supplemented by material gleaned from intervening chronicles), as if Cavendish were vainly trying to complete some unfinished business.[5] It is the text, finally, that even in its imperfection constitutes a necessary link between Bede and Roper, and in a sense prophesies both More and Roper.

The latter point, admittedly, is not made by Anderson or by the equally hagiographic Yale editors of *Two Early Tudor Lives*, for whom the glaring contrast between Wolsey/Cavendish and More/Roper remains uppermost. No prophetic continuity, let alone a disturbing one, is apparently suspected, yet the continuity is as inescapable as the contrast, and it is emphasized by More's succeeding Wolsey as Lord Chancellor. While interpreting that continuity is not my purpose here, one possibility embodied in it can relevantly be identified at once with the help of Wyatt's first satire. In that poem, the Wyatt speaker somewhat disingenuously complains, perhaps not without reference to Thomas More, that he, Thomas Wyatt "cannot speke and loke lyke a saynct, / Vse wiles for witt and make deceyt a pleasure"(185).[6]

Contra Anderson, we may wonder whether saintly appearances and pleasures are what the manifestly power-hungry, epicurean Cardinal Wolsey and/or his confused biographer also miss, while those appearances and pleasures are achieved by More/Roper in a scenario of perverse stoicism. In that case, Wolsey/Cavendish may logically constitute a negative-prophetic *exemplum* to be "corrected" by successors operating in the same field. Indeed, we might wonder whether the real break between naivete and sophistication comes not between Bede and Cavendish, but between Cavendish and Roper. At all events, it would be risky to suppose that any breach with naive sanctity can be healed as effortlessly and completely as Anderson imagines Roper to do—least of all, it might be added, under the theatrical rubric of "conscience" or through the application of various restorative arts.[7] Nor does the ostensibly perfect life so readily escape the forms of imperfection that prophesy it as a triumph of superior, pleasurable artifice. If More's life, as recorded by Roper, instantiates any single thing, it may not be sanctity but the inescapable bad faith of the secular-political *belle âme* or incipient Tartuffe. That bad faith is what Wyatt arguably acknowledges in a satire of which he inexorably becomes the only subject in the end.[8]

All this brings us back to the question of the paradigm, and of the paradigmatic argument as an alternative to Christian witnessing (whether as a commitment or a mere interpretive premise is immaterial). I will suggest that Anderson's reading of Cavendish, both in general and in some details that remain to be considered, can be reconstrued in terms not her own as the unintended confirmation of a paradigm shift. In other words, her bracketing of Cavendish between the "medieval" Bede and the "Renaissance" Roper, her sense of the text's strangeness and/or deficiency in relation to full, normal texts coming before and after it, and her characterizations of the text's behavior all tend in spite of themselves to identify Cavendish's *Life* as the one in which a paradigm shift is occurring. And in so identifying it, they make it into the prefiguratively anomalous text, rupturing and departing from an existing paradigm, but also prophesying the new.

I should emphasize that the paradigmatic view of Cavendish's text is not altogether novel. Greenblatt's work implies the paradigmatic utility of this text, and much previous discussion of it, including Anderson's, has drawn attention to Cavendish's recurrent and apparently failing effort to contain Wolsey's life and his own act of authorship within medieval norms or forms: principally those of a Boethian *contemptus mundi* and of Fortune's Wheel.[9] (If Cavendish could conceive of Wolsey's life as tragedy, it would presumably be in those terms, but to little avail since they are terms that, in their privative emphasis on human vanity and shortsightedness, are fundamentally hostile to any notion of authentic tragedy.) Implicitly, then, the weakening of a medieval paradigm is widely recognized in discussion of Cavendish's *Life*, but the recognition of a paradigm *shift* does not necessarily follow, if by that we rigorously mean a historical shift entailing strong anticipations of the new within the old, incommensurable difference as well as reconstructive continuity in the sociocultural "text," and a historical temporality, even if not necessarily a uniform, unidirectional, or irreversible one. In these terms, which represent a conception of paradigmatic discontinuity that is less than complete, it is possible to see Cavendish's *Life* as a bearer of paradigmatic Renaissance novelty.

～～～

Cavendish's text refers to events during the reign of Henry VIII and bears its own witness to the princely—meaning also centralizing, nationalizing, and antifeudal—power-politics of that reign. In that context of Renaissance as well as English politics, the career of Wolsey as the son of an Ipswich butcher—an "honest, poor man" (5) to Cavendish—rising to the Lord Chancellorship becomes a glittering instantiation of *la carrière ouverte aux talents*, of the rise of the literate and gifted, and of the corresponding, perspicuous marginalization of a hereditary aristocracy whose "crisis" is already upon it.

Cavendish insists, of course, on the life and *death* of Wolsey— More will have only a "life" in Roper's representation—as if Wolsey's history were finally one of exemplary humiliation and misfortune. What the reader sees, however, is the dazzling, prolonged success, conferred not by Fortune but by Wolsey's prodigious energy and brilliant management. What makes Cavendish's Wolsey different, in a way that can be regarded as paradigmatic, is his almost unlimited social mobility and achievement, uninhibited by any premature concern about ends. If that Cardinal Wolsey also looks to Cavendish like a shockingly unprecedented monster of vanity and appetite, all the more does the monster show forth what is in the process of becoming. Wolsey is paradigmatic of the Renaissance life of ambition that has so widely been perceived in recent criticism, and also perhaps of the transformation of the medieval Catholic prelate into a secular, Renaissance master of ceremonies as power-broker.

Another prima facie instance of the paradigmatic in this text is its acknowledgment of pleasure as a motive or even a principle. Wolsey's success with the king, beginning while he is in the relatively humble position of royal almoner, is partly explained for Cavendish by his "secret intelligence of the King's natural inclination . . . so fast as other counsellors advised the King to leave his pleasure and to attend to the affairs of his realm, so busily did the almosyner persuade him to the contrary . . . thus the almosyner ruled all them that before ruled him, such did his policy and wit [that is, not Fortune] bring to pass" (13). The identification of princeliness with unlimited pleasure-seeking has already occurred in Book 4 of Castiglione's *The Courtier*, in which it becomes the good courtier's purgatorial vocation to guide the prince as libidinal infant monster into paths of responsibility and righteousness:

> Besides never hearing the truth about anything at all, princes are made drunk by the great license that rule gives; and by a profusion of delights are sunk in pleasures, and deceive themselves so and have their minds corrupted . . . the courtier will be able to lead his prince by the austere path of virtue, adorning it with shady fronds and strewing it with pretty flowers to lessen the toil of the journey for one whose strength is slight.[10]

Far from experiencing pleasure himself, the good courtier allegedly manipulates it for pedagogic ends only, making it merely a "veil" (294) under which subtle princely mortification can be pursued. At best, the chances of success are slim—the courtier's manipulative control of pleasure is no less questionable than the prince's willingness to be divorced from it—and courtly pedagogy is utterly subverted when any particular courtier recognizes, as one surely always will, that the way to power consists in *not* thwarting the "natural inclination" of the prince. Acting on his own secret intelligence of Henry's natural inclination, which is that of Renaissance princes as a class rather than of Henry Tudor in particular, Wolsey goes all the way. This way includes recognizing Henry's lust for Anne Boleyn at an early stage and virtually acting as pimp; he simply browbeats her betrothed out of an existing engagement so that he may present her for the king's delectation.

In Cavendish, admittedly, Wolsey's breaking of this engagement makes Anne Boleyn his mortal enemy, and places her in conspiratorial alliance with an offended traditional nobility, all of which leads to Wolsey's eventual downfall and humiliation. Admittedly, too, Wolsey cannot deliver, try as he may, Henry's divorce from Catherine of Aragon and consequent freedom to marry Anne Boleyn; this failure is the beginning of the end for Wolsey. The principle of Wolsey's success thus appears to be one that implies eventual failure as well, and to *become* a principle of failure as soon as pleasure ceases to be magically deliverable on demand. From a paradigmatic standpoint, however, the issue is not just the particular courtier's success or failure—important though both those possibilities may become for later poets and playwrights possessed of the same "secret intelligence" about princes—but the manifestation of a "pleasure principle" as such. It is this principle that triumphs in Wolsey's death as in his life. When Cavendish comes to court to report the death of the Cardinal, no doubt hoping thereby to gain some favor, he waits until the king has finished his shooting:

> And repairing to the King, I found him shooting at the rounds on the backside of the garden. And perceiving him to be occupied in

shooting, thought it not my duty to trouble him, but leaned to a tree, intending to stand there and to attend his gracious pleasure, being in a great study. At the last, the King came suddenly behind me where I stood and clapped his hand upon my shoulder. And when I perceived him, I fell upon my knee. To whom he said, calling me by my name, "I will," quod he, "make an end of my game, and then I will talk with you." (188)

Chillingly, no doubt, nothing, including the death of Wolsey, for whose well-being the king has continued to profess concern, must interrupt the king's "gracious pleasure." The Cavendish who knows this has learned his lesson in principle well.

The paradigmatic emergence of this pleasure principle—which will place the courtier in a stoic position in which pain may have to become his pleasure—as well as the reconstruction of political order around this principle is not apparent only in this text. It is the principle that Thomas More renders explicit even as he seeks to displace it into his Utopia, where it will also be disciplined and made accountable: "For they are somewhat more inclined to this attitude of mind: that no kind of pleasure is forbidden, provided no harm comes of it."[11] In Utopia, natural inclination will no longer be the manipulable object of secret intelligence but will openly be avowed, while by the same token it will be disowned and expunged in More's own life of stoic self-mortification. Yet More's capacity to disown pleasure—to make it the principle of the Utopian other rather than his own—becomes questionable precisely in Roper's *Life*, as we have seen.

The paradigmatic ascendancy of the pleasure principle in Cavendish's text is fundamentally transforming inasmuch as it results in that aestheticization and staging of life to which writers on the Renaissance as a cultural epoch have testified at least since Burckhardt. (Conversely, the recognition of a governing *principle* of pleasure may necessitate or even constitute a reinterpretation of the existing world, here meaning principally the medieval world, of which, for example, the monastic asceticism and "childlike" innocence may be seen always and already to have been in the secret service of pleasure.) Yet this pleasure principle apparently does not generate an autonomous category of the aesthetic in the Renaissance. On the contrary, it is a principle that without contradiction coincides with that of power in the key figure of the prince, whose power is his power to take his pleasure. Since, however, neither power nor pleasure are ever self-identically embodied in the prince, whose powerlessness and misery may indeed be apparent (as are Henry's in dealing with Rome, with Catherine of Aragon, and even with the "wild" Anne Boleyn), it is only the *staging* of princely power that without contradiction coincides with the staging of pleasure. That is what may paradigmatically be seen in Cavendish's text, and that is what brings us to the most often discussed aspect of the text, namely its tireless reporting of grandiose public spectacles:

> [Wolsey] would issue out into [his chambers] apparelled all in red in the habit of a Cardinal; which was either of fine scarlet or else of crimson satin, taffeta, damask, or caffa, the best that he could get for money; and upon his head a round pillion with a neck of black velvet, set to the same in the inner side . . . there was also borne before him first the Great Seal of England, and then his Cardinal's hat by a nobleman or some worthy gentleman right solemnly, bareheaded . . . thus passing forth with two great crosses of silver borne before him, with also two great pillars of silver, and his sergeant at arms with a great mace of silver gilt. Then his gentleman ushers cried and said: "On my lords and masters, make way for my lord's grace!" (25)

> And when it pleased the King's majesty for his recreation to repair unto the Cardinal's house . . . there wanted no preparations or goodly furniture with viands of the finest sort that might be provided for money or friendship. . . . The banquets were set forth with masques and mummeries in so gorgeous a sort and costly manner that it was an heaven to behold. . . . I have seen the King suddenly come in thither in a masque with a dozen of other maskers all in garments like shepherds, made of fine cloth of gold and fine crimson satin paned, and caps of the same with visors of good proportion of visonamy; their hairs and beards either of fine gold wires or else of silver, and some being of black silk, having sixteen torches bearers besides drums, and other persons attending upon them with visors and all clothed in satin of the same colors. And at his coming and before he came into the hall, ye shall understand that he came by water to the water gate without any noise, where

against his coming was laid charged many chambers. At whose landing they were all shot off, which made such a rumble and thunder in the air that it was like thunder. (26–27)

The French guard and the Scots had all one livery, which were rich coats of fine white cloth, with a guard of silver bullions embroidered an handful broad. The King came riding upon a goodly jennet. . . . Then was word brought my lord that the King was coming to encounter him; with that, he, having none other shift, was compelled to alight in an old chapel that stood by the highway and there new apparelled him into more richer apparel. And then mounted upon a new mule very richly trapped with a footcloth and trapper of crimson velvet upon velvet, purled with gold and fringed about with a deep fringe of gold, very costly, his stirrups of silver and gilt, the bosses and checks of his bridle the same. (55–56)

For Anderson, this endless theatrical pageant, from which Wolsey's ostentatious celebrations of High Mass are far from being excluded, constitutes the peculiar emptiness or opacity of Wolsey's life and Cavendish's text. Both life and text begin to assume significance for her only after Wolsey's fall from power, when Wolsey begins to enact his belated, anticlimactic, but strangely affecting version of Christian mortification and passion. (About this phase, Anderson writes with a penetration altogether lacking in her discussion of Roper's *Life*, a fact which might suggest that the "failed," embarrassing imitation of Christ is at once more authentic and moving than More's supposedly successful one.) For Greenblatt, in contrast, such is the spectacle of Renaissance power, deliberately orchestrated as such. If Wolsey has a life it is continuously being improvised in scenes like those quoted—but no less so in the "failed" scenes after Wolsey's fall—and this spectacle is constitutive of a world of theatricalized power.

In the light of recent discussion, particularly of the Elizabethan and Jacobean reigns, it would be possible to develop and refine the paradigmatic claim. If, for example, we might suppose that this is Wolsey's peculiar spectacle, that is, the spectacle of an upstart without hereditary claims to the position he occupies and therefore in special need of this machinery of self-aggrandizement, we would have to recall that it is a spectacle in which Henry VIII fully participates. He evidently plays himself no less than Wolsey does, and no doubt for comparable reasons: as the son of a dynastic usurper, his power is scarcely more hereditary or self-embodied than Wolsey's. Wolsey and Henry VIII are thus complicitous and even interchangeable players, each periodically speaking in the king's name, while Wolsey is also the grand Master of the Revels in a staging of power that is to be repeated throughout the Elizabethan and Stuart reigns.

This theatricalization of power is also its antifeudal centralization in the royal court and its satellites. In Cavendish, one role for the marginalized traditional nobility is to serve the "honest, poor man's son" who is Wolsey: "of gentleman waiters in his privy chamber he had six; and also he had of lords nine or ten, who had each of them allowed two servants; and the Earl of Derby had allowed five men" (21). Among the gentry serving the upstart is the gentleman-usher George Cavendish. Hereditary nobles may also become palace conspirators and guerilla saboteurs, as some do in conspiring with Anne Boleyn against the Cardinal whom she hates. In seeking to compass Wolsey's death, however, they miss the point about the disembodied nature and indeterminate location of the new theatricalized power that eludes them. For them, the death of Wolsey will not change anything fundamentally.[12]

In Cavendish, then, power is symbolized and enacted, not embodied, in a world increasingly reconstituted as theater, not only in England but during all Henry VIII's minutely described progresses, campaigns, and self-dramatizing appearances in France; in the trial of Catherine of Aragon (who refuses to "play" and resolutely withdraws from the stage); and in the final acts of the discredited Wolsey, belatedly playing the feudal patron, saint, martyr, and expiring prophet. Insofar as elements of material power continue to appear in Cavendish's account—for example, those of money, law, and military-diplomatic action, as well as brute coercion of the weak—they seem increasingly to be subsumed within an order of spectacular representation without ground or substance. Such is the Wolsey paradigm.

Yet is it the *Wolsey* paradigm? It may escape notice that while Cavendish tends to perceive and report everything as spectacle, punctuating his fascinated accounts with obligatory, self-excluding denunciations of vanity, he also *constitutes* everything as theater through his relentless act of beholding. This form of constancy is arguably more important and masterful than his explicit interpretations or his critically recognized vacillation between faith and infidelity, love and loathing, towards his master. No doubt an invidious psychology of the servant-betrayer motivates his act of spectatorship; no doubt, too, it is the inconspicuous gentleman-usher who can become the privileged, telltale witness to his master's doings, just as "son Roper" can become the intrusive witness to More's life. At one level, however, it is enough that Cavendish does *constantly* witness—possibly altering the meaning of "bearing witness" in a telltale direction—and thus render as spectacle all that passes before him. He beholds the public scenes, but also the scenes behind them, as in the quoted example in which he sees Wolsey turn an old chapel into an impromptu tiring-house, hurriedly preparing for his next scene with the king. It is also Cavendish who sees the act right through to the end, at which point Wolsey dons a hairshirt (he typically has three of them!) as his final costume. This is the spectatorship that at once mediates and constitutes Wolsey's life as a paradigmatic one, the paradigm being that of endless Renaissance theatricalized power and mobility.

Conceivably, then, the Wolsey paradigm is as much or more the Cavendish paradigm, at once mediated and constituted for us by an author whose overt intentions are irrelevant here; it is enough that his text behaves in a certain way. Yet inasmuch as we recognize the paradigmatic utility of this text, we may increasingly wonder about the role(s) of its author. The perspicuousness of Cavendish's spectatorship rather than its inconspicuousness—his constantly identifying himself through the pronoun "I" as the privileged witness—begins to displace attention from Wolsey. As in Roper's *Life of More*, the spectatorial position thus increasingly becomes one within the circuit of power and pleasure, not one external to it, as that of the unreconstructed traditional aristocracy has become. And the position of the privileged witness is incipiently that of the author, who will retroactively determine the spectacle as that of power and render it paradigmatic *avant de la lettre*.

As spectator Cavendish repeatedly plays the awed, wondering onlooker, possessed of a humble, limited mind unable to take in the unheard-of novelties that shock and fascinate it: "It was an heaven to behold" (27); "And thus the world began to grow into wonderful inventions, not heard of before in this realm" (39); "Also they sent for all the expertest cooks besides my lord's that they could get in all England, where they might be gotten, to serve and garnish this feast. The purveyors brought and sent in such plenty of costly provision as ye would wonder at the same" (71); "I do both lack wit in my gross old head and cunning in my bowels to declare the wonderful and curious imaginations in the same invented and devised" (75); "Which was the strangest and newest sight and device that ever was read or heard in any history or chronicle in any region—that a King and Queen to be convented and constrained by process compellatory to appear in any court as common persons" (81). Cumulatively, this wondering testimony to unprecedented and uninterpretable novelty, to "imaginations" and "inventions" of a new world, may constitute evidence for us of a paradigm shift, but it is hardly neutral evidence or pure data, since its source is a highly interested onlooker. Cavendish has his own stake in participating in these allegedly novel forms of power and pleasure, however much he may seemingly cling to old norms and old forms, and also in reconstructing his marginalized gentry situation.

Cavendish's stake in the "new world" becomes apparent at many points in the text. His name and authorship depend on this novelty, for one thing, and he, like Roper, like Plutarch, seeks to appropriate the life he records—a general feature of biography not noted by Anderson. (Whose "life" is it finally?) Nowhere does Cavendish's stake more strikingly appear than in an ostensibly digressive episode, in which he breaks cover. This "chance" (58) episode is one in which he is received into a French castle, virtually as a Wolsey-surrogate: "There came to me one of the servants of the castle, perceiving me to be the Cardinal's servant and an Englishman, who required me to go with him into the castle to my lord his master, whom he thought would be very glad of my coming and company" (58). The host, "Monsieur Crequi, a nobleman born and very nigh of blood to King Louis," warmly receives Cavendish, shows him the military secrets of the castle, and presents him to his wife and other ladies, whom he is allowed to kiss. Throughout this inset narrative, Cavendish is his own man, a first-person subject with a narrative of his own, this freedom and subjecthood conferred on him by his taking the place of Wolsey. Throughout this episode, it is of course possible to see Cavendish being feted as one who is known to represent a threatening English military presence in the neighborhood, but it is also in this digressive episode that Cavendish benefits from the mobility and interchange of place that a theatricalized world allows, and in doing so recovers—and greatly enhances—his own "lost" gentry status.

I shall conclude by suggesting, then, that we can indeed regard Cavendish's *Life* as a text that behaves as if a paradigm shift were occurring, and that it is critically useful to regard it as such in our ongoing effort to conceptualize the Renaissance as a historico-cultural phenomenon. Equally, however, we need to consider the extent to which Cavendish is the self-interested, rather effective, mediator of our own paradigmatic conception. Furthermore, we need to consider just how far the Cavendish paradigm extends. In this regard, I will suggest that the Cavendish paradigm, as distinct from the Wolsey paradigm, is one in which the spectatorial dependent as privileged witness becomes profoundly complicit in the circulation and exchange of power and pleasure. In doing so, he emerges as a type of the Renaissance author—as one who progressively emerges from dependent obscurity to acquire a name, a public position, and his own more or less modest story. More importantly, perhaps, he acquires the power at least of retroactive determination and reconstruction in a world given as spectacle. Cavendish thus prophesies some of his most illustrious successors even while he bears witness to a new order. After Cavendish, Spenser and Shakespeare are possible, including the Shakespeare who pillages scenes from Cavendish's *Life* in *Henry VIII*.

Finally, in terms of the *Gestalt* being produced in this book, I will suggest that Cavendish's text can be read not just as constituting a Renaissance paradigm but also as enacting an oppositional discontinuity with the Middle Ages. That that opposition and discontinuity are not complete or fundamental, and cannot be so, continues to be implied in the larger undertaking of this book.

5

Gascoigne's Woodmanship:
Antioedipal Poetics

In general, it might be said that the strange case of George Gascoigne is that of an appreciable poet of the English sixteenth century with whom, since Yvor Winters, no one has known quite what to do.[1] It is true that Gascoigne inserts himself into the major poetic genealogies of the period, as we shall see, and also practices tight, courtly lyric forms, albeit not predominantly so. Yet readers have usually failed to recognize Gascoigne as having affinity with Wyatt and Surrey, or with his later Elizabethan lyric successors. Where he fits in remains a problem.

I don't intend to dispute the widely held belief that the dominant lyric forms I discuss in earlier chapters don't work for Gascoigne, though it might be suggested that they do work insofar as they enable him to create a poetic persona for entrepreneurial exploitation; the work isn't necessarily being done in the poems, but *with* them when Gascoigne becomes a self-anthologizer.[2] My main concern, however, is not with Gascoigne's place in the general scheme of things, but in the limited scheme of this book. In this scheme, it would be tempting and consistent to argue that the reason why these forms don't work for Gascoigne, and why he therefore fails to be a poet as Wyatt and Surrey are poets, is that they are inherently masculinist, overdisciplined forms that cease to be viable, or to *do* work, under the "feminized" and somewhat liberalized conditions of Elizabethan culture.

Formal and generic impasses of that kind are widely represented in *The Shepheardes Calender*, in which even "the perfecte paterne of the poete" appears to have become a recipe for pure disaster (October eclogue). Poetry, it would seem, has virtually to be reinvented. If one of the E. K. footnotes to the October eclogue is to be credited, the theoretical enabling act for poetry has to be rewritten as well; this rewriting is promised when E. K. speaks of a volume forthcoming from the anonymous author of *The Shepheardes Calender* entitled *[The] English Poete*.[3] As far as we know, however, that document was never produced.

My own choice to discuss a prose text and a rather free "verse" by Gascoigne in this chapter may seem to reinforce the supposition of a breakdown in "inherently" masculinist representation under the altered conditions of Elizabethan symbolization. More radically, one might speculate that symbolization as such (the complex interaction of simulacra), as well as the construction of an elaborate symbolic *order*, occurs only under "anomalous" conditions of cultural feminization, and does not necessarily constitute the cultural norm. Indeed, the career of the prodigiously symbolizing Elizabethan Shakespeare might constitute major evidence of this possibility. What then becomes problematical, and will remain so in my argument, is the supposition that the construction of culture is *always* synonymous with the construction of a complex symbolic order.

Admittedly, this line of speculation may seem to be contradicted by other data of this period: first, by the manifest likelihood that the Elizabethan moment merely renders perspicuous a complex symbolic order always and already constituted within the culture, and, second, by the sheer expansion of sonneteering and lyric production in the 1580s and 1590s, which seems to extend rather than transform the undertakings of Wyatt and Surrey. I would suggest, however, that persistence in "anterior forms" of the lyric becomes part of the conspicuous Sidney-and-Puttenham *defense* of poetry, explicitly conceived as a traditional stronghold of masculine privilege, during the 1580s and 1590s. "Restoration" is anticipated, and the forms can be practiced defensively as well as "symbolically," thus requiring no strictly new enabling act to be written. Moreover, these forms are practiced with a revealing difference. If there is one critical distinction of the Lewis-Winters era that remains workable, it is that between Henrician Drab and Elizabethan Golden. The dazzling success of the latter is partly a function of the poems' *figurative* ostentation, their seemingly enforced tribute to a different order of things. Finally, in addition to being heavily ornamented, the golden sonnets are typically anomalous, a contradiction in terms that may be indispensable for the characterization of Elizabethan writing.

The anomalously self-deconstructing excess and "peculiarity" of Elizabethan sonnets and their speakers has increasingly been recognized in recent criticism, partly since the taboo on saying why Shakespeare's Young Man sonnets are "peculiar" was lifted. (A further disclosure of radical "peculiarity" might be effected if, instead of always genteelly speaking of Shakespeare's Dark Lady sonnets, we could bring ourselves to call them the Black Woman sonnets.)[4] Shakespeare's apparent production of Jacobean as well as Elizabethan sonnets—or at least the "mysterious" Jacobean publication of the sonnets volume in 1609—is another anomaly from which full value has yet to be extracted. But it is not only Shakespeare's "ill-timed" sonnets and their misplaced personae that are peculiar. There is the self-deconstructing excess of Sidney/Astrophil, anxiously producing and withdrawing every imaginable textual warrant for his own existence, and producing numerous poems that are so effectively censored that they are not allowed to begin even by the time they have ended. There is the oddity of the "Amoretti" speaker who evidently has no father but three synonymous mothers, one of whom is apparently his prospective wife. There is the speaker of the Daniel sonnets who can apparently never rise to the occasion; there are the speakers of the grimly and knowingly unsuccessful Greville sonnets. Despite the pervasive consciousness of Petrarch and the French sonneteers, Elizabethan sonnet projects are all marked by differences that can be construed, and are now often construed, as the product of Elizabethan political and symbolic reconfiguration.

In this chapter, I try to consider ways in which Gascoigne prefigures some of the paradoxes, crossings, and double crossings, of

Elizabethan writing. The differences that characterize this writing can to some extent be brought under the rubric of an "antioedi-pal" poetics, while my recourse to the specific term "oedipal" gives a more definitive and dialectical turn than I have given so far to the notion of phallomorphic representation. I thus allow the oe-dipal to have its moment as the putatively definitive instance of phallomorphic representation without committing the book as a whole to that self-fulfilling premise.

~~~

Gascoigne writes:

> I venter my good will,
> Yn barren verse to do the best I can,
> Like *Chaucers* boye, and *Petrarch's* journeyman.[5]

In this moment of apparent self-deprecation, the versifier seem-ingly foreswears any oedipal designs on his masters, or any ca-pacity to effect such designs if he had them. Subject to more (or less) than a profound anxiety of influence, he is evidently recon-ciled to perpetual emasculated boyhood in relation to Chaucer and perpetual apprenticeship in relation to Petrarch. His modesty as well as his incapacity places him out of contention with these unassailably preemptive figures, whose position he uninvidiously acknowledges. No overreaching conceit or suicidal poetics here. Innocence of any usurping desire or intent is attested by the "good will" with which he cheerfully plods along. In short, he will remain a good-natured practitioner and instructor in "verse," not a Poet.[6]

All this is disarming enough, and no one who has attempted a sustained reading of Gascoigne's lyric poems will necessarily dis-pute his self-evaluation. Only in Winters's inverted hierarchy of poetic merit is Gascoigne a Major Poet of the English sixteenth century. Yet this is not Gascoigne's only self-characterization, nor is this puerile limitation always professed. On the contrary, the Gascoigne who appropriates for himself the tag *Tam Marti quam Mercurio* sometimes emerges as a self-consciously macho figure, soldiering in the Low Countries, present and assiduously scribbling as eyewitness reporter at the siege of Antwerp in 1569, and so on.[7] Indeed, "Gascoigne" parades himself in an unusually large number of guises for a sixteenth-century author. Fictional ones in the poems include those of the Green Knight, Dan Bartholomew of Bath, the Reporter, and a feminine Philomel, but there is also the Gascoigne who asserts his third-person existence in the world through the odd, proprietary titles of such poems as "Gascoigne's woodmanship." (This self-alienated, third-person Gascoigne is periodically replaced in the writings by a lovingly self-addressed "George.") Finally, there is the Gascoigne who plays the man of letters with considerable brilliance, his parts including those of translator, apologist, satirist, reporter, playwright, prose-fiction author, moral essayist, editor, self-anthologizer, and instructor in versification. All this implies something more martially aggressive and mercurially devious than Gascoigne's credible self-characterization as a weak poet might lead one to expect.

In fact, the lines quoted above are not as candidly innocuous as they seem or possibly want to be. Apart from their mock-modesty and their repetition of a humility *topos* all too reminiscent of the low-lying Chaucer, their structural oppositions (boy/man; journeyman/master) invidiously reify figures of paternal power while the violent consequences of doing so are blandly denied. And even or especially if spoken in all innocence, Gascoigne's language embodies a scenario of repressed desire; the language itself, one might say, is more knowing than its innocent speaker. Professed boyish "good will" anticipates the time in which "will" must acquire its connotation of sexual desire and cease to be (or to think itself) quite so good. The term "barren" imports a desirable and threatening maternal-feminine participant into a scenario of poetic production that is overtly masculine, and that is (mis)conceived as one structured solely by master-servant, master-apprentice, or father-son relations. (Being Chaucer's "boye" need mean no more than being his youthful retainer.) If it remains unclear whether the lines are "barren" because their author lacks paternal potency or because they are being produced from a naively reified masculine position without recourse to a constructed feminine-generative one, they are still lines that know more of desire than they admit. Their denial of invidious participation therefore seems at once premature and belated. In fact, the lines suggest not so much a resigned nonparticipation as a compulsive yet failing, hence humorously denied and deferred, participation in the oedipal action.

Once that possibility is recognized, it also becomes possible to discern a certain *anti*oedipal impulse in Gascoigne's work. Under this term I include not only forms of attempted humorous denial or release, but stratagems through which oedipal failure can be compensated, through which the "classic" unfolding of the oedipal script can be circumvented, or through which the burden of inheritance can be refused. Perhaps these will all be stratagems of failure, remaining captive in the last resort to the dominant oedipal paradigm of cultural production. They do, however, permit significant departures from "classic" authorship.

The text in which Gascoigne's antioedipal undertakings may most readily be apparent to us is the prose work *Master F. J.* This work, in the subaltern form of "Elizabethan prose fiction," is also the supremely ironic and metapoetic text of its time, more open to postmodernist recognition than anything else Gascoigne wrote. In *Master F. J.*, poems as iconic "primary" texts are incorporated into a humorously demystifying prose narrative. No poem in *Master F. J.* is free-standing; the primacy of social context and/or occasion is implied there as it is in many of Gascoigne's own "lyric" poems, which are typically introduced, as we shall see, by elaborate prose scenarios.[8] Not only can no poem in *Master F. J.* have a stable or immanent meaning, but each one circulates as a message to be read, along the lines and between the lines, according to divergent interests, albeit generally erotic ones in the sexual hothouse of Gascoigne's fictionalized aristocratic domain. In that setting, moreover, the poem becomes an instance of the letter in social circulation, not an ontologically distinct entity or

iconic form as virtually all contemporary treatises in humanist poetics would have it.[9] In *Master F. J.*, the authentic scene of the
poem is that of its social production and reading as a message,
not that of its "empty" cultural *Aufhebung*.

Correlatively, the prestigious figure of the aspirant courtier-
poet (represented, however, as naive in the sentimental education
of *Master F. J.*) is virtually displaced in the book's scheme of things
by the quintessentially Gascoignian figure of the Secretary. This
official is no person of name but a scribal functionary in and of
the system. As such, he emerges as the figure of the writer as opposed to that of the poet, yet he also demystifies the poet inasmuch as he occupies the servant position repeatedly idealized in
courtly-love poems. The real servant is not a courtly wooer but
one who knows his place and function, performing anonymously
in both.

In keeping, however, with the double-playing irony of *Master
F. J.*, both place and function turn out to be a little more complicated than might initially be supposed. (The comedy of incorrect
"supposes" is Gascoigne's major legacy to the English theater and
above all to Shakespearean comedy.) The place of the Secretary,
we discover, is behind the scenes as well as on the scene, while his
"anonymous" function—in the guise of virtual ambulatory phallus as well as scribe—appears to be that of enabling the ladies, as
one critic has put it, "to get [their] sexual business done."[10] In the
society world of *Master F. J.*, dominated by powerful, experienced
women whose "dictation" requires servants rather than masters,
the Poet is at once differentiated from and reductively subsumed
in the Secretary, whose potency becomes *inter alia* a physiological
function of those women's requirements.

Not only does all this imply a significant critique of classic conceptions of paternal poetic identity and inheritance, but the implicit anti-Petrarchanism of *Master F. J.* is also antioedipal in the
terms previously proposed. A matriarchal poetics of women who
do not write, and whose culturally constitutive power consists
rather in dictating what is written, is thus at once conceived and

seemingly upheld in this text. It is possible to regard the prose narrative of *Master F. J.*, then, as the paradoxically strong outcome of Gascoigne's poetics of failure, and as an outcome, moreover, in which a countercultural critique of the courtier-poet and of the ontological primacy of the poem is brilliantly effected. Under these circumstances, devoted close reading of Gascoigne's lyrics begins to look like a litmus test of stupidity, while Gascoigne's insistence on the term "verse" begins to take on a resolutely heuristic appearance.

It should be admitted, however, that the current accessibility of *Master F. J.*, as well as its paradoxical "mastery," may facilitate critical misrepresentation of Gascoigne's performance. The account I have given could certainly be faulted as a narrow, dehistoricizing assimilation of *Master F. J.*, and hence of the historical Gascoigne, to a postmodernist aesthetic. A better test might be "Gascoigne's woodmanship," the autobiographical verses in which Gascoigne represents his own "failing" career under the figure of so-called woodmanship, the aristocratic practice of a woodcraft that comprises mainly hunting and archery.

Before turning to that text, which represents a somewhat baffling and seemingly irrational state of affairs, some reorientation and further historical priming is necessary. Perhaps most importantly, it is necessary to recall that the term "woodmanship" is subject to punning Elizabethan transformations that include the signification of madness: "woodman" = "madman." For example, the excessively "crossed" lovers in *A Midsummer Night's Dream* are crazy when they are "wood within the wood" (2.1.192). The punning conflation of literal woods with forms of confusion and self-alienation tantamount to madness is common in Gascoigne's period. (Can we be sure that Milton is unaware of this, or can't be thinking of it, when he speaks of Shakespeare's "native woodnotes wild?") In Spenser's *Faerie Queene*, madness increasingly characterizes the donkey-worshipping (also ass-worshipping) "saluages" or wood-people of Book 2. It less comically characterizes these "saluages," Una's erstwhile saviors, when they are transmuted into the sacrificial murderers of Book 6. Finally, it constitutes the "character" the autobiographical speaker of the December eclogue assumes when he starts turning into a tree— literally becoming wood—near the end of *The Shepheardes Calender*.

These states of "woodmanship" can to some degree be regarded as the bad outcome of an oedipal poetics, or as that poetics gone wrong. They will then imply compulsive failure as well as a lack of integral identity and/or the splitting of the normative phallic subject into figments of so-called multiple personality. They may also, however, be reclaimed as subversively antioedipal—as another poetics or poetics of the "other"—while their emergence may facilitate the theatrical brilliance, versatility, and multiscriptedness of character to which Gascoigne's career also testifies. Any part, including that of the woman or of the woman writer who ipso facto cannot be a Poet, becomes playable in the absence of an integral self—a self for the construction of which, however contradictorily, our culture admits only one definitive script, namely that of oedipal accession and succession.[11]

The point, even at this broad cultural level, is not that this integral or centripetal identity is ever necessarily attainable, but that it remains a guise in which a succession of ipso facto seminal figures continues to be recognized, retroactively as a rule. Thus from Gascoigne's standpoint, Chaucer or Petrarch may be so recognized—or practically must be so recognized and resisted—while from the standpoint of both those authors, especially the diffuse Chaucer, it is Dante who must be so recognized. This genealogical (mis)construction after the fact, which often or always entails the reduction of a heterogeneous *oeuvre* to a single awe-inspiring name (Homer, Virgil, Dante, Milton, et al.), may, however, function as a shaping myth of authorship. The projection of that genealogical line into the future enables a self-fashioning commitment to this identity to be pursued as part of authorial appropriation and self-construction. At least on the face of it, authors differ significantly in the extent of their commitment to this formation of identity, and it is partly on this account that it is possible to distinguish, though perhaps not in the very final analysis, between an author of the egotistical sublime and one of negative capability. The title of Poet may, however, belong definitively to the former only.

Granted this broad cultural problematic to which Gascoigne appears subject but also highly and unusually resistant, the possibility of self-production in the guise of the Poet, and as one possessed of integral identity, is not, I would argue, a historical constant. If we regard Gascoigne as the first of the Elizabethans, his work prefigures the untenability of, as well as resistance to, that integral mode for the duration of the reign, if for no other reason than the obvious one of symbolic and "genealogical" disruption effected by the ascent of a powerful queen (one who, unlike her elder married sister, Mary, occupies a symbolic as well as a political position). It is more than just circumstantial that Spenser's "weakly" vast metapoetics and Shakespeare's theatrical multi-scripting remain the premier literary achievements of the reign. If Major Poet identity is nonetheless conferred on Shakespeare by broad, or perhaps just bad, cultural tradition, that ascription of identity has regularly been accompanied by apparently enforced recognition of Shakespeare's difference, and by differing conceptions of the "seminal" that his work sponsors.[12] Shakespeare thus tends to remain the exception that proves the rule of oedipal succession, but he is also the one who, as author of the Elizabethan-into-Jacobean *Hamlet*, problematically reinstates the rule. Not all of this is in Gascoigne's work by any means, and his status as harbinger of the Elizabethan is itself a retroactive construction, yet his texts give their own special access to the broader Elizabethan situation.

～～

Typically, "Gascoigne's woodmanship" begins with some "extrapoetic" preliminaries:

Gascoigne's woodmanship written to the L. Grey of Wilton upon this occasion, the said L. Grey delighting (amongst many other good qualities) in chusing of his winter deare, & killing the same with his bowe, did furnish the Aucthor with a crossebowe *cum pertinenciis* and vouchsaved to use his company in the said exercise, calling him one of his woodmen. Now the Aucthor shooting very often, could never hitte any deare, yea, and oftentimes he let the heard passe by as though he had not seene them. Whereat when this noble Lord tooke some pastime, and had often put him in remembrance of his good skill in choosing, and readinesse in killing of a winter deare, he thought good thus to excuse it in verse.[13]

This prose text typically threatens to forestall and replace the poem as primary text. It dramatizes the occasion, but also the fundamentally occasional, "ontologically" extemporal (*ex tempore*) genesis of the verse text. Yet in identifying the verse text as a begging letter to Lord Grey, it also situates it within the now-familiar Elizabethan system of patronage and self-advancement. It accordingly anticipates historicist reading of the text as one produced and, as it were, fully consumed in that patronage system. (In other words, Gascoigne may be said to foreground the sociocultural subtext that a certain historicism regularly unearths.) The prose narrative thus appears to function in a manner comparable to that of the prose narrative in *Master F. J.*, establishing the priority of context and message over poetic form or genealogy.

Gascoigne cannot be said to reverse these priorities or fully to reauthorize poetic discourse in the verse text of "Gascoigne's woodmanship," yet he evidently does reinvest something in the writing of verse there. (Not coincidentally, "Gascoigne's woodmanship" is regularly identified as a poem by readers and anthologists.) One way in which he effects this reinvestment is by structuring the verse text as allegory or extended metaphor, thus bringing it under what one critic has called "Gascoigne's master trope" of allegory.[14] The autobiographical character of the verse text also implies self-investment on Gascoigne's part, and this text becomes the locus of a subjectivity or even of a putative subjecthood absent or repressed in the prose text. Instead of merely forestalling such developments as these, the prose text turns out subtly to facilitate them as well. In it, a subdued conflict of wills is already being staged between the patron who dubs Gascoigne one of his "woodmen," thus seeking to appropriate him and determine his place in the scheme of things, and the Gascoigne who not only names (signs) himself in claiming title to the poem, but reappropriates "woodmanship" as his own term.

In one view, Gascoigne's anomalously explicit foregrounding of his authorial "entitlement" may signal the advent of bourgeois authorship, and thus an incipient, fundamental change in the form of property and hence in the forms of cultural production and self-production. (As a work in the "minor" form of Elizabethan prose fiction, *Master F. J.* may do likewise, signaling the advent of the novel as dominant bourgeois form.) In the overdetermined view I wish to maintain, however, this "anomalous" prose text foregrounds a conflict of wills, Gascoigne's no longer being quite so "good," that is more often latent or better-masked in the literature of patronage. This conflict is then subsumed, undercut, and displaced in the verse text, in which a more complex scenario emerges than one of direct masculine subordination and rivalry. Nor is the scenario merely one of negotiation occurring in the implicitly pastoralized yet still fully masculinized sphere of Lord Grey's woodmen.[15]

What, then, is this scenario? Circumstantially, the verse text confirms (and supplies) certain biographical data that appear in Charles Prouty's *George Gascoigne: Elizabethan Courtier, Soldier, Poet*.[16] It contributes to the representation of Gascoigne as a superior jack-of-all-trades, failing in the pursuit of any unified, upwardly mobile career. Gascoigne's forays into law, military service, and courtiership are all included in the allegorical narrative:

> First if it please your honour to perceyve,
> What makes your woodman shoote so ofte amisse,
> Beleeve me L. the case is nothing strange,
> He shootes awrie at almost every marke,
> His eyes have bene so used for to raunge,
> That now God knowes they be both dimme and darke.
>   (11–16)

The verse text thus speaks candidly to the facts, which may indeed speak for themselves, requiring only acknowledgment; yet the text hardly presents these facts transparently or unselectively. Gascoigne's up-to-the-minute representation of his life is also a retrospective and prospective reconstruction of it. The temporal and representational maneuvers of the text accordingly align it with other sixteenth-century projects of self-writing, enabling us to identify it, with a sidelong glance at the Montaigne of the *essaies*, as a somewhat innovative autobiographical essay in verse. More importantly, Gascoigne's represented vocational failures constitute *displacements* of successive careers and "selves" that allow the analogical possibilities of the literary career and the textual self to emerge.

This paradoxical work of failure is being done in a context in which certain other broad revisions are being effected. An important precursor of "Gascoigne's woodmanship" is Roger Ascham's *Toxophilus*. In that pedagogic text on archery, not only are shooting straight and hitting the mark unequivocal goals of a particular, gender-coded, athletic discipline, but they become hugely invested as emblems of masculine aristocratic virtue and performance within an ideology of *mens sana in corpore sano*. The construction of an empowered yet disciplined phallomorphic subject, political rather than individual in the first instance, is manifestly at stake in this pedagogy of the unerring bowman, conducted, for whatever the ironies are worth, by one who was also Queen Elizabeth's tutor. (Thus if Elizabeth is the *diva virago* rather than the *diva virgo* of the period, tutorial discipline, including discipline in archery, may have something to do with the fact.) It is in the service of this discipline that Ascham writes his justly admired and highly sensitive passage on the effect of crosswinds:

> To se the wynde, with a man his eyes, it is vnpossible, the nature of it is so fyne, and subtile, yet this experience of the wynde had I ones myself, and that was in the great snowe that fell .IIII. yeares agoo: I rode by the hye waye betwixt Topcliffe vpon Swale, and Borowe bridge, the waye beyng sumwhat trodden afore, by waye fayrynge men. The feeldes on bothe sides were playne and laye almost yearde deepe with snowe, the nyght afore had ben a little

froste, yt the snowe was harde and crusted aboue. That morning the sun shone bright and clere, the wynde was whistelinge a lofte, and sharpe according to the tyme of the yere. The snowe in the hye waye lay lowse and troden wyth horse feete: so as the wynde blewe, it toke the lowse snow wyth it, and made it so slide vpon the snowe in the felde which was harde and crusted by reason of the frost ouer nyght, that thereby I myght se verye well, the hole nature of the wynde as it blewe yt daye. And I had great delyte & pleasure to marke it, which maketh me now far better to remember it. Sometyme the wynde would not be past .II. yeardes brode, and so it would carry the snowe as far as I could se. An other tyme the snowe would blowe ouer halfe the feld at ones. Sometyme the snow woulde tomble softly, by and by it would flye wonderfull fast. And thys I perceyved also that ye wind goeth by streames & not hole togither.[17]

This virtual prose poem, a tribute to "delyte and pleasure," is a digression in Ascham's text prompted by the entrancingly digressive and indeed magical spectacle of the wind, yet all the digressive or dilatory promise of the writing is quickly subordinated again to the real point (for the toxophile, there will always be a real point), which is that the bowman must learn to compensate for crosswinds. Thus when Gascoigne begins to tell an autobiographical story that is virtually all about missing the mark, repeatedly going astray, and self-proliferation, he is doing so in a primed situation. His representation is countercultural with respect to *Toxophilus*, a text that derives its own authority from classical sources, and also covertly so with respect to the system of order, value, and identity manifested in Lord Grey's "pastoral" recreations.

The verse text begins by merely making excuses for failure, with reference directly to Lord Grey's commands:

> My woorthy Lord, I pray you wonder not,
> To see your woodman shoote so ofte awrie,
> Nor that he stands amased like a sot,
> And lets the harmlesse deare (unhurt) go by.
> Or if he strike a Doe which is but carren,*
> Laugh not good Lord, but favoure such a fault,
> Take will in worth, he would faine hit the barren,†
> But though his harte be good, his happe is naught.
>
> (1–8)

carren: with young and hence unfit to eat
†*barren*: does without fawns (Sylvester)

The speaker appears to be claiming (again!) that he means well ("take will in worth") but has recurrent bad luck ("his happe is naught"). These rationalizations don't, however, account for everything that is happening in the passage. The deferential speaker implies in the second line that he is speaking in the drastically *self-alienated* person of one of Lord Grey's woodmen, in which case the self-excusing voice is not fully his own; a subversive counterdiscourse is also audible. In this discourse the reasonableness of shooting "harmlesse" deer, whether carren or barren, isn't self-evident, nor is it clear whether good heartedness would result in submission or resistance to Lord Grey's commands. As in the Wyatt satire I discussed earlier, the speaker's failure or rebellious naughtiness of will can be implied under the term "naught"; the prose text has already claimed that the speaker deliberately misses the mark. Here too, as in Wyatt, the hart/heart and deer/dear puns conflate erotic pursuit with the violence of the chase in general, and here again these puns necessarily suggest a certain natural or a priori sympathy between those cast in the roles of hunter and hunted.

To have been made one of Lord Grey's "woodmen," then, can mean having been made answerable to authorized demands for brutal, gender-coded performance, and ones so powerfully authorized as to preclude any simple or putatively emancipated resistance. Even the passive resistance of the persistently failing "woodman" will make him look like a fool or a madman ("amased like a sot"). At best, perhaps, a "humorous" (humoring) deferral of these requirements can be attempted, and that is evidently part of what Gascoigne undertakes in his jocular, protracted allegory. Yet in the space of this deferral, alternative possibilities proliferate.

First, Gascoigne's career of failure as a lawyer, soldier, and courtier is retroactively subsumed and justified under this scenario of the failing woodman:

> For proofe, he beares the note of follie now,
> Who shotte sometimes to hitte Philosophie.
> ·
> Next that, he shot to be a man of lawe,

And spent sometime with learned *Litleton*,
Yet in the end, he proved but a dawe.
. . . .
From thence he shotte to catch a courtly grace
And thought even there to wield the world at will,
But out alas he much mistooke the place,
And shot awrie at every rover still.

(17–36)

In establishing the putative justification for all these failures, Gascoigne can and does invoke various well-established terms of countercultural humanistic enlightenment and sympathy. It is virtually a satirical truism of the period that success in law, the court, or the military entails personal degradation. Moreover, English Renaissance love poetry regularly invokes the commonplaces of natural ("kind") affection and sympathy against forms of culturally authorized violence. Inasmuch as that violence emanates from the schooled and directed will of the "princely" masculine subject, sensitively taking the part of the woman / hunted / other, including that "part" of the self, becomes programmatically thinkable. This subtext of sympathetic enlightenment becomes highly overt in More's *Utopia*, for example, in which princes and the aristocratic chase are excoriated, in Erasmus's *Praise of Folly*, and in Montaigne's essay on cruelty. Furthermore, the philosophical justification of folly—which is also to say the pursuit of philosophy in a vein other than that of male scholastic dogmatism—is widely disseminated in the period. Gascoigne's trope of dim-sighted old age permits the reclamation of more philosophical second sight. In short, there are any number of terms, including finally those of a widely disseminated neoplatonism, under which "failure" to conform to heartless and mindless dominant criteria can be regarded as desirable. Such appears to be the case in Gascoigne's praise of (his own) folly.

It is hardly necessary to point out just how problematic these forms of "good will" are, or how problematic is any attempt to sustain a cultural / countercultural coding of the forms of will that circulate in Gascoigne's vacillating, discontinuous, and generically unstable text. The belatedness of the text with regard to the facts and its status as rationalization cannot be disguised, while its drift towards making its subject into the figure of the one just man—that is, into the intolerably narcissistic subject of an interminable satiric diatribe against the world—is already anticipated in the Wyatt satire I have discussed, and which Gascoigne may also be imitating when he writes that:

> He cannot climbe as other catchers can
> To leade a charge before himselfe be led;
> He cannot spoile the simple sakeles man,
> Which is content to feede him with his bread.
> He cannot pinch the painefull souldiers pay,
> And sheare him out his share in ragged sheetes,
> He cannot stoupe to take a greedy pray
> Upon his fellowes groveling in the streetes.
> . . . .
> And now adayes, the man that shootes not so,
> May shoote amisse, even as your Woodman dothe.
>   (73–86)

In a word, the profoundly self-centered, retrograde drift of this countercultural discourse—its being the site of endless bad-faith investments—becomes apparent in the poem, as does the accompanying construction of a highly inauthentic ego-ideal through the device of the alienated third-person. The subjected "he" who speaks at Lord Grey's bidding progressively but dubiously becomes invested with the characteristics of an ideal other with which the self may finally become fully identified—and with respect to which endless denial of a "bad" or complicit self can be maintained. Although active self-denial and an ethical posture can be said to possess value in the stoic frame of satire, what emerges in the quoted lines is more like a ridiculous, secularized *imitatio Christi*. The radical duplicity of this self-construction gets exposed when the poem takes a confessional turn, which is also a pleasurable homecoming to the all-engrossing plenitude of the first person:

> Yet therewithall I can not but confesse,
> That vayne presumption makes my heart to swell,

For thus I thinke, not all the world (I guesse)
Shootes bet than I, nay some shootes not so well.
(97–100)

This confession of the crypto-toxophile seemingly enables him to
have his duplicity both ways. More tellingly, however, it implies
the at least *crypto*-toxophilic signification of the "I" as such, from
whatever position in the text (or perhaps the culture itself) it is
spoken. The ostensibly deviant and recalcitrant aspects of the performance thus appear all along to have been in the secret and inescapable service of the self-empowering autobiographical subject,
never other but always the same in whatever resistant or disarming
guise. Indeed, what seems to emerge as the most authentic anxiety
of the Gascoigne speaker is that premature narcissistic arrest or
excessive deferral might cause him *really* to miss out on the action,
and thus on self-construction:

And whiles mine eyes beholde this mirrour thus,
The hearde goeth by, and farewell gentle does.
(121–22)

~~~

In dealing with the verse text, I have perhaps too problematically conflated the antioedipal with the countercultural, and have
done so at the risk of allowing the latter term to displace the former. Yet in fact this apparent displacement is no more than a de-
tour, and the conflation is unavoidable for as long as the thematic
of cultural production and inheritance continues to be pursued,
as it is so often is, under the aspect of a dominant oedipal scenario—one that can anticipate and contain at least some of its
own most problematic features. "Gascoigne's woodmanship" implies that any devices that appear to contest, retard, or transform-
ingly supplement this "master" script will merely support it in
reality; similarly, every form of deferral or counterrepresentation
recognizable within the culture may be virtually foredoomed to
failure and/or dissimulating complicity. In this of all spheres,
good intentions will count for nothing.

Never for a moment having departed from it, the ending of the verse text enacts the eventual return of/to the "classic" script. This ending does not of course explicitly confirm any oedipal thesis, partly because, whether in profession or fact, the poem's rationale escapes its speaker in the end, when he simply gives up on his "tedious tale in rime, but little reason" (150). In other words, this ending does not propound a retroactive thesis, nor can it propound an "oedipal" one in our sense of the term inasmuch as that would require historically unavailable analytical access to the Freudian Unconscious. Not even the Shakespeare who wrote *Hamlet* possessed that, and only within a structure of *Nachträglichkeit* can *Hamlet* assume its psychoanalytic status as the supreme "anatomical" text of the culture.[18] Yet the scenario finally produced in "Gascoigne's woodmanship" in an apparent attempt at self-decoding is an incompletely precipitated oedipal one:

> Let me imagine in this woorthlesse verse
> If right before mee, at my standings foote
> There stood a Doe, and I should strike hir deade,
> And then shee prove a carrian carkas too,
> What figure might I finde within my head,
> To scuse the rage whiche rulde mee so to doo?
> . . . .
> I say *Jehova* did this Doe advaunce,
> And made hir bolde to stande before mee so,
> Till I had thrust mine arrowe to hir harte,
> That by the sodaine of hir overthrowe,
> I might endevour to amende my parte,
> And turne myne eyes that they no more beholde,
> Such guylefull markes as seeme more than they be:
> And though they glister outwardely like golde,
> Are inwardly but brasse, as men may see:
> And when I see the milke hang in hir teate,
> Me thinks it sayth, old babe now learne to sucke,
> Who in thy youth could never learne the feate
> To hitte the whytes that live with all good lucke.
>
> (127–48)

Let us recognize one more time that there is still a subtext of Elizabethan patronage in these lines inasmuch as the doe can emerge as a potentially nurturing mother, materially "carren" even if physiologically "barren," while shooting at the "barren" may suddenly have become highly counterproductive. Yet the historical circumstance of female rule facilitates a shift within rather than away from the paternal-patrilineal construction of culture. Admittedly, it legitimizes at least the appearance of narcissistic regression rather than oedipal progression in the construction of the masculine subject, and may indeed temporarily forestall that progression, requiring it to be historically suspended or dissimulated within a more "civilized" order of things. It apparently undermines fixed hierarchy and gender-identity, constituting the feminine and the androgynous as powerful roles to be played. Finally, it allows the return of/to a repressed maternal origin and genealogy to be powerfully and opportunistically troped, and also threateningly troped at least for the male author inasmuch as it infantilizes him. Like the Gascoigne speaker, this "author" may find himself, as old babe, back where it all began. The appearance of antioedipal poetics in all this, however, is less convincing than the evidence of a crossed-up oedipal script—one that becomes virtually the normal script of Elizabethan authorship.

~~~

By now the conclusion to my discussion, like the ending of Gascoigne's text, is practically foregone. This double foregone conclusion, which attests to the constraining power and elasticity of the oedipal plot, remains only to be drawn explicitly. The strange final "imagining" that ends the poem (lines 127–48) is brought on by the speaker's continuing inability to account for his own perverse, failing woodmanship. What he then produces is, in effect, a mysterious emblem through which he finally attempts to read himself. Switching as well from an inductive to a deductive approach, he imagines himself having shot a doe that turns out to be "carrian," and thus unfit to eat. How is this mysterious rage to be construed?

Three incompatible readings of the imaginary event are produced in the poem: (1) his hitting the doe is simply a further instance of his perverse misfortune in a world governed by fortune, since even the mark he hits is the wrong one; (2) the doe is a heuristic device employed by "Jehova" to teach the speaker once and for all to stop aiming at unworthy marks implying false values; (3) that the truly instructive emblem is the maternal-feminine one of the *carren* doe, which may teach the speaker about sources of power and nourishment to which he had better attach himself for the duration of his limited future. The poem thus finally and inconclusively rehearses a fairly standard Elizabethan interpretive repertoire.

From our own standpoint, this historic repertoire calls for recognition, but it is practically impossible to inhabit its perspectives for reasons that are no less historic. The unexpected intrusion of Jehova into a scene from which he has not only been absent, but might have been expected to remain so, gives the game away. The *imagining* of the doe, which is also its apparent symbolic sublation as the Doe, triggers or makes manifest a desire that has hitherto been absent or denied in the poem. While this rage to "strike hir deade" implies a contradictory violence of separation, mastery, and masculine (re)identification, the continuity of desire is nonetheless implied in the speaker's toxophile figures of thrusting and overthrowing. This imagined release of "rage," which is inseparable from the figurative sublation of its object, simultaneously triggers the prohibitive "return" of the hitherto absent Father. The speaker's utterance of the ultimate, archaic *nom du père* is practically indistinguishable from his hearing the *non du père*, albeit a "*non*" expounded in a language, peculiarly forced even in its historic context, of stoic edification.

The speaker's bizarre fantasy that he has been presented with the Doe as a moral emblem by Jehova implies Jehova's continuing possession of the Doe and the speaker's never more than imaginary access to her. The Doe's being offered as a virtual scapegoat for the speaker's guilty desire also seemingly arrests his rage before any of it can be turned against the lawgiver Himself. At the same time, any prohibitive power of the woman (*diva virago*, phallic mother) is reconstrued as a function of the father's possession and investment of her. The moment of imagined "rage" and renewed prohibition having passed, the speaker is apparently left to enjoy a more innocuous form of access to, and dependency upon, the maternal-nourishing Doe.

Recalling now the starting point of this discussion, we still have a speaker whose language may know more of desire than he does, yet something closer to knowledge or recognition has surfaced at the end of this text. What appear to be present, though arguably misrecognized by their interpreter in the poem, are the elements of an oedipal scenario that has not yet crystallized into one or more of the forms it can take in modern psychoanalytic interpretation—for example, that of the "classic" Oedipus Complex, of the Lacanian "fallen" Oedipus Complex, or of an oedipal scenario that emphasizes the maternal-preoedipal phase.[19]

While it might be possible for us to read the poem's ending into one of these "fulfilled" scenarios, the imperfectly elicited master script of this autobiographical verse is indeed the oedipal one, and the position of the speaker in it continues be that of the one who fails—either with reference to an unassailably reified lawgiving "father" or to one who, as "[m]other," no less unassailably occupies the same position. In either case, the poem's counterdiscourses, to the extent that they exist, remain failed or dissimulating instances of an oedipal discourse. This is what makes Gascoigne's script an unusually valuable diagnostic one for the Elizabethan period—and for consideration of what Gascoigne's poetic successors have to contend with.

6

Shakespeare's Figure of Lucrece: Writing Rape

I suggested in my introduction that the Shakespeare of "Lucrece" remains within the frame of this book although with differences that include more complex mediations, an at least incipient inter-activeness in representation, a new emphasis on forms of exchange, a capacity for shifting reified antitheses and fixed alignments, and an evident commitment to the socialization of the poetic. All this could add up to a marked capacity for producing difference even within parameters that do not necessarily change. These forms of difference will be highlighted in my discussion, yet their capacity to *make* a difference remains somewhat questionable here. I have already implied that the Jacobean Shakespeare is far from escaping the consequences of the "restoration" anticipated at various points in this book, and in some ways the parameters of representation that have been evident throughout this discussion are even more starkly exposed in "Lucrece" than in the work of any of the poets treated so far. The poem could thus give a specially disconcerting twist to the cliché *plus ça change, plus c'est la même chose.* My account could also parallel a view of the sonnets advanced by Joel Fineman's *Shakespeare's Perjur'd Eye*, which is that the Shakespearean break with what might there be called homomorphic representation can only be a break into aggressively heteromorphic (misogynistically heterosexual) representation. The attempted representation of otherness or difference, including gender difference, will, in other words, be *structurally* proprietary and alienating, double and contradictory, but never "just." Moreover, the attempted representation of difference may

140

overtax or introduce intolerable contradiction into the system of neoclassical rhetoric, in which difference is regularly suppressed while the ratios and substitutions that permit resemblance to be claimed are specified (metaphor, metonymy, synecdoche, and so on).

The capacity of Shakespeare or anyone else to institute difference, not just systematically but systemically, in traditional representation is accordingly questionable—it has been so throughout this book—but that is the question that I take to be principally and appropriately at stake in our current reading of Shakespeare. If "Lucrece" is far from being a text that can bear the entire "Shakespearean" burden—or the full charge of what is at issue in our reading of Shakespeare—it is nonetheless a text that enables the effect of cumulative differences, including their displacement of anterior forms, to be considered. It is thus a text that particularly lends itself to consideration in the frame of this book, but is also a text that resists this framing.

~~~

In more than one sense, Shakespeare is repeating history when he rewrites the narrative of Lucrece. Her story is first related in Livy's larger history of Rome, in which, however, it is not precisely her story, since she is not heard. It is then frequently retold in historical, literary, and other texts. Ovid, Augustine, Chaucer, and Machiavelli may be the most notable repeaters of the Lucrece story before Shakespeare, but they are far from being the only ones. The history of Lucrece thus comes to include the history of its textual repetition.[1]

It might be suggested that what motivates or corresponds to this textual repetition is the sociohistorical recurrence of rape, in which case the repetition at every level of Lucrece's history threatens to be endless and identical. Moreover, the mere fact of this repetition may seem to imply the existence of a stable, transhistorical fatality of political life and/or gender relations in which rape is virtually predestined to keep on occurring identically, perhaps as the negatively defining nexus of masculine and feminine identity. The actuality of this threat of repetition reveals itself at the authorial and critical level as well as in the narrative; "writing rape" ("the violence of the letter") threatens merely to reinstantiate rape, as we shall see, and it is difficult at least for any male critic to avoid repeating the action, at once pusillanimous and relentless, of Tarquin in the poem. It is also difficult for the male critic not to repeat the abusive cliché that rape is the secret desire of the female victim, betrayed by her body language. Indeed, this cliché, which is also that of the masculine observer, *is* repeated in the poem, but with a difference.

Here I shall argue that Shakespeare, while far from escaping repetition and in some ways only intensifying it, tries to stake out a field of conscious reflection, and possibly of conscious sociopolitical interest and representation, in "Lucrece," doing so within and against this seemingly fateful repetition. This repetition with a difference is at once facilitated by and manifested in Shakespeare's expansion of the usually brief Lucrece story to "minor epic" proportions. Among other things gained through this expansion, I will suggest, is this space of putative reflection, volition, and maneuver. This gain constitutes part of the distinctively Shakespearean interest of the poem, just as it reveals a distinctively Shakespearean interest in the story of Lucrece. Correspondingly, the poem has something to lose from simply being assimilated to its textual predecessors.

A corollary to this claim (or perhaps it is just another way of making the claim) is that Shakespeare's poem enacts a sustained problematization of the abstraction, reification, or totalization of rape. It accordingly enacts a sustained interrogation of the totalization of gender differences, of the accompanying totalization of violence and abuse, and of the representation of rape as a violation of essence. Correspondingly, rape does not emerge as the constitutive thing unequivocally signified by the poem or in the poem.[2] Nor can rape be regarded as an extratextual phenomenon, an ideal Aristotelian action, or a pure social fact that the poem merely imitates or reflects.[3] In none of these ways is the poem simply "about" rape, though the assumption that it is so (or must be so) is encouraged by the 1616 Folio, in which "The Rape of" was added to the poem's 1594 quarto title, "Lucrece."

All these differences, many of them between the poem and its textual predecessors, notably including those of Livy and Augustine, render "Lucrece" somewhat insusceptible to totalizing criticism of the kind that has been practiced, sometimes in relation to it, but perhaps more often in relation to Richardson's *Clarissa*.[4] Furthermore, it makes an issue not just of reading rape but of writing it—of writing rape, that is to say, as literature, as law, and as social or even sociobiological fact. The question of difference, or of the capacity to make a difference, is thus posed at the level of writing. It becomes a question of the level at which rewriting could hope to begin, or would have to begin.

~~~

We can begin—but only begin—to consider the poem's repetition with a difference by noting that Shakespeare does not identify rape with the single or punctual act of physical penetration. Nor does he fully identify the crime with Tarquin, who increasingly emerges as the problematic scapegoat-rapist of the poem. In Shakespeare's poem, Tarquin's penetration of Lucrece—or whatever—occurs between two stanzas, not in any one stanza, and it is therefore "censored," meaning that only one thing can be understood to occur there—or that nothing definitively occurs *there*. One stanza ends with the lines "The spots whereof could weeping purify / Her tears would drop on them perpetually," and another begins "But she hath lost a dearer thing than life."[5] What actually happens in the relevant blank—a blank in which Tarquin's action may or may not coincide with something Lucrece has already been dreaming as he watches her sleep—is left, as the saying goes, to the reader's imagination. Yet if penetration must be supposed to occur in, or unequivocally to be signified by, this blank space, it is anticipated in the preceding stanza and also temporally displaced, possibly to the occasion of marital deflowering, in which the consent and even the desire of the woman is rightly or wrongly assumed by the law. Temporal displacement to an even earlier psychic or literal violation by the father (or dream of it) cannot be ruled out.[6] As a result of this apparent temporal displacement or indeterminacy, an internal scenario of repetition with a difference is introduced into the poem. Lucrece's sense of being tainted or unchaste is thus related to more than one possible scenario of rape, including that of its unfulfilled dream-recurrence in her mind.

Admittedly, one could say that this particular "deletion" principally confirms that rape is not a sexual crime and that physical penetration is not constitutive of it. Rather, it is a crime of violence, which the penetration merely instantiates, and that is what we see it to be in Lucrece's bedroom, in which Tarquin's violence *is* represented and which thus remains definitively the scene of a rape. What is constitutive, legally and phenomenologically, is Tarquin's threat of violence and his defamatory plot. This possibility is doubly marked in the poem inasmuch as there is evidence of Lucrece's willingness to sleep with someone other than her husband without being threatened, and hence at least of his choosing to *make* it a rape. Tarquin recalls the moment in which Lucrece received him:

> "she took me kindly by the hand,
> And gaz'd for tidings in my eager eyes,
> Fearing some hard news from the warlike band
> Where her beloved Collatinus lies.
> O how her fear did make her colour rise!
>   First red as roses that on lawn we lay,
>   Then white as lawn, the roses took away.
>
> "And how her hand in my hand being lock'd,
> Forc'd it to tremble with her loyal fear!
> Which strook her sad, and then it faster rock'd,
> Until her husband's welfare she did hear;
> Whereat she smiled with so sweet a cheer
>   That had Narcissus seen her as she stood,
>   Self-love had never drown'd him in the flood."
>   (253–66)

These two stanzas are part of the poem's endless rereading of the mingled red and white in Lucrece's face. Here the colors are read into the best possible construction of Lucrece's behavior as loving wife, namely that she is concerned for nothing but her husband's safety. Yet it is Tarquin the would-be rapist who effects this reading—he precisely does not claim that she secretly desires him—and who construes Lucrece's trembling handclasp and sweetly enigmatic smile as evidence of pure concern about Collatine. To say that there is a sign or body language here that can be read otherwise is *not* to say that Tarquin, in raping or attempting to rape Lucrece, enacts her secret desire, but rather that his nonrecognition of any alternative to rape seems to be a function of his own ironically betrayed narcissism. Nothing but rape, it would seem, of an empowered, married woman who also "belongs" to her husband can effect the competitive male autonomization he desires. In this critical moment, Tarquin as rapist paradoxically becomes the ideal reader of Lucrece as chaste, loving wife. His reading denies her the natural ("kind") motive of wanting a lover rather than a husband who is always literally or figuratively in the wars with other men. It also denies her the "unkind" but not socially or culturally insignificant one of masochistically exposing herself to a putative figure of masculine power. We are thus made aware of avenues not explored at this point in the poem, at least by Tarquin; in Shakespeare's "Lucrece," like *Clarissa*, a rape scenario is not the only possible one between adult principals. Nor does there seem to be any moment in the poem in which that scenario can be the sole or self-identical one.

Yet even if rape is to be construed here as a crime of violence rather than as a sexual one, it apparently takes its place in a violent continuum without a clear origin or end. The violence begins in the poem with the siege of Ardea; continues when Collatine invidiously boasts of his possession of Lucrece and thus exposes her to danger; continues when Tarquin arrives at her house while her husband is away, in a manner that may already, as the poem implies, taint her in the eyes of her servants; continues when the (prose) siege is replayed as (poetic) rape, just as it does when (poetic) rape is folded over and replayed as (prose) siege; continues when Lucrece "gratuitously" commits suicide, thus effecting an intensified repetition as well as attempted annulment of rape after everyone has declared her innocent; continues when the men in her life competitively seek to appropriate her in a grieving contest; arguably continues when the Brutus of the poem exploits the situation to reveal himself as a hitherto unsuspected political contender. Within this continuum of violence, rape can mean physical assault on Lucrece's person, but as an act of seizure (*raptus*) it can also be regarded as that which nonexclusively instantiates an originary violent desire for and crime against private property, not excluding textual property:

> why is Collatine the publisher
> Of that rich jewel he should keep unknown
> From thievish ears, because it is his own?
> (33–35)[7]

If the rape remains unlocated as a sexual crime, then, it also seems unlocated as a crime of violence. This diffusion of rape in the text might seem to constitute part of Shakespeare's problematization of it, as well as resistance to its reification, yet this diffusion also threateningly generalizes it. Moreover, abusive masculine spectatorship as well as originary masculine violence seem to be displaced "upward" towards the reader and/or the author: indeed, the tendency of the poem to relocate all violence in writing, reading, and the acquisition of textual property, hence "authorship," has previously been remarked by critics including Dubrow. In other words, resistance to reification alone constitutes an insufficient political-representational strategy.

Thus far, however, we have not considered the extended representation of Lucrece as a site of potential difference, both in her problematic capacity to act against the repetition and totalization of rape, in her capacity to act for or against the Shakespearean "interest," and in her capacity to facilitate the forms of mediation and exchange that might be capable of instituting difference.

An impulse to regard rape as an elementary form or originary event is at once manifested and resisted by Lucrece herself. She attempts to trace her own victimized situation back to that of fateful, "originary" rape in the Troy story, where it has frequently been located, and her victimization—or rather, her conflicted desire to be and not to be in the victim position—appears when she seeks out the abducted married woman, Helen, in the Trojan picture she eventually confronts. In identifying Helen, however, not as the victim but as the whorishly culpable cause of her own undoing, Lucrece as chaste Roman drastically separates herself from infamous Greek Helen, and perhaps from certain temptations of power. (The negative differentiation and positive identification effected through rape thus reemerge between women as well as between men and women.) Yet her momentary recognition of Helen as alter ego does allow her to recognize the possible power or complicity of the woman as passive-aggressive cause of Troy's fall, an event in which, incidentally, the cultural *translatio* in which Rome is founded begins. In this drama of power and violent inheritance, it is not quite clear whether the man or the woman comes first—or who desires to occupy the originary position. Lucrece's subjective/objective genitive, "Helen's rape" (1369), lodges this indeterminacy in the poem and locates a certain doubleness or even duplicity at the origin of cultural violence and inheritance. After surveying the entire scene, however, Lucrece fails to recognize herself or originary rape in Troy—or resists doing so.

The refusal of identification with Helen does not, however, fully or differentially identify the chaste Roman Lucrece, but rather makes her a baffling and self-baffled figure, while it contributes to the generic instability of the poem that bears her name. If this refusal sets Lucrece up to be the tragically abused victim, no less does it enable her to subvert tragic (or reified) high seriousness. Not only is Shakespeare's figure of Lucrece assimilated to a Renaissance dialectic of will and wit, tragic high seriousness and deflating humor, but the figure of Lucrece becomes the eponymous one in Shakespeare's ironic "Ovidian" poem, in which tension is periodically reduced by a garrulous narrator (the rape narrative is not identical with the poem). Moreover, the poem will not sustain high seriousness as it transforms itself finally into a humorous etiological one to explain why Lucrece's spilt blood splits into three fractions. In short, neither Lucrece nor the poem will sustain anyone's critical high seriousness, or will do so only on the rather ironic condition of being critically silenced.

It is Lucrece who, lamenting in isolation after the departure of Tarquin, avowedly finds her own complaints tedious in the end, and cuts them off before turning to more economical and productive use of her resources.[8] And it is she, the figure in the poem most entitled to do so, who may find the whole overwrought, impossible situation ludicrous in the end. When she is asked to identify her assailant, she does not successfully name Tarquin, but can only manage a repeated "He, He—" (1717, 1721). (Tarquin's name is produced as that of the definitive rapist by Lucrece's furiously proprietary father.) In Lucrece's own locution, we may hear the echo of a Chaucerian giggle. Or rather, we can undeniably hear this even while we hear Lucrece, like Clarissa, incriminate Man in general rather than any particular man: it is He, *He*, who is responsible. The point is that Lucrece's final utterance will not *sustain* the reification of her rape or of Tarquin as the definitive figure of the rapist.

This failure of definition or final identification is accompanied by the extraordinary tinctures and crossings of Lucrece's representation in general, and specifically in her extended, multiphase blazon, that feature of the poem that is so often discussed. It is within this hugely expanded field of indeterminacy that tinctures, crossings, and mergers of "interest" become important, while identities become virtually untraceable.

At one level, the blazon of Lucrece is the utterly conventional one of the Elizabethan poet, which Louis Montrose among others has read in terms both of a conventional Petrarchanism and of the iconography of Queen Elizabeth, to which Spenser notably contributes.[9] On Shakespeare's part as "woman's poet," and no doubt on Spenser's as well, a certain identificatory interest in the Petrarchan queen and a sympathetic view of her threatened position among violent Elizabethan noblemen can be inferred. An unsuspected Shakespearean interest in the queen's successfully maintained character of chastity, all the ugly "tainting" Elizabethan rumors notwithstanding, may also disclose itself in due course. Something other than identificatory sympathy is present in the blazon of Lucrece, however, since one of those who produces it is Tarquin as beholder, intent on penetrating the shield of chastity which Lucrece, as Roman wife rather than Virgin Mary, mysteriously still possesses.

This reminds us that the blazon is conventionally the product of the masculine master-perspective or objectifying gaze, which at once fixes and anatomizes, composes and decomposes, its object.[10] In this poem, however, the gaze of the observer is itself fractured and distributed among successive observers—even if it is also displaced "upward"—and forms of reciprocal exchange between gazer and object begin to assume increased significance.

The prolonged blazoning of Lucrece begins when her husband, Collatine, is reported as praising the "clear unmatched red and white / Which triumphed in the sky of his delight" (11–12). This crudely self-serving appropriation of Lucrece in the act of praising her coincides with, but is simultaneously exposed as, a very simple reading of her, that of naively totalized self-interest. For Collatine, Lucrece's red and white are stable, stably opposed and distinct, and uncontradictorily combined. This figure of pure Petrarchan triumph is one that Collatine also assimilates to an immaculate *purity*, not cosmetic beauty, when he goes on, like a witless Astrophil, to stellify Lucrece along with other "mortal stars as bright as heaven's beauties" (13)—stars that are there, however, only to do him "peculiar duties." Ironically, just as the "ideal" reading of Lucrece as dutiful wife comes from her would-be rapist, so the "ideal" Petrarchan reading of her comes from the crudely possessive husband, exposed as such.

From Collatine's point of view, Lucrece's possible interests, which are not necessarily undivided, remain unacknowledged, nor is any interest manifested in her. A more complex and arguably more interesting as well as interested figure of Lucrece succeeds this one. It is the developing figure of Lucrece in the criminal/incriminating eye of Tarquin, but then also of Tarquin in the eye of Lucrece. (The question of who has the superior or more encompassing eye, Tarquin or Lucrece, is played out through a series of grotesque "eye/I" puns akin to those of the sonnets.) For Tarquin, Lucrece is the property of another, but by the same token one who acquires the properties of another, properties not fully identical to those of the self:

> When at Collatium this false lord arrived,
> Well was he welcome'd by the Roman dame,
> Within whose face beauty and virtue strived
> Which of them both should underprop her fame.
> When virtue bragg'd, beauty would blush for shame;
>   When beauty boasted blushes, in despite
>   Virtue would stain that o'er with silver white.
>
>   (50–55)

The stable, distinct red and white of Collatine's description have been destabilized (or mobilized) here, and have entered, as Joel Fineman has claimed in the related instance of "Venus and Adonis," into an increasingly complex pattern of chiastic crossing, in which separate identities, original positions, and determinate significations are rapidly effaced.[11] (Silver and gold later take the place of white and red, but not respectively so, since each color can fight with the other color, fight under the other color, or blend into it.) Distinctions between background and foreground, face and mask, surface and depth, are equally undone, and so therefore is the topography that would enable any moral determination to be made about Lucrece's complicity or otherwise in the rape, or perhaps about the respective positions of the participants.

Moreover, with the introduction of all these chiastic figures, a new form of representation enters the field of the poem. This is what I shall call the cross-representation of individual subjects' material interests that would otherwise remain merely opposed, incommensurable, irreconcilable, or even unrepresented. Not only does this pattern of cross-representation become more marked as the poem continues, but it is a form of representation of which Lucrece becomes the key figure by being "blazoned." (This process renders more complex and generally *representative* the figure of the Petrarchan woman as well as of the queen who unites the houses of York and Lancaster.)

This blazon is one in which the interest of Lucrece appears to be not simple, but divided or reciprocal inasmuch as virtue and beauty constitute two possible and antithetical grounds of fame, the former being the claim of the iconically chaste wife, akin to that of the stoic Roman man of virtue, and the latter being the claim of the more glamorously infamous beauty, figured for Lucrece by Helen of Troy. Yet these putative interests coincide inasmuch as they imply a common interest in fame, and yet again they divide inasmuch as "fame" can mean good reputation or notoriety. What we have in the figure of Lucrece, then, is a model of actual or potential unity as well as conflict of interest, but also a model of one in whom antithetical interests may be cross-represented—for example, that of virtue by beauty and vice versa, or that of Greek Helen by Roman Lucrece and vice versa. While the crossing may remain incomplete, the possibility of cross-representation also applies to the interaction between Lucrece and the increasingly reciprocal figure of Tarquin—an interaction in which each beholder sees him/herself figured in the other. Not for nothing does Lucrece say at one point, "In Tarquin's likeness I did entertain thee," thus identifying herself, no doubt inadvertently, with her rapist—or with the King Tarquin who is the rapist's namesake elder brother, the original rather than the likeness already found wanting. This reciprocation, in which the non-self-identify of the identified, gendered principals is increasingly implied, leads up to the final moment of the blazon, in which Lucrece's blood is finally spilt—or "let," to adopt one of the poem's favored locutions. The spilt blood immediately splits into three fractions.

We may have imagined, as we have often been led to do in the poem, that there is a "bottom line," and that the redness of blood is (at last!) a primary color or determinate signifier, on the one hand of masculine violence, or on the other of feminine passion and guilt, betrayed by an uncontrollable blushing.[12] Yet Lucrece's spilt blood splits into the three fractions, a red, a black, and a pale, watery corona or "rigol" (1745). The blood of the living Lucrece is thus shown to have been a tincture all along, not a primordial entity, signifier, or natural cause. If this paradoxical "clarification" is part of what makes Lucrece's death the cathartic one of the poem—makes it a therapeutic bloodletting that renders her own figure and everything else in the poem dis-tinct—what it makes distinct is, ironically, the non-self-identity of Lucrece as well as of her interest.

There are now three colors or tinctures to which Lucrece may be assimilated: the pale, virtually pure "rigol," red, which is now indeterminately a primary color and a tincture (whole and part at once), and an unexpected dark tint/taint close to black. This un-suspected dark fraction, identified in the poem as the Tarquin strain, implies Lucrece's partial internalization of the Tarquin fig-ure and hence her ability to cross-represent him up to a point (it is through her action that King Tarquin is deposed). It is also, however, the strain or tincture in which the ink can most readily be identified. We are made to see that Lucrece's "character" and fate are—or have been—written all along, yet not exclusively in black as the color of her doom and/or "hidden" criminality, or in blood as the color of irrepressible natural passion, or in the ethe-real "rigol" of endless (or only *slightly* tinted) purity.

The final exposure of Lucrece's tainting writtenness not only implies the "crossing" complexity of the Shakespearean invest-ment in her figure, but also the possibility of her being rewritten, ultimately even by her own hand. It implies the possibility of her being rewritten right down to the biological level that may seem to constitute destiny in the final analysis.[13] In his figure of Lu-crece, Shakespeare foregrounds even the biological determina-tion—or that one above all in the end, since it is equally the de-termination of the male author as perpetual rapist-manqué. While no full, specular interchange can ever be said to occur between Shakespeare as author and the represented figure of Lucrece, a certain crossing of "selves" and material interests can now be considered, as can the displacement of primary identities and gender determinations.

~~~

In an almost uncanny way, we may be brought to the recognition of a Shakespearean interest in the figure of Lucrece as woman by the feminist discourse that seems most antipathetic to it. This is the now arguably "primitive," foundational feminist discourse in which rape is not just reified, but projected in the most primordial, elementary form. Such a projection is contained in a work by Susan Brownmiller with the suitably anti-Shakespearean title *Against Our Will: Men, Women and Rape*.[14]

Brownmiller reimagines prehistory such that rape constitutes the sole, universal, and absolutely differential nexus of relation between the sexes. (One can hardly speak of constructed genders at that stage.) By virtue of man's biological advantage in strength over woman, he is able to turn his penis into an offensive weapon and to assert his power at his will. It is open season on rape. Brownmiller also imagines a primordial moment in which the woman is "fighting like hell to preserve her physical integrity" (22), but because of her biological disadvantage she must strike a "risky bargain," namely that of placing herself under the protection of a particular man.

This first form of the social contract in a hitherto Hobbesian world of endless rape is the one in which the institution of marriage is born. For Brownmiller, however, the primordial state of affairs, which is biologically determined, is mitigated but not radically changed in any subsequent version of the social contract. The implied threat against women, or against any particular woman, is that of recourse to rape in the final analysis; in principle, furthermore, every married woman is still a raped virgin, the only difference being that she is the private property of a single rapist rather than the common possession of an entire rapist community. Every social formation, material practice, and representation will betray the continuation of originary rape, which also remains the unalterable content of social life and gender relations. Rape is the signified in which all signifiers originate, and to which they inevitably return.

Confirmation of this thesis might be claimed from the notorious figurative overload of Shakespeare's "Lucrece," in which "the violence of the letter" is sufficiently foregrounded.[15] In the scene of rape, moreover, Tarquin's displayed sword is metonymically his penis (and vice versa). Neither this assumed figurative telos nor this figurative equivalence, however, is the same as primordial identity. The sword, after all, is no more nor less a cultural artifact than is the mythic phallus, and neither is an inalienable form or function of alleged male biological supremacy. In the poem, moreover, sword, spear, phallus, engraving tool, pen, embroidery needle, gauntlet, and glove are all within the same substitutive chain, as are various senses of the word "pricking." Among other things, it is the woman's power to alienate ostensibly male tools and signifiers that Lucrece's entry into writing and her eventual suicide reveal. It is by these means that she penetrates (or always and already inhabits) masculine order in both the critical and political senses of the word, and it is by these means that she inserts herself into the poem's circulation of power and violence, though to what eventual avail and in whose ultimate interests is debatable.[16]

Correlatively, it appears to be Tarquin's unrealizable desire in the poem to reestablish primordial male identity by explicitly willing or intending rape. Yet after the blank in the poem, Tarquin seems to find not only that he has not been authenticated or taken the place of his own elder brother, but that he has been penetrated himself. This also constitutes his own discovery of himself in the place of the female other rather than of the authenticated male self:

> his soul's fair temple is defaced,
> To whose weak ruins muster troops of cares,
> To ask the spotted princess how she fares.
>   (719–21)

A voice within, now that of Lucrece as internalized governing "other," replies, condemning Tarquin, her subject, to "living death and pain perpetual." The end of Tarquin's story in the poem is one in which he is reduced (or elevated) to a figure of penitence, having in effect become Lucrece's imagined, powerful reading of him. As the fool who rushed in, he becomes a strong negative exemplum for the aspiring Elizabethan writer; he is also a telling instance of one who is read by the woman, whose "literacy" apparently prevails.

The effect of all this is to render highly dubious any claim to identity or uninterrupted series between the phenomena of the poem and those of primordial or biologically determined rape and sexual difference. Even if these primitive "origins" remain uneffaced, they are at once attenuated and redistributed through a far more complex system than any envisaged under Brownmiller's social contract, or perhaps under any possible social contract. This, too, becomes clear as Brownmiller articulates her vision of the contemporary primitive:

> On the shoulders of these unthinking, predictable, insensitive, violent young men there rests an age-old burden that amounts to an historic mission: the perpetuation of male domination over women by force. The Greek warrior Achilles used a swarm of men descended from ants, the Myrmidons, to do his bidding as hired henchmen in battle. (174–75)

According to Brownmiller, it is these "police blotter rapists," repeatedly convicted in an act of bad faith by patriarchal society, who do the dirty work of male terrorism. Yet we may wonder how the secondary distinction arises between Achilles and his Myrmidons. It is not enough to rehearse their mythic origin in an ant swarm as that which differentiates them from Achilles. In Brownmiller's scenario, it is hard to imagine how the distinction could be produced except by the very same means used to subjugate woman, namely violence culminating in and signified by homosexual rape. And insofar as Brownmiller is testifying to a continuity between the primordial condition and immediate social fact, we may recognize—as Brownmiller certainly does—that these same "police-blotter rapists" will continue to rape and be raped in the primitive power struggles in the prisons to which they are sent. Indeed, the threat of such rape and of contingent degrading dependencies is a highly publicized and seldom-challenged unofficial deterrent in the modern criminal justice system.

It is precisely the possibility of masculine power asserted through homosexual rape that is figured by Achilles in Shakespeare's *Troilus and Cressida*. If Achilles is the hypermale figure, he is so by virtue of a violence that does not appear to discriminate between men and women, or may functionally rather than chivalrously discriminate in favor of women. Shakespeare's Achilles is the alleged pining lover of a Trojan woman but the dominant male in his relation to Patroclus, who has arguably entered into Brownmiller's risky matrimonial bargain with Achilles as protector. For what it is worth, too, the only damage we see being done by the Myrmidons in *Troilus and Cressida* is to Hector. And if the violence of Achilles is directed primarily against men, Brownmiller will have given us the reason for it, which is that women are biologically *hors de combat* before the struggle really begins. None of this, however, is either unequivocally supported by or fatefully written into Shakespeare's play. Indeed, it is the Achilles of Shakespeare's "Lucrece" who emerges as a better candidate for hypermale rapist than the feeble performer in *Troilus and Cressida* or the almost comically pusillanimous Tarquin in the poem.

The hitherto unconsidered figure of Achilles in "Lucrece" is conspicuously *not* pictured in the otherwise rather full Trojan tableau that Shakespeare's Lucrece eventually confronts:

> For much imaginary work was there—
> Conceit deceitful, so compact, so kind,

> That for Achilles' image stood his spear
> Gripp'd in an armed hand; himself behind
> Was left unseen, save to the eye of mind:
> A hand, a foot, a face, a leg, a head
> Stood for the whole to be imagined.
>
> (1422–28)

Compelling an imaginative presence as Achilles may be, he is also just not "there" in the poem—the "whole" is a "hole" in the text—any more than is punctual rape. His absence, which is also the lack of any image other than that of the synecdochic spear as big prick (which may nevertheless be what the fantasized hypermale always comes down to in the end), makes it impossible for Lucrece to find the mythical hypermale rapist in the picture. Tarquin, by the same token, is no more than the player of Achilles' mythical part in a rape that apparently cannot be total in the absence of Achilles. Certainly, neither Paris nor Helen, neither Greeks nor Trojans, participate in any "ideal" action of rape, either in *Troilus and Cressida* or in "Lucrece."

The figure on whom Lucrece herself becomes most intensely fixated in the end—or looks at most "advisedly" (1527)—is that of the traitor, Sinon. He, rather than Helen, is the one who promises or threatens most perfectly to represent her, and by the same token to represent her crossing with the "impotent" Tarquin. On one hand, he is the weak though womanishly "fair" (1530) man, virtually the eunuch, whose only power (albeit an enormous power) is that of the smooth-spoken betrayer or rhetorical rapist who penetrates the paternal domain of Troy. He is also the figure of the perfect hypocrite in whose face truth appears. For all these reasons, he is putatively the figure by whom Lucrece can be cross-represented, but by whom Tarquin may also be represented, just as Ajax and Achilles cross-represent each other when Lucrece says of them that "the face of either ciphered either's heart" (1396). (Perhaps, however, it is only through the neuter figure of Sinon that Tarquin and Lucrece can fully cross over.) Yet Sinon is also the figure in whom Lucrece may least be represented, since he is a weak *man*, a Greek, and a seducer from without, none of which characteristics is literally hers. As a hypocrite's, moreover, his is the self-cancelling image that may simply be another blank in the representation or limit to it. After an enormous effort to decipher this baffling figure, Lucrece furiously attacks it in an attempt to distinguish herself from it and force it definitively upon Tarquin as *his* image:

> Here all enrag'd, such passion her assails,
> That patience is quite beaten from her breast.
> She tears the senseless Sinon with her nails,
> Comparing him to that unhappy guest
> Whose deed hath made herself herself detest.
>   At last she smilingly with this gives o'er:
>   "Fool, fool," quoth she, "his wounds will not be sore."
>
> (1562–68)

Lucrece's humorously recognized failure to discover any figure in the painting, male or female, who satisfies her demand for effective, punitive identification of rapist or victim may lead to her making *herself* that figure in the end, possibly in the androgynously "whole" guise of the woman effectively raping and punishing herself in a single action. She cannot, however, fully possess and autonomize herself as the raped woman even in that moment, since what she is doing will also look like stoic suicide, a publically virtuous action that makes her the noblest Roman of them all.

What therefore seems to be lacking in the representation, or unrepresentable in it, is the definitive figure of the rapist as the actor of an "originary" masculine violence against the woman. This absence does not, however, mean that the parameters have finally changed. One reason why Lucrece cannot definitively locate the figure of the rapist is that he is to be found, if anywhere, in the authorial position, in keeping with the "upward" displacement of violence in the poem. The compelling imaginative presence of Achilles is marked by the spear held in a mailed fist, but this figure is also the Shake-spearean signature in the poem. It is with the power of Achilles that "Shakespeare" is thus identified, all the more so for its being an invisible but imaginable omnipotence, never compromised, as is that of Tarquin or Lucrece, by its own theatrical representation. Yet at the same time it is a power, which is also an imagined power of sole authorship, never capable of being wholly embodied or possessed. Arguably, the attempt to do so could be only an act of folly or of abomination that would turn William Shakespeare—if these expressions may be forgiven—into the biggest prick known to history—or, more advisedly considering the Achilles emblem, the biggest jerk. Failing, and always failing, this impossible self-identification, Shakespeare too must participate in the poem's field of more complex and restricted interest.

To say this is tantamount to saying that the only representable Shakespearean interests or positions in the poem participate in, or cross-represent, those of represented others, including those of Lucrece and Tarquin. And even (or above all) in relation to the self-totalizing Achilles figure, another Shakespearean interest in the poem's schemes of reciprocation may disclose itself. The Achilles position may be one in which Shakespeare is under a compulsion to sign himself, yet that signature is not his only one in the text, and the Achilles position is one from which he is also socially displaced. Another Shakespearean signature appears on the title page, subscribed (the term is important) to the poem's dedication to the Earl of Southampton. A particular form of impotence or emasculation, not merely feminine, is the reciprocal one of Achillean domination, and the name of that powerlessness is Patroclus. The name is not spoken in the poem, yet the relevant form of powerlessness is not necessarily unrepresented in it; indeed, it is inherent in the very situation to which the poem's dedication draws attention, namely its being produced under patronage, and specifically under the patronage of the powerful Earl of Southampton. It is being produced, in other words, in a setting of domination and dependency between men, and a specific one of which (thanks to the advertising of Shakespeare among other authors) the homoerotic "taintedness" has become a commonplace of literary history. The authorial position is accordingly one in which Shakespeare can be more than a little interested in the violated, shamed, and incipiently silenced woman, who is also the "property" of another. Moreover, "disadvantaged" class and gender positions, both qualified, however, by the singular privilege of literacy, can evidently be cross-represented up to a point.

The reason for suspecting that a Patroclus is implied in the figure of Lucrece and in the patronage setting has already been anticipated in my discussion of Brownmiller's primordial scenario and specifically in my identification of Achilles as the fantasized hypermale warrior-rapist of the poem. A further reason for supposing that there is a Patroclus inside the figure of Lucrece is given by the ordinary conventions of the Shakespearean theater, in which there is a boy actor inside every represented woman. It is this which makes every heterosexual courtship on the Elizabethan stage a masked homosexual courtship as well, and "taints" at least any man with an interest in that stage; crossings between the social text of drama and the more withdrawn poetic text are ubiquitous in Shakespeare's writing.[17]

The question of why Shakespeare's interest crosses with, and is also masked by, that of Lucrece in the poem may now seem practically to answer itself, but let us briefly spell it out. It is a participatory interest in Lucrece's struggle, whether vain or successful, for self-inscription in a political world in which she is threatened with marginalization, objectification, and the performance of others' scripts, including their erotic ones. Identification with this "woman's condition," already effected by Ovid and Chaucer as "women's poets" or male poets as women, is vastly extended by Shakespeare in "Lucrece." Her effort to establish her will, meaning in every sense *her* desire rather than that of others, leads to her entry into writing and the attempt literally to write her own will as a master text of the future.

Shakespeare's quasi-identificatory interest in the figure of Lucrece presumably includes an interest in her as the Philomel-figure of the raped woman who is also the silenced woman. This silenced condition seems compatible not just with garrulousness but with brilliant lyric performance, yet it remains the imagined or felt condition of having or being allowed no voice in which the self is recognizable, or by which it feels authentically constituted. The role of Philomel, however, is one that Lucrece plays to comical excess, in a way that increasingly implies its possessive, autistic inauthenticity. The poignant, classical Philomel lives only to name her rapist before relapsing into silence and death, whereas Lucrece spends 265 lines denouncing Night, Opportunity, Time, and other reified agents (belonging, indeterminately, to scenarios of rape and assignation) before even she gets bored with the sound of her own voice. She ends her life, as we have seen, without naming her rapist to her would-be avengers, thus paradoxically reclaiming her autonomy but failing, like Richardson's immaculately self-totalizing Clarissa, Queene of Grub Street if not of the shepherds, to be the touching Philomel.

Shakespeare's "Lucrece," as I have suggested all along, is far from resolving questions of gendered representation fundamentally, or from decisively negating "primitive" determinants of representation. Yet it does constitute a socialization of representation in comparison with the texts previously discussed, and it does incorporate in and through the figure of Lucrece a field of reciprocation, exchange, and differing potentiality, even if that potentiality remains in many if not all respects unfulfilled in the poem.

There is, however, a clear sense in which Shakespeare's figure of Lucrece is Shakespeare's figure *as* Lucrece, or is Shakespeare fighting for, and under, her (rhetorical) colors. Similarly, Lucrece's drama of self-recognition and attempted self-embodiment in front of the Trojan painting may in some respects be taken as a reciprocal miming of Shakespeare's own, while her attempted movement into the position of the interpreting subject from that of the female "cipher"—or that of the endlessly tainted ("tinted") woman—constitutes a significant moment of attempted self-inscription:

> "Make me not object to the tell-tale day:
> The light will show character'd in my brow
> The story of sweet chastity's decay,
> The impious breach of holy wedlock vow,
> Yea, the illiterate that know not how
>   To cipher what is writ in learned books,
>   Will quote my loathsome trespass in their looks.
>   (806–12)

The fear of being objectified by being powerfully or determinately read into an unfavorable scenario—including an historical one of "chastity's decay"—is evident here, and it is a "feminine" anxiety to which there is a suggestive masculine counterpart in the Elizabethan antitheatrical reading of the male actor/poet/playwright as homosexually tainted, complicit, or passive. Yet the fear of such objectification must not make Lucrece *object* to exposure, and to being read, hence "attainted," by anyone in the literate domain, since that is the only condition on which she can write herself. It is the condition on which she can enter into writing, as distinct from remaining in the private condition of a Philomel; it is also the condition on which she can seek to escape the prophecy that the writing of the "good" woman will be done by others, canonically by men, or will, in effect, be no writing at all, either remaining undone or being done only in "chaste" invisible ink.

It would be presumptuous to suggest that the Shakespearean difference and the difference it makes is that of establishing common cause or fully representing the sociopolitical interest of the woman as other, as if it were identical to his own interest. For one thing, difference is always that which remains to be produced, not that which has its own a priori grounds in representation. For another, the exemplary fate of "Shakespeare's" Lucrece and his continuing self-inscription in the Achilles position might seem to betray the lack of any difference in the final analysis; indeed the strategic incorporation by the male author of the woman's part (the synecdochically reduced woman) could be regarded as masculinist business as usual, here conducted by Shakespeare as the supreme businessman. Yet in emphasizing the writtenness of rape through the nonfatal "posthumous" emblem of Lucrece's blood, the poem does establish the field of difference as one of unforeclosed possibility in the rewriting of sociocultural scripts. In this respect, it differs from many of its predecessors in the Lucrece tradition, as it does from most of the previous representations in this book.

Notes

INTRODUCTION

1. Stephen J. Greenblatt, ed., *Representing the English Renaissance* (Berkeley and Los Angeles: University of California Press, 1988).

2. For example, Shoshana Felman, ed., "Literature and Psychoanalysis: The Question of Reading: Otherwise," *Yale French Studies* 55/56 (1977).

3. If the phallus constitutes the ur-form, it is possible that, as Stephen Greenblatt has implied, it does not definitively belong to the man, since the same form reversed and internalized constitutes the Renaissance anatomy of the woman. So if part of the self-consciousness of Renaissance representation consists in its dialectical interplay between a repertoire of forms and the imaginary phallic uni-form, which is also putatively that of ultimate power, a possibly more repressed aspect of its consciousness admits this doubleness, indeterminacy, or female (feminine) instantiation of the ur-form. All the latter possibilities, including appropriation of the feminine in these terms, will be evident in the texts I discuss. See Stephen Greenblatt, "Fiction and Friction," in *Shakespearean Negotiations: The Circulation of Social Energy in Renaissance England* (Berkeley and Los Angeles: University of California Press, 1987), 66–93.

4. Hayden White, *Metahistory: The Historical Imagination in Nineteenth-Century Europe* (Baltimore: Johns Hopkins University Press, 1973); *Tropics of Discourse: Essays in Cultural Criticism* (Baltimore: Johns Hopkins University Press, 1978). In more recent work, White has developed and modified his earlier positions, but that is irrelevant to the point I am making here. His tendency to make form prescriptive of, or identical to, content is one repetition of neoplatonic poetics that I wish to avoid.

5. Producing this "romance" stereotype of critical representations of the Renaissance entails the double risk of misrepresenting the broad work of scholarship and criticism in this field and of doing justice to no-

body's work in particular. No offense is intended; what is at issue here is only the broad shape of Renaissance *representation* at present, not the state of knowledge or research. Nostalgia for the Renaissance as the empowering origin of the modern world has recently given way to a still-nostalgic critical reading of it as an already belated and self-mourning epoch, self-consciously suspended in the afterglow of the classical world: see Thomas Greene, *The Light in Troy: Imitation and Discovery in Renaissance Poetry* (New Haven: Yale University Press, 1982), and Jonathan Goldberg, *Voice Terminal Echo: Postmodernism and English Renaissance Texts* (New York: Methuen, 1986). A nostalgically renewed "cult of Elizabeth" is also evident in a good many recent critical essays and book-jacket illustrations. Yet nostalgia is far from being ubiquitous: recourse to the Renaissance not just as a storehouse of exempla but as a putative reservoir of energy for effecting change in the present (usually as regards the construction of the subject or self, and as regards political and/or gender constructions) is quite widely apparent: see, for example, Jonathan Dollimore and Alan Sinfield, eds., *Political Shakespeare: New Essays in Cultural Materialism* (Ithaca: Cornell University Press, 1985); Jonathan Dollimore, *Radical Tragedy: Religion, Ideology and Power in the Drama of Shakespeare and His Contemporaries* (Chicago: University of Chicago Press, 1984); Stephen J. Greenblatt, *Renaissance Self-Fashioning: From More to Shakespeare* (Chicago: University of Chicago Press, 1982), and *Shakespearean Negotiations*; Jonathan Goldberg, *James I and the Politics of Literature* (Baltimore: Johns Hopkins University Press, 1983); John Drakakis, ed., *Alternative Shakespeares* (London: Methuen, 1985); Margaret Ferguson, Maureen Quilligan, and Nancy Vickers, eds., *Rewriting the Renaissance: The Discourses of Sexual Difference in Early Modern Europe* (Chicago: University of Chicago Press, 1986); Patricia Parker and Geoffrey Hartman, eds., *Shakespeare and the Question of Theory* (New York: Methuen, 1986); Peter Stallybrass and Allon White, *The Politics and Poetics of Transgression* (Ithaca: Cornell University Press, 1986); Leonard Tennenhouse, *Power on Display: The Politics of Shakespeare's Genres* (New York: Methuen, 1986). The charge of misrepresenting the Renaissance in the interests of renewed authoritarian control has explicitly been leveled from various quarters at Stephen Greenblatt as a seminal figure, and by implication at those who have been influenced by his work. The text most often incriminated is the frequently reprinted "Invisible Bullets," now chapter 2 of *Shakespearean Negotiations*.

6. Many of the texts I cite to instantiate one aspect of romance could as well be cited to instantiate any one, or all, of the others I list. I have tried to avoid excessive repetition. The title of one book cited above, *Rewriting the Renaissance*, implies something more than revisionary reinterpretation of the Renaissance; it implies rewriting in order to change history. This implication of "rewriting" applies to most of the works cited in the previous note, but also, for example, to some of the essays in Patricia Parker and David Quint, eds., *Literary Theory/Renaissance Texts* (Baltimore: Johns Hopkins University Press, 1986); and in Arthur Kinney and Dan S. Collins, eds., *Renaissance Historicism* (Amherst: University of Massachusetts Press, 1987).

7. Reappropriating the unfixed energies of the Renaissance is, once again, a strategy of many of the books cited above, especially those most influenced by deconstruction. Repeated attacks on any notion of fixed Renaissance hierarchy or of a stabilized Elizabethan World Picture have been intended to mobilize the Renaissance both as an object of representation and for continuing political action. Misrepresenting or misusing these unfixed energies has been part of the charge leveled against Greenblatt and those he has influenced. Magisterial restabilization with a difference has been pursued—almost uniquely so—by Joel Fineman, *Shakespeare's Perjur'd Eye: The Invention of Poetic Subjectivity in the Sonnets* (Berkeley and Los Angeles: University of California Press, 1986), and "The Turn of the Shrew," in Parker and Hartman, eds., *Shakespeare and the Question of Theory*, 138–59. In these discussions, the Jacobean Robert Fludd's concentric, hermetic, universal diagrams constitute a bigger and more imperturbable world picture than Tillyard's Elizabethan ones. Fineman is, however, reading these reconstructed world pictures back into Elizabethan texts.

8. Greenblatt must be credited as the prime inaugurator of this anthropologism—and of a taste for exotica—in which the work of Clifford Geertz has been an important influence. Anthropological discourse, including that of Victor Turner and Jack Goody, has been invoked by Louis Adrian Montrose, most notably in "Shaping Fantasies: Figurations of Gender and Power in Elizabethan Culture," in *Representing the English Renaissance*, 31–64. See also Steven Mullaney, "Strange Things, Gross Terms, Curious Customs: The Rehearsal of Cultures in the Late Renaissance," in the same volume, 65–92. "The culture" tends to emerge in these anthropologized representations as the plane of successful action, or even

as the successful actor, throughout history. It also tends to emerge as the realm of authentic causation.

9. Most of the terms cited here have appeared repeatedly in discussions of Renaissance culture, often as terms putatively defining that culture. The syncretism of these representations, many of which include historical, anthropological, epistemological, psychoanalytic, and linguistic components, has often gone under the name of cultural studies and/or of interpreting the cultural text.

10. White, *Metahistory*, 251.

11. Systematically so, for example, by Karl Schorsky in discussion at The Johns Hopkins University, 1985. There is of course a side to Burckhardt and to the Renaissance that is not going to be represented here. This is what might be called the Black or Evil Renaissance so memorably captured in some of Burckhardt's accounts of princely rulers, and which has been rather significantly forgotten in recent discussions of Burckhardt.

12. White, *Metahistory*, 250–51.

13. Elaine Scarry, *The Body in Pain: The Making and Unmaking of the World* (New York: Oxford University Press, 1985), 247. The sweeping undoing and/or reversal of pain constitutes the at once admirable and highly problematic romance project of this book.

14. To which, among others, Fredric Jameson testifies in *Marxism and Form: Twentieth Century Dialectical Theories of Literature* (Princeton: Princeton University Press, 1971).

15. I recall, though I cannot find in print, an anthropological anecdote retold by Stephen Greenblatt in which a particular tribe showers its idol with excrement and verbally abuses it. This anecdote can serve as an allegory of negative relationship to objects of cultural veneration.

16. One example of this bondage is supplied by Jonson's *Epigrammes*. Beginning by establishing the medical alibi of the satirist in the prose preface, and then going on to produce regular, brief epigrams at the start of the sequence, Jonson finally writes the 196-line "The Famous Voyage" as a prolonged, excremental inversion of romantic epic (one that may also testify to the effects of all the satirical purging that has preceded it). This poem suggests the tendency of satirical representation eventually to shift attention from anterior to "posterior" forms, at the same time eliciting the biological potentialities of those terms—as when "fame's posterior trumpet" blows in *The Dunciad*, or when Swift's yahoos perform their

distinctive act of critical depreciation. While "anterior" forms may be gender-indicative, "posterior" forms evidently are not. These satirical developments remain, however, on the horizon in my account as conventionally post-Renaissance ones in English literary history.

17. Jacqueline Miller, *Poetic License: Authority and Authorship in Medieval and Renaissance Contexts* (New York: Oxford University Press, 1986).

18. Margaret Ferguson's work in this area has not yet been published. See, however, Heather Dubrow and Richard Strier, eds., *The Historical Renaissance: New Essays on Tudor and Stuart Literature and Culture* (Chicago: University of Chicago Press, 1989); Margaret Hannay, ed., *Silent But For the Word: Tudor Women as Patrons, Translators, and Writers of Religious Works* (Ohio: Kent State University Press, 1985).

19. Michel Foucault, "What is an Author?" in *Language, Counter-Memory, Practice* (Ithaca: Cornell University Press, 1977), 121.

20. Richard S. Sylvester, ed., *English Sixteenth-Century Verse: An Anthology* (New York: Norton, 1984); Richard S. Sylvester and Davis P. Harding, eds., *Two Early Tudor Lives* (New Haven: Yale University Press, 1962); H. E. Rollins, ed., *Tottel's Miscellany* (1557), 2 vols. (Cambridge, Mass.: Harvard University Press, 1928–29).

21. Some recent discussions of "Lucrece" that represent the state of the art are not taken into account in this discussion, either because they appeared after it had substantially been completed or because they do not affect my reading of the poem in what I have to emphasize is the framework of this book. See, however, Heather Dubrow, *Captive Victors: Shakespeare's Narrative Poems and Sonnets* (Ithaca: Cornell University Press, 1986); Joel Fineman, "Shakespeare's *Will*: The Temporality of Rape," *Representations* 20 (1987): 25–76. I should also like to acknowledge in a general way Clark Hulse, *Metamorphic Verse: The Elizabethan Minor Epic* (Princeton: Princeton University Press, 1981).

22. Jonathan Goldberg, *James I and the Politics of Literature* (Baltimore: Johns Hopkins University Press, 1983).

23. In addition to repeatedly restaging the oedipal scenario in his works and also rereading the Oedipus story, in *The Wisdom of the Ancients*, as the great mythic authorization of knowledge and power, Bacon contributes importantly to the process of making woman, as Luce Irigaray has put it, into "science's unknown." For an account of Woman's being reduced to the object-type of scientific discovery, and of Bacon's

part in this, see among others Carolyn Merchant, *Women, Ecology and the Scientific Revolution* (New York: Harper & Row, 1983).

24. Arthur Marotti, *John Donne: Coterie Poet* (Madison: University of Wisconsin Press, 1986), paradigmatically establishes an approach that will be applicable to, and is already strongly informed by, texts and manuscripts of the sixteenth century.

CHAPTER 1: WYATT'S CRAFT

1. In the most recent as well as the best and most theoretically informed book on English prosody of which I am aware, Derek Attridge writes that "Wyatt's metrical intentions remain one of the most enduring of prosodic mysteries, and I have no solution to offer." An account is nevertheless given of what makes some Wyatt lines seem irregular (*The Rhythms of English Poetry* [London: Longman, 1982], 374–77). The discussion of these meters, likewise of Wyatt's intentions (or mysterious lack of intentions), is complicated by the almost universal claim that "rhythm," "the natural rhythms of the English language," or even "the ring of truth" take precedence over metrical regularity in all good English poetry, including Wyatt's. Whether Wyatt is metrically deficient or is obeying higher, intuitive laws thus remains in contention; implicitly, however, we are often led to believe that Wyatt's poems are metrically regular constructions in which strains of natural language are periodically and thrillingly audible. I am aware of no discussion in which it is recognized that the many oppositions that structure the debate about Wyatt's meters (wild/tame, art/nature, savage/civil, voluntary/involuntary, regular/irregular) are problematized, as are the borderlands between them, in the very poems under consideration.

2. The metrical issue intersects with exceedingly vexed and difficult editorial problems, including those presented by Wyatt's handwriting and practices of revision. See, however, R. A. Rebholz, *Sir Thomas Wyatt: The Complete Poems* (New Haven: Yale University Press, 1978), 33–58, which includes extensive notes on Wyatt's meters; Joost Daalder, ed., *Sir Thomas Wyatt: Collected Poems* (New York: Oxford University Press, 1975), xi–xiii; H. A. Mason, *Editing Wyatt: An Examination of Collected Poems of Sir Thomas Wyatt* (Cambridge, Eng.: Cambridge University Press, 1972).

3. Sylvester, ed., *English Sixteenth-Century Verse*, 130, 139.

4. A significant opening up of the sociocultural and ideological determinants of sixteenth-century anthologies has been made in published and unpublished work by, for example, Arthur Marotti. See " 'Love is not love': Elizabethan Sonnet Sequences and the Social Order," *ELH* 49 (1982): 396–428.

5. *Tottel's Miscellany* 1:2.

6. In this context, the use of a modernized edition of Wyatt is unthinkable, since spelling modernizations frequently suppress crucial implication, homonymic/homophonous kinship, and atavistic elements in the poems. The state-of-the-art texts from Yale and Oxford, cited above, are thus excluded. No edition of Wyatt will be ideal—nothing about Wyatt ever seems to be—and no claim is being made here about the superior authority or fidelity to Wyatt's "intentions" of unmodernized editions. I have in fact decided to cite here the lightly edited though overpunctuated Kenneth Muir, ed., *Collected Poems of Sir Thomas Wyatt* (London: Routledge and Kegan Paul, 1949), supplemented by Sylvester and by Kenneth Muir and Patricia Thompson, eds., *Collected Poems of Sir Thomas Wyatt* (Liverpool: Liverpool University Press, 1969). "What vaileth trouth" is cited from Muir, *Collected Poems*, 3.

7. Stephen Greenblatt, "Power, Sexuality and Inwardness in Wyatt's Poetry," *Renaissance Self-Fashioning*, 115–56. See also Annabel Patterson, *Censorship and Interpretation: The Conditions of Writing and Reading In Early Modern England* (Madison: University of Wisconsin Press, 1984).

8. Guild-identity, constructed in a setting of apprentices, master-craftsmen, closed guilds, and protected "mysteries," may seem to have been oppressively and exclusively masculinist as a historical fact, yet the symbolic possibilities (which may also be impossibilities) of the tool-bearing craftswoman are a common trope in traditional literature.

9. Henry Howard, Earl of Surrey, in Sylvester, ed., *English Sixteenth-Century Verse*, 214.

10. There are several accounts of Wyatt's career, including his possible involvement with Anne Boleyn (a number of whose alleged lovers were executed along with her) and his well-documented defense on the charge of treason in 1541. A good chronological summary appears in Rebholz, ed., *Complete Poems*, 19–32.

11. I use the term "emissary" advisedly, taking cognizance both of Wyatt's public role as diplomatic go-between and of the term *bouc émissaire*, recently given critical currency by René Girard, *Bouc émissaire*, trans-

lated as *The Scapegoat* (Baltimore: Johns Hopkins University Press, 1986). The failure of mediations is implicitly or explicitly considered by, among others, Greenblatt in *Renaissance Self-Fashioning*, Alexandra Halasz in "Wyatt's David," *Texas Studies in Literature and Language*, 30 (1988): 320–44, and Peter Sacks, in "Interpreting the Genre: The Elegy of Mourning," in *The English Elegy: Studies in the Genre from Spenser to Yeats* (Baltimore: Johns Hopkins University Press, 1985), 1–37.

12. The two accounts I have principally in mind are Stephen Greenblatt's seminal one, cited above, and Marguerite Waller's belated review, "Academic Tootsie: The Denial of Difference and the Difference It Makes," *Diacritics* 17 (1987): 2–20. Both these arguments call for detailed attention in their own terms, and I claim neither to do justice to them nor to adjudicate their differences. I should merely like to emphasize the key strategic role in Greenblatt's argument, and in the empowering of a referential new historicism, of "Whoso list to hunt."

13. A fifteenth-century Italian imitation, cited by Rebholz, ed., *Complete Poems*, 343, may intervene. One achievement of this edition is to suggest the huge extent and complexity of Wyatt's intertexts.

14. Waller, "Academic Tootsie," extensively surveys the sources and implications of this allusion in Petrarch and Wyatt, also privileging its implied invocation of the Christ figure in his interactions with women. (In Waller's argument, Christ becomes a figure, and perhaps the only one, who deconstructs the constitutive but denied differences of masculinist ideology.) For my purposes, it is enough to cite Rebholz, ed., *Complete Poems*, 343 n. 13: "Whatever Wyatt's immediate source, [*noli me tangere*] derives ultimately from a Latin motto, *Noli me tangere quia Caesaris sum*, supposedly inscribed on the collars of Caesar's hinds. That motto in turn was probably derived from a conflation of John, xx, 17 and Matthew, xxii, 21. In the first, the risen Jesus tells Mary Magdalen not to touch his body. In the second, Jesus tells the Pharisees to render unto Caesar the things that are Caesar's." A detail omitted in this account, but cited by other commentators, is the highly pertinent "romantic" one that Caesar's deer were still being found with their collars on long after Caesar's death.

15. Wyatt's banishment is noted by Sylvester, ed., *English Sixteenth-Century Verse*, 173.

16. Puttenham's chapter on the "courtier" figure of allegory or extended metaphor, with its allusion to Tiberius as the figure of the hidden, absent, and dissimulating ruler, has attracted a great deal of recent notice,

starting with Daniel Javitch's seminal *Poetry and Courtliness in Renaissance England* (Princeton: Princeton University Press, 1978). It has been discussed, *inter alia*, by Louis Montrose, "'Of gentlemen and shepheardes': The Politics of Elizabethan Pastoral Form," *ELH* 50 (1983): 415–60. Invisible, dissimulating, "emissary" Tiberian rule, reflexively instantiated in Jonson's "stoic" *Sejanus*, has been discussed by Jonathan Goldberg in *James I and the Politics of Literature*.

The stoic aesthetic is well discussed by Gordon Braden in *Anger's Privilege: Renaissance Tragedy and the Senecan Tradition* (New Haven: Yale University Press, 1985). Braden draws attention to both the capacity for negation (not "negative capability"!) and the incipiently boundless, inordinate antiromance of Latin stoicism.

CHAPTER 2: THE SUICIDAL POETICS OF THE EARL OF SURREY

1. As in *Re-membering Milton: Essays on the Texts and Traditions*, ed. Mary Nyquist and Margaret Ferguson (New York: Methuen, 1987).

2. My approach to Surrey and my sense of the Surrey personal history and persona are influenced, perhaps inordinately so, by the essay of S. P. Zitner, "Truth and Mourning in a Sonnet by Surrey," *ELH* 50 (1983): 59–80. This essay constitutes an integral reading of the sonnet, in which formal, generic, historicist, and literary-historical data are skillfully processed. I have also, however, consulted Edwin Casady, *Henry Howard, Earl of Surrey* (New York: MLA, 1938). My *Gestalt* for this period, as well as the reintegrating criticism of Surrey I am attempting in the wake of Zitner, depends, in ways I can only incompletely acknowledge, on the work of historians, editors, and literary critics dealing with the Tudor period.

3. *Tottel's Miscellany* 1:32, 39.

4. Two crucial and fairly general treatments of the politics of Tudor sonneteering on which I depend here as elsewhere are Louis Adrian Montrose's "'Of gentlemen and shepheardes'" and Arthur Marotti's "'Love is not love.'" But the dark story is now quite widely told.

5. We need to keep in mind that Surrey's autobiographies are always those of a subject whose doubleness is inescapably engraved in the difference between his Howard name and Surrey "style." Understandably, if absurdly and misleadingly, the *MLA Bibliography* lists the author under

his style. Listing Sidney under Astrophil would not be so very different from listing Howard under Surrey. Stephen Foley, in "The Honorable Style of the Earl of Surrey," Ph.D. diss., Yale University, 1980, anticipates my argument in some respects. He recognizes suicide as one among a range of options in the gentleman's repertoire (or rhetoric), though obviously I differ from him in establishing a suicidal *telos* in Surrey's work.

6. Zitner, "Truth and Mourning," amusingly elaborates a Monty Python version of Surrey, but it must be recalled that this version, which includes Surrey's hellraising in London with his servant (*pour épater le bourgeois*, a point on which Nashe picks up), is part of *Surrey's* self-presentation in his "satirical" poems. And when Surrey puts himself on the battlefield as Monty Python, something less than fully comic ensues.

7. Sylvester, *English Sixteenth-Century Verse*, 185.

8. Sylvester avowedly depends on Emrys Jones, ed., Henry Howard, Earl of Surrey, *Poems* (Oxford: Clarendon Press, 1964), which I have periodically consulted, and from which Sylvester takes some notes verbatim. He is also aware of several earlier editions of Surrey's poems. In response to my claim that many poems by Surrey are misidentified as Petrarchan imitations, a friend has written that "the attribution [of "Thassyryans king"] is not from the Jones edition. . . . I have also found that both the Oxford and the Norton (third and fourth editions) *Anthologies of English Literature* consistently . . . misattribute Wyatt and Surrey poems to Petrarch, following a numbering that I have not been able to find anywhere in Petrarch editions. Something funny is going on . . ." Whatever is going on, with the preposterous results we see, it reveals the blind determination of literary-historical commentators to assimilate Wyatt and Surrey fully to "Petrarchanism."

9. "The Ascent of Mont Ventoux," in *The Renaissance Philosophy of Man*, ed. Ernst Cassirer et al. (Chicago: University of Chicago Press, 1948), 36–46.

10. Robert Durling, ed. and trans., *Petrarch's Lyric Poems: The "Rime sparse" and Other Lyrics* (Cambridge, Mass.: Harvard University Press, 1976): 258.

11. My discussion here, including some of its locutions, is indebted to the excellent first chapter of Gordon Braden's *Anger's Privilege*.

12. I am indebted to something like a common critical lore of the English sonnet form, some of which Zitner, "Truth and Mourning," re-

hearses, but for which considerable originality can be claimed by J. W. Lever, *The English Sonnet* (London: Methuen, 1965).

13. Zitner gives a fairly detailed account of Surrey's miseries in the Muttrell (Montreuil) engagement, in which Clere was mortally wounded. Henry's military exploits have been variously assessed, though it seems clear that the most decisive military conquest of his reign was the defeat of the Scots at Flodden, an engagement in which the Scottish nobility was practically wiped out for a generation. This defeat was inflicted while Henry was absent from the country in France, and while Catherine of Aragon and Wolsey presided. A highly parodic recall of Henry's French "conquests," resulting primarily in syphilis, is included in *The Unfortunate Traveller*.

14. I take this account mainly from J. J. Scarisbrick, *Henry VIII* (Berkeley and Los Angeles: University of California Press, 1968).

15. My characterization of Sidney here owes a lot to Richard McCoy, *Rebellion in Arcadia* (New Brunswick, N.J.: Rutgers University Press, 1979).

16. Greenblatt, *Renaissance Self-Fashioning*, 121. Alexandra Halasz suggests in "Wyatt's David" that, for Wyatt, Henry VIII might redeem himself by public confession and penitence, in which case as "David" he might be assimilated to a New Testament dispensation of poetic and public righteousness. (Dante among others supplies the model for this assimilation.) Failing Henry's acceptance of this generously offered role, which does more than justice to the royal poetic gift, Wyatt as royal poet is left to act it out himself.

17. It may be asked what else Surrey could have done than expose himself to danger. If, as seems to have been the case, Henry VII and Henry VIII followed standard Machiavellian procedure under which usurpers must cut down all possible rival claimants, Surrey's lying low would not necessarily have helped, and might have attracted suspicion in itself. Whatever the victim does may not work since, in Braden's acute formulation, imperial paranoia always verifies itself (*Anger's Privilege*).

18. Suggested by Joel Fineman in *Shakespeare's Perjur'd Eye*.

19. For the "homosocial" structure, I am indebted to Eve Kosofsky Sedgwick, *Between Men: English Literature and Male Homosocial Desire* (New York: Columbia University Press, 1985). What I would want to emphasize is the antithetical interlocking of the homosocial and oedipal

scenarios, each of which gives a different though perhaps ultimately reconcilable account of the production and transmission ("between men") of sociocultural power. While the oedipal is seen from the side of the masculine observer/participant, the homosocial is seen from the side of the feminine observer/nonparticipant. Shakespeare in *Hamlet* may see it both ways.

20. I am influenced here by Peter Sacks, *The English Elegy*.

21. For a suggestive account of the represented relationship between Surrey and Wyatt, see R. B. Twombley, "Surrey's Fidelity to Wyatt," *Studies in Philology* 77 (1978): 376–87.

22. The crossover point between the oedipal and the homosocial may be the figure of the empowered male, indeterminately the father who owns the mother or the one whom Milton calls the Elder Brother. This is the one who by law of primogeniture is doomed, in every sense, to succeed unless displaced by a younger sibling, and who, again by unfair virtue of primogeniture, enjoys privileged possession of the mother for a certain time. In the homosocial scenario, fathers effectively don't exist except in and through empowered mothers, and the structure of male relationships is one of pure sibling affection and rivalry.

23. Freudian biography has increasingly emphasized though perhaps not yet sufficiently interpreted Freud's own lifelong stoicism and preoccupation with Rome. What my argument implies is that Freud, as erotic psychologist, willy-nilly replays a certain Petrarchanism. In this context, one can enter a protest against the ongoing foolishness of having Freud's basic subject-terminology Latinized in the English translation: ego, id, superego, etc. The overpraised Strachey translation, self-described as "standard" and representing a particular institutionalization of psychoanalysis, looks like it's becoming the "eternal" monument to a possible misreading.

CHAPTER 3: REMEMBERING THOMAS MORE

1. Endless fascination with the "life" or enigmatic figure of More can be inferred from the repeated attempts of biographers to capture both. The most recent, highly ambitious attempt is that of Richard Marius, *Thomas More: A Biography* (New York: Alfred Knopf, 1984).

2. William Roper, *The Life of Sir Thomas More*, in *Two Early Tudor*

Lives, 197–254. While one can appreciate Marius's attempt, referred to above, modern biography reciprocally enables one to appreciate Roper's attempt. Its spareness implies extreme selectivity—whole areas of More's life are simply ignored—and a capacity to make the smallest detail count. Indeed, Roper's text, which is also *Roper's* "life," demonstrates an ability to distinguish between structure and circumstantial clutter. Judith Anderson, *Biographical Truth: The Representation of Historical Persons in Tudor-Stuart Writing* (New Haven: Yale University Press, 1984), has written about Roper's text as one ideally instantiating a bio-hagiographic merger of art and life (40–51). This particular act of faith or ultimately of Christian witnessing is necessarily opposed in my reading. The "folly" reading of More is already launched by 1555, when the chronicler Edward Hall, cited by Marius (518), observes that More is either "a foolish wise man or a wise foolish man."

3. Stephen Greenblatt, "At the Table of the Great," *Renaissance Self-Fashioning*, 29–30.

4. The hagiographic representation of constancy is more than just a Christian undertaking in the sixteenth century, just as the "virtue" in question is more than just a Christian one; its stoic provenance is well known. The hagiographic impulse asserts itself strongly in sixteenth-century secular contexts; Sidney, for example, construes the *epic* hero as a figure of ideal constancy in all the vicissitudes of the narrative: "Only let Aeneas be worn in the tablet of your memory . . . how in storms, how in sports, how in war, how in peace, how a fugitive, how to strangers, how to his own; lastly how in his inward self . . . he will be found in excellency fruitful." The hero of epic action thus becomes the stoic *par excellence* (Philip Sidney, *An Apology for Poetry*, ed. Geoffrey Shepherd [London: Nelson, 1965], 119–20). Spenser, whose Book 1 of *The Faerie Queene* gives more than a casual nod in the direction of the hagiographic *Golden Legend*, published in English by Caxton in 1483, overtly attempts hagiography in his "legend" of Redcrosse/St. George, though what ensues is a portrayal of one whose great lack seems to be stoic constancy or "singleness." As legend succeeds legend in *The Faerie Queene*, constancy seems capable of being marked only as the virtue that is always absent, whatever the gender of the protagonist. In the "Mutabilitie" cantos its lack is formally marked, since we have only the fragmentary cantos of Mutability, not the purported Legend of Constancy to which they belong.

5. More not only entertains Henry VIII but apparently instructs him in astronomical lore and calculations. What More rejects along with the role of the entertainer is that of the natural philosopher, skilled in material phenomena.

6. It has been suggested by J. J. Scarisbrick, for example, in *Henry VIII*, that all the major personages of More's "life" are politically significant while he is not: Wolsey as gifted and tireless administrator-diplomat seriously committed to the ideal of European peace; Thomas Cromwell (More's successor as chancellor) as a bureaucratic genius who developed stable administrative procedures for a centralized state; Henry VIII as one who, despite his vagaries, contributed significantly to the development of English national power and visibility. For Scarisbrick, each of these figures has an intelligible political agenda and some ability to carry it out; More has none, and he is a scarcely appreciable figure in the larger picture. The most systematic reading of More's political career as such is given by J. J. Guy, *The Public Career of Thomas More* (New Haven: Yale University Press, 1980), and even it must conclude with the remark that More failed at last: "his ship had sunk with all hands" (201). The point made by Guy is that More does not just fail, but is outmaneuvered politically by Thomas Cromwell.

7. Thomas More, *Utopia*, trans. Edward Surtz (New Haven: Yale University Press, 1964), 49–50. It is impossible to track here the endless criss-crossing between Roper's "life" and More's self-representations in *Utopia*. It should be noted, however, that in Cardinal Morton's "family," various filial roles are rehearsed, including those of clown, lawyer, and philosopher (9–57).

8. "Failing political conversion More's continued presence in Henrician England undermined forces of social constraint which buttressed the revolutionary morality of blameless conformity and obedience to parliamentary and royal authority," Guy, *Public Career*, 202. "Political conversion" is a significant locution in the context of my argument as well as Guy's, since it implies that conversion (like revelation) does not go only one way.

9. *Two Early Tudor Lives* presents powerfully antithetical figures in More and Wolsey, with Wolsey, of course, the overt figure of monstrous vanity, worldliness, and empty show. It is ironic, however, that Wolsey too wears a hairshirt, a fact discovered only when his corpse is stripped, not "accidentally" beforehand.

10. The question of More's sexuality and even of the "special" relation to Margaret has always hovered in discussions of his life and career, including Greenblatt's, in ways to which the Marius biography gives partial access. Critics have noted not just More's hairshirt but his self-flagellations, and have connected his controversial violence and persecution of heretics with a certain sexual obsessiveness. (It is in the register of obsessiveness and sadomasochistic violence that More's sexuality has most often been construed.) For my argument, More's own remark is significant: at a time when Margaret was severely ill, More observed that if she had died he "would never have meddled with *worldly* matters after" (Marius, *Thomas More*, 226; my emphasis). During this illness, More performs what Roper records as his one miracle. When the doctors give Margaret up for lost, More goes into a kind of vatic trance, from which he emerges with the suggestion that she be given an enema ("clyster," 213) while sleeping. This having been done, she recovers miraculously. An imagined, then literal, penetration of her body becomes the miracle cure. What has to be recalled in all readings, including hagiographic ones, is the extent to which terms like "life" and "spirit" are bawdily contaminated in the period in which this biography is written. When Guy, for example, lugubriously concludes that More "earned his place among those who have enlarged the horizon of the human spirit" (*Public Career*, 203), one wants to respond with something more complicated than the pious "amen."

11. Making this strong—perhaps exorbitant—claim for Roper's very "slight" text may seem implausible. What I would suggest, however, is that the text bears witness to a still imperfectly comprehended cultural moment, from which exorbitant consequences may indeed flow. It is characteristic of various slight, "artless" Renaissance texts to produce just this excess: *Lazarillo de Tormes, The Prince, The Praise of Folly, Utopia* itself.

12. Processes of displacement and construction are occurring all over Roper's text. "Son Roper," constructed by More and displacing the biological son, also reconstructs himself in this text, even contesting More's possession of his "life." More's choice of the less attractive of two potential brides who are also sisters (198–99) saves his own sexual energy from being inwardly consumed in the family and at the exogamous, homogenerational level; it thus frees it from a politically and culturally predetermined end, enabling both it and its objects to be reconstructed. The

clever, educated Margaret, constructed by More in his own image, displaces the vulgar, ignorant, and rebellious wife (Dame Alice is More's second wife, which may explain his paranoia about family unfaithfulness should *he* die); she also displaces the other sister, whose laughter at the hairshirt may be more than a sign of her worldliness. The pattern of reconstruction is also visible outside the text: More begins reconstructing Roper by converting him from Lutheranism, while a not-so-naive Roper may "seduce" More as an object of conversion.

13. My connecting Roper's *Life* to the Jacobean Shakespeare depends somewhat on the story being told in this book, which is one of eventual symbolic restoration. This story implies that the phase from Edward VI through Elizabeth I is an interregnum in which one boy and two women rule, distorting if not suspending the patriarchal construction of power. As soon as James is king, history begins to repeat itself. In *Lear*, it may be said that Goneril and Regan immediately take up their options on power within the patriarchy, embarking on a highly competitive stripping, humiliation, and final emasculation of patriarchal figures. Cordelia reserves her option, apparently exercising it, however, when she returns at the head of an army to restore the kingdom and absolve Lear. Perhaps Edmund, the "natural" son and thus rival of the "natural" (that is, most political?) daughter, intuits something like this when he "gratuitously" orders her execution.

14. Stephen Greenblatt, "Psychoanalysis and Renaissance Culture," in *Literary Theory/Renaissance Texts*, ed. Parker and Quint, 210–24. The scenario I have outlined of course combines the Freudian daughterly seduction and oedipal ones, and turns the repetition of the former into the undoing of the latter. In Freud's own intellectual chronology, daughterly seduction comes before oedipal theory and is annulled by it; in this scenario, daughterly seduction is postoedipal as regards the patriarch and pre- or antioedipal as regards the son. Its repetition and inversion allow it to reappear in these different guises and positions. Daughterly seduction also "successfully" repeats the oedipal son's thwarted impulse towards maternal incest and paternal displacement, allowing him to be reborn as a father indeed. Shakespeare translates Dante's "Vergine madre, figlia del tuo figlio" (*Paradiso* 33) into the secular chiasmus "Thou that beget'st him that did thee beget" (*Pericles* 5.2.197).

CHAPTER 4: REMEMBERING
CARDINAL WOLSEY

1. C. S. Lewis, "New Learning: New Ignorance," in *English Literature in the Sixteenth Century, Excluding Drama*, vol. 3 of *The Oxford History of English Literature* (Oxford: Clarendon Press, 1962), 1–65.

2. Ernst Cassirer, Paul Oskar Kristeller, and John Herman Randall, Jr., eds., *The Renaissance Philosophy of Man* (Chicago: University of Chicago Press, 1971).

3. Notably Thomas Kuhn, *The Structure of Scientific Revolutions*, 2nd ed. (Chicago: University of Chicago Press, 1970). At present, the term "paradigm" continues to be used in interpretation, though seldom with Kuhnian technicality. I assume the continuing usefulness of the term, which predates Kuhn even in its somewhat "Kuhnian" sense, yet I also recognize that the term is no longer useful insofar as it implies a model of absolute discontinuity and a unidirectional temporality of change.

4. Judith H. Anderson, *Biographical Truth*, 27–39.

5. Wolsey died in 1530 and Cavendish evidently completed his *Life* in 1558. Comparably, More was executed in 1535 and Roper's *Life* was completed ca. 1557. The publication of both these "redeeming" Catholic lives at that time must be regarded as somewhat opportune.

6. Thomas Wyatt, "Myne owne John Poyntz," in Sylvester, *English Sixteenth-Century Verse*, 170–73.

7. Perhaps it would be fairer to say "incipiently theatricalized" in this context, in which a paradigm shift is being claimed. The theatricalization of conscience proceeds apace during the English Renaissance, however, and by the seventeenth century, according to Jonathan Goldberg, conscience has become a theatrical motif in itself ("The Theatre of Conscience," in *James I and the Politics of Literature*, 113–63). Questions of the kind raised by More's performance and Roper's representation of sanctity are articulated, for example, by Donne in *Pseudo-martyr* and *Ignatius his Conclave*. The failure of death to signify authentic martyrdom (true witnessing) is bound up with the theatricalization even of the saintly end.

8. Part of what distinguishes Wyatt from More (and from Catholic hagiographers) is a nascent and highly iconoclastic "Protestant poetics." Producing the image of the saint in life or letters becomes a highly problematical (indeed, suspect) undertaking in these new Protestant terms, as

witness, among others, the Spenser of *The Faerie Queene* and the Milton of *Eikonoklastes*. In "Wyatt's David," Halasz interestingly contrasts Wyatt's iconoclastic and nonrecuperative representation of David in the *Penitential Psalms* with Dante's recuperative one in *Purgatorio* and *Paradiso*.

9. Greenblatt has not extensively referred to Cavendish in print as far as I know, yet his references to Cavendish in teaching and discussion imply this utility of the *Life* of Wolsey.

10. Baldessare Castiglione, *The Book of the Courtier*, trans. Charles Singleton (New York: Anchor Books, 1959), 293–94.

11. Thomas More, *Utopia*, 81; 91–101.

12. The disembodied quality of this power is definitively identified by Jonathan Goldberg as the problem for the conspirators in Shakespeare's *Julius Caesar*. See *James I and the Politics of Literature*, 164–76. One might suggest that it is part of Coriolanus's madness to attempt ideal reembodiment of that power in himself, thus detaching it from all opportunistic appropriations, failing representations, and theatrical mediations. The attempt doesn't make him any less a "Roman actor," in Goldberg's phrase, than his Shakespearean predecessors, and his stupendous negations invest him with a negative theatrical charisma unequalled on the Shakespearean stage—at least until his collapse before Volumnia, an even more stupendous Roman actor. On a slightly different point, Cavendish suggests that one reconstructive possibility for the disenfranchised traditional nobility is that of becoming the political "prophets," contra Wolsey, of Henry's Reformation. Hence the startling moment in which the Duke of Suffolk, prompted by the king, confronts Wolsey with the words: "'It was never merry in England whilst we had Cardinals among us.' Which words were so set forth with such a vehement countenance that all men marvelled what he intended" (93).

CHAPTER 5: GASCOIGNE'S WOODMANSHIP

1. Yvor Winters, "Aspects of the Short Poem in the English Renaissance," in *Forms of Discovery* (Chicago: The Swallow Press, 1967); 1–20. This is not to say that Gascoigne has received no attention in recent criticism, only that he has not functioned as a particularly significant exemplum. See, however, Joseph Loewenstein, *Responsive Readings: Versions of*

Echo in Pastoral, Epic, and the Jonsonian Masque (New Haven: Yale University Press, 1984), 57–73.

2. The Gascoigne anthologies are *A Hundreth Sundrie Flowers* [1573], revised, reissued, and self-censored, partly in response to complaints, as *The Posies* [1573].

3. Edmund Spenser, *Poetical Works*, ed. J. C. Smith and E. de Selincourt (Oxford: Clarendon Press, 1959), 456.

4. This is not a step to be taken lightly, fraught as it is with possibilities of misconstruction, as well as of offense to and appropriation of black women. Yet without taking this heuristic step, it is hard to imagine a way of eliciting the significance of these sonnets, which may be even more deeply disconcerting, liberalism notwithstanding, than the homoerotic Young Man sonnets. A double crossing in idealized masculine representation is being effected when the Black Woman becomes its subject: it is a simultaneous crossing of "color" and gender that dislocates the epideictic conventions of the fair Young Man sonnets as well as of Petrarchanism generally. The dislocation may additionally be one of social class (the woman in place of the lady) and bodily representation (the diseased, deficient body in place of the whole one). The very act of writing becomes conceptually inverted in this sonnet sequence; instead of being an instrument that marks the chaste white paper, the pen becomes figuratively a stylus penetrating the cosmetic whiteness of the page to expose a dark "primary text" and/or primary object of desire below. Without purporting to summarize all the effects of these amazing sonnets, including their equivocal praise of miscegenation, I will suggest that they constitute a singularly radical attempt to conceive of the "other," which is also the repressed primary text, of any representation in which the White Man is explicitly or implicitly the idealized subject. My term "double crossing" implies the complex chiasmus involved as well as the possibility of further betrayal *of* rather than by the Black Woman in this representation. She is the one who will repeatedly be excluded from *any* order of "likeness."

5. Cited from Gascoigne's "The Griefe of Joye," in Ronald C. Johnson, *George Gascoigne* (New York: Twayne Publishers, 1972).

6. See the frequently and deservedly reprinted minor classic *Certayn Notes of Instruction Concerning the Making of Verse*, in Gregory Smith, ed., *Elizabethan Critical Essays*, 2 vols. (Oxford: Clarendon Press, 1904), 1:45–47.

7. On the strength of his siege reporting, Gascoigne has sometimes

been taken as a precursor of the modern journalist or even war correspondent. It is noteworthy that Gascoigne projects various authorial functions including those of the Secretary and the Reporter, thus implying both a skepticism about "authorship" and ongoing difficulty in assimilating these dispersed functions to any construction of integral authorship to which he might lay claim.

8. In this connection, see especially the important essay by Jane Hedley, "Allegoria, Gascoigne's Master Trope," *ELR* 11 (1981): 148–64.

9. The constitutive scene of the poem's *reading* as real or imagined social message is a staple of Shakespearean comedy, notably in *As You Like It*. This constitutive scene is also well discussed by Hedley.

10. Hedley, "Allegoria, Gascoigne's Master Trope," 156.

11. If this seems unduly sweeping or arrogant, particularly in the wake of feminism, it testifies to the virtual impasse at which we arrive when our thinking of the subject as a cultural phenomenon is either Freudian or nothing at all. I do not underrate the power or interest of the Kristevan conception of a proto-subject prior even to narcissistic determination, and partaking only of a nondifferential dyadic relation to the mother that is at once constitutive and annihilating. (It is from this dyad that the subject as such requires to be abjected, perhaps repeatedly through the agency of so-called purification rituals.) It is not yet clear what systematic cultural rethinking along these lines would entail, or how feasible it would prove. See, however, Julia Kristeva, *Powers of Horror: An Essay in Abjection*, trans. Leon Roudiez (New York: Columbia University Press, 1982).

12. By broad cultural tradition here I mean international tradition, in which Spenser doesn't necessarily count as a Major Poet. It is easy to recall as well a New Critical dispensation under which Spenser wasn't even a Major English Poet. His metapoetic situation is implied in the tradition according to which he is "the poet's poet," not a primary "maker."

13. "Gascoigne's woodmanship," in Sylvester, *English Sixteenth-Century Verse*, 268–72.

14. Hedley, "Allegoria, Gascoigne's Master Trope."

15. Thanks to the work of Montrose and others, the represented pastoral scene has been converted from one of apparent retreat into one of intense, displaced, political negotiation. Pastoral *otium* is thus recharacterized as strenuous *negotium*. The "invasion" of masculine pastoral negotiating space, which is also a hunting space, by the woman is defini-

tively though of course incompletely staged by Shakespeare in *As You Like It*.

16. Charles Prouty, *George Gascoigne: Elizabethan Courtier, Soldier, Poet* (New York: Columbia University Press, 1942).

17. Roger Ascham, *Toxophilus*, in *English Works of Roger Ascham*, ed. W. A. Wright (Cambridge, Eng.: Cambridge University Press, 1970), 112.

18. How it is read as that text varies considerably, even under the psychoanalytic dispensation since Ernest Jones. For a very strong feminist reading, see Jacqueline Rose, "Sexuality in the Reading of Shakespeare," in *Alternative Shakespeares*, 95–118. My "excluding drama" clause notwithstanding, it is hardly irrelevant that Gascoigne coauthored an English translation of Ludovico Dolce's *Jocasta* and was also the author of masques, including one presented for the queen's entertainment at Kenilworth in 1575.

19. An excellent discussion of these variants with special reference to Shakespeare's simultaneously anomalous and seminal position is contained in work forthcoming by Julia Lupton of the University of California at Irvine and Kenneth Reinhard of the University of California at Los Angeles.

CHAPTER 6: SHAKESPEARE'S
FIGURE OF LUCRECE

1. The historical legend of Lucrece is discussed by Ian Donaldson in *The Rapes of Lucretia: A Myth and Its Transformation* (Oxford: Clarendon Press, 1982). Textual predecessors of Shakespeare's poem include: Livy, *Ad Urbe Condita* (trans. Philemon Holland, 1600) 1:57–60, 3:44–49, in a version conceivably pertinent to the Folio "Rape of Lucrece"; Ovid, *Fasti* 2:721–852; Augustine, *City of God* 1:19; Chaucer, *Legend of Good Women* 1680–1885; Gower, *Confessio Amantis* 6.4593–5130; Painter, *Pallace of Pleasure* (1556). More remote impingement might be traced to versions by Dionysius of Halicarnassus; Servius; Plutarch; Diodorus Siculus; Valerius Maximus; Florus; Dio Cassius; Emporius; Seneca; Jerome; Tertullian; Salutati; Machiavelli; Tyndale; Edward More; John Case. See also Heather Dubrow, "The Rape of Clio: Gender and Genre in Shakespeare's *Lucrece*," *Shakespeare Newsletter* 34 (1984): 3.

2. I have been positively and negatively influenced by William Beatty

Warner, "Reading Rape: Marxist-Feminist Figurations of the Literal," *Diacritics* (Winter 1983): 12–32. Warner criticizes the notion that rape is purely signified in Clarissa: he antithetically conceives of rape as a circulating figure in the text, which such critics as Terry Castle and Terry Eagleton aggressively literalize. My main differences with Warner arise from his constituting antithetical realms of textual circulation and free play on one hand and of inert sociolegal fact on the other. I wish to emphasize writing rape rather than reading it, and to insist that writing goes between these antithetical realms, if such they are.

3. As significantly "entitled" women, protagonists like Lucrece and Clarissa are hardly instances of broad social fact, nor do they self-identically and exclusively instantiate the feminine. It could be suggested that my account, unlike those of Terry Castle, *Clarissa's Ciphers: Meaning and Disruption in Richardson's "Clarissa"* (Ithaca: Cornell University Press, 1982), and Terry Eagleton, *The Rape of Clarissa: Writing, Sexuality and Class-Struggle in Richardson* (Minneapolis: University of Minnesota Press, 1982), dehistoricizes the issues. For Eagleton especially, the figure of Clarissa is a function of a particular, determinate shift from aristocratic landowning to bourgeois property relations. Clarissa acts for the latter against the former, yet her "excessive" adherence to the codes of the latter disrupts the codes. A very similar argument could be made, however, about the Shakespearean Lucrece in her earlier historical setting; in fact, the argument practically makes itself.

4. Under reifying criticism, I include the work of Eagleton and Castle, and of Warner inasmuch as he antithetically reifies a free text and a fixed world of sociolegal fact. In relation to "Lucrece," the reifying tendency is represented, for example, by Coppélia Kahn, "The Rape in Shakespeare's *Lucrece*," *Shakespeare Studies* 9 (1976): 45–76; Katherine Eisaman Maus, "Taking Tropes Seriously: Language and Violence in Shakespeare's *Rape of Lucrece*," *Shakespeare Quarterly* 37 (1986): 66–82.

5. William Shakespeare, "Lucrece" in *The Poems*, ed. F. T. Prince, Arden Shakespeare (London: Methuen, 1960), 80. Prince represents one limit in regarding the poem as virtually pure, unmotivated, and tiresome figuration from start to finish.

6. I make no claim about what women dream, yet the claim that they dream *inter alia* of rape is made by Helen Hazan, *Endless Rapture: Rape, Romance and the Female Imagination* (New York, 1983), cited in Warner, "Reading Rape," 13. Nothing new or different is proved about rape even

if that is the case, and it is certainly no argument either for women's social complicity in rape or for any sociolegal tolerance of it.

7. Needless to say, the woman's property in her body or self is virtually a contradiction in terms in the poem and elsewhere in Shakespeare. Such property is property in the no-thing (*res nulla*) that woman must be in phallocentric representation. Yet even that negative ownership or property is not immune to invidious appropriation, as Shakespeare equally suggests. In the invidious eye of the beholder, that paradoxically unownable property may become the most desirable of all.

8. In unpublished work, Mark Rasmussen of Johns Hopkins University has interestingly discussed Catullus's lament of Ariadne abandoned by Theseus, in "The Marriage of Peleus and Thetis," as a model for such extended complaint in Latin and neoclassical poetry. The problematic of such prolonged complaint includes that of its solitariness—its lack of, and lack of any desire for, a social audience or participation.

9. On the blazon and its implications, see Louis Adrian Montrose, "'Eliza, queene of the shepheardes' and the Pastoral of Power," *ELR* 10 (1980): 153–82; Nancy Vickers, "'The blazon of sweet beauty's best': Shakespeare's 'Lucrece,'" in *The Woman's Part: Feminist Criticism of Shakespeare*, ed. Caroline Lenz, Gayle Greene, and Carol Thomas Neely, eds. (Urbana: University of Illinois Press, 1980): 95–115; and Catherine R. Stimson, "Shakespeare and the Soil of Rape," in the same volume, 56–64.

10. There is now a very extensive critique, largely feminist, of the master-gaze of the male beholder in Western painting, film, and visual representation generally. A summary of the issues and some of the criticism is included in Michael Fried, "Courbet's Femininity," forthcoming. I am not aware of any extensive comparable discussion of the reciprocal gaze that is troped in "Lucrece." It also needs to be recalled that reading is not "gazing."

11. I acknowledge the usefulness of Joel Fineman's discussion of colors and tints in "Venus and Adonis," Johns Hopkins University, 1986.

12. Reading the woman's blush as the undecidable sign of her innocence or guilty complicity is too widespread in literature and criticism to need particular citation. Suffice that the reading of the blush is an issue in "Lucrece," as in *Much Ado* and *Clarissa*, to name only those. Frequently in the criticism, but *not* in Shakespearean representation, "reading rape" seems to come down to a reading of the blush.

13. Jonathan Goldberg has emphasized that the biological is always and already written, subject only to revision as the (auto)biographical. See "Milton's Prose Autobiographies," *English Renaissance Prose* 1 (1987): 3.

14. Susan Brownmiller, *Against our Will: Men, Women and Rape* (New York: Simon and Schuster, 1975).

15. In work forthcoming, Jonathan Goldberg systematically and powerfully examines writing (writtenness) as the material matrix of all Renaissance constructions of universal anthropology, of privileged and repressed subjecthood, and of representation generally. He also gives a landmark account of "the violence of the letter" in Renaissance representation.

16. The question *cui bono?* could somewhat tediously be thrashed out with reference to the action of the poem, yet the point I would rather make is that the action of Lucrece—both figure and poem—is not just inconclusive but unconcluded inasmuch as it continues in our criticism.

17. I acknowledge the forthcoming work of Laura Levine of Wellesley College on the homoerotic "taintedness," in the eyes of Elizabethan antitheatricalists, of the theater and all who participate in it. The claimed emasculation of the actors and, by extension, their imitative audiences, makes them virtually equivalent to depraved women in this antitheatrical discourse.

Index

Abjection, 27–28, 184n11
Achilles (in "Lucrece"), 155–60, 162
Ab Urbe Condita, 185n1
Aeneas, 71, 177n4
Aeneid, 52
Alice, Dame (wife to Thomas More), 91–92
Allegory, 38–39, 43, 128, 132, 172n16
Alterity, 55–56. *See also* Identity
Amoretti, 120
Amorphousness, 10–11. *See also* Forms
Anderson, Judith, 102–7, 116, 177n2, 181n4
Anteriority. *See* Forms, anterior
Anthology, as object of criticism, 16–17
Anthropologism, 8, 167n8
Apology for Poetry, An, 19, 177n4
Aragon, Catherine of, 14, 87, 109, 111, 113, 175n13
Archetypes, 3, 6. *See also* Forms
Arte of English Poesie, The, 4, 46, 172n16
Ascent of Mont Ventoux, The, 55, 174n9
Ascham, Roger, 130–31, 185n17; *Toxophilus*, 130–31
Astrophil, 60, 62, 120, 149
As You Like It, 185n15
Attridge, Derek, 170n1
Augustine of Hippo, Saint, 55, 141, 143, 185n1; *City of God, The*, 185n1
Austen, Jane, 12
Author, 2, 13–15, 18–21, 83, 98, 107, 114–17, 123, 126–27, 129, 137, 146, 152, 159, 169n17, 173n5, 184n7

Autobiography, 51, 70, 73, 125, 128, 130, 135, 173n5

Bacon, Francis, 21, 169n23; *Wisdom of the Ancients, The*, 169n23
Bede, 103, 106
Biography, 13, 17, 79, 81, 93, 99, 103–6, 177n23
Biology [-logical], 99, 152–53, 155, 188n13
Black Knight, The (Man in Black) (*Book of the Duchess*), 69, 77
Black Woman, 120, 183n4. *See also* Dark Lady
Blazon, 148–53, 187n9
Boleyn, Anne, 37, 64, 83, 87, 90, 97, 109, 111, 113, 171n10
Bond, male, homosocial, 65, 72, 77, 175n19
Bondage, 33, 41, 168n16
Book of the Courtier, The. *See Courtier, The Book of the*
Book of the Duchess, The, 69. *See also* Black Knight
Braden, Gordon, 173n16, 174n11, 175n17
Browne, Anthony, 60
Brownmiller Susan, 153–56, 160, 188n14
Brudermord, 52, 56, 74, 76–77
Bruderschaft, 52
Burckhardt, Jacob, 2, 6, 10, 12, 102, 110, 168n11
Burke, Kenneth, 6

Caesar, 38, 40–44, 172n14
Canon[-ical], 16–17, 46, 162

Capital, 91
Casady, Edwin, 173n2
Cassirer, Ernst, 2, 174n9, 181n2
Castiglione, Baldessare, 108, 182n10; *Book of the Courtier, The*, 108, 182n10
Castle, Terry, 186n3
Catullus, "Marriage of Peleus and Thetis, The," 187n8
Cavendish, George, 18, 21, 101–18, 181n5, 182n9; *Life and Death of Cardinal Wolsey, The*, 101–18
Certayne Notes of Instruction Concerning the Making of Verse, 183n6
Character, 12, 18, 41, 98, 126, 149, 152
Chaucer, Geoffrey, 53, 58, 62, 67–68, 71–72, 77, 122, 141, 148, 160, 185n11; *Book of the Duchess, The*, 69; *General Prologue*, 67; *Knight's Tale, The*, 53, 71; *Parliament of Fowls, The*, 46, 67; *Troilus and Criseyde*, 53
Christ, Jesus, 31, 44, 92, 104, 112, 172n14
City of God, 185n1
Clarissa, 20, 143, 145, 148, 161, 186n3, 187n12
Clere, Thomas, 64–66, 175n13
Confessio Amantis, 185n1
Complex, Oedipus, 139
Conscience, 81–82, 86–88, 103, 106, 181n7
Constancy, 80–84, 114, 177n4. *See also* Stoic[-ism]
Contemptus mundi, 107
Contract, social, 153, 155
Counterculture [-al], 6–7, 21, 125, 131, 133–35
Courtier, The Book of the, 108, 182n10
Craft, 23–47, 171n8
Criticism, 25–26; New, 15, 16, 24, 31, 33, 45, 47; satirical, 7–13
Cromwell, Thomas, 178n6
Cross-representation, 150–63
Culture, 3, 10, 13, 15–18, 44, 47, 51, 54–55, 65, 77, 118–21, 124, 127, 133–37, 147, 167n7, 168n9, 179n11; Renaissance, 1–8, 20, 116–17, 168n5

Daalder, Joost, 170n2
Dan Bartholomew of Bath, 122. *See also* Gascoigne, George
Daniel, Samuel, 120
Dante, 36, 126, 175n16, 180n14; *Paradiso*, 180n14, 182n8; *Purgatorio*, 182n8
Dark Ages, 102
Dark Lady (Shakespeare's sonnets), 120, 183n4. *See also* Black Woman
Death-wish [-drive], 56, 57, 74, 77
Deconstruction, 2, 9, 17–18, 29–31, 49, 120, 167n7
Decorum, 3, 87–88. *See also* Forms
Degeneracy, 56–57
Deniability, 27–29, 63. *See also* Dissimulation
Dictation, 51, 76, 124
Difference, 102, 140–41; representation of, 146–63
Discontinuity, 101–2. *See also* Paradigm
Dissimulation, 27–29, 36, 38, 45, 137, 139, 172n16. *See also* Doubleness
Dolce, Ludovico, 185n18
Dollimore, Jonathan, 166n5
Donaldson, Ian, 185n1
Donne, John, 181n7; *Ignatius his Conclave*, 181n7; *Pseudo-martyr*, 187n7
Doubleness, 29, 32, 43–46, 93, 147, 165n3. *See also* Dissimulation
Dubrow, Heather, 146, 169n21, 185n1
Dunciad, The, 168n16
Durling, Robert, 174n10

Eagleton, Terry, 186n3
Edward VI, 180n13
Eighteenth Brumaire of Louis Bonaparte, The, 11
Eikonoklastes, 182n8
E. K. (in *The Shepheardes Calender*), 119
Elegy [-giac], 53, 64–66, 69. *See also* Pastoral
Eliot, Thomas Stearns, 82
Elizabeth I, 14, 60, 130, 148, 166n5, 180n13; era of, 2, 13, 18–20, 48–50,

77, 112, 118–21, 125, 127, 129, 136–
39, 148–49, 155, 162; cult of, 166n5
Emissary, 35–36, 171n11, 173n16
Empson, William, 16
Encomium moriae, 79–100, 101. See
also *Praise of Folly*
English Poete, The, 119
*English Sixteenth Century Verse: An
Anthology*, 16, 24, 169n20, 170n3,
181n6, 184n13
Epigrammes, 168n16
Erasmus, Desiderius, 79–80, 84, 93,
101, 133; *Encomium moriae (Praise
of Folly)*, 79–100, 101, 133

Faerie Queene, The, 125, 177n4, 182n8
"Famous Voyage, The," 168n16
Fasti, 185n1
Faultiness, 25–26, 47
Felman, Shoshana, 165n2
Feminism, 2–3, 18, 187n10. See also
Gender; Subject
Feminization, 119. See also Culture
Ferguson, Margaret, 14, 169n18, 173n1
Fineman, Joel, 19, 140, 150, 167n7,
169n21, 175n18, 187n11
Fitzgerald, Elizabeth, 59–61. See also
Geraldine
Fitzroy, Henry (Duke of Rich-
mond), 60, 70–71
Flodden, 175n13
Fludd, Robert, 167n7
Foley, Stephen, 59, 174n5
Folly, 80, 84–85, 88–89, 92–93, 95,
97, 177n2; praise of, 79–100, 133
Form[s], 10–11, 79–80, 94, 101, 115,
123, 165n3; anterior, 3–4, 17, 101,
119, 141, 168n16; critical, 4–13; cul-
tural, 3–4; poetic, 3, 15, 47, 128;
Renaissance, 79–80, 94; rondo,
26, 30, 33–37; sonnet, 39–45, 68–
69
Formalism, 3, 7
Foucault, Michel, 14–15, 169n19
Freud, Sigmund, 77, 176n23, 180n14
Fried, Michael, 187n10
Frye, Northrop, 6

Gascoigne, George, 18–19, 118–39,
182n1, 183n2, 183n5, 183n6, 184n7;

"Gascoigne's woodmanship," 122,
125, 127–39, 184n7; *Certayne Notes
of Instruction Concerning the Making of Verse*, 183n5; "Griefe of Joy,
The," 121, 183n2; *Hundreth Sundrie Flowers, A*, 183n2; *Jocasta*,
185n18; *Master F.J.*, 123–25, 128,
129; *Posies, The*, 183n2; *Supposes*,
124
Geertz, Clifford, 167n8
Gender, 8, 13–14, 18–19, 37, 151–54,
160, 165n3, 183n4; construction of,
42–44, 132, 137–39, 140–42
Genealogy, 4, 58, 118, 126–27, 137
Genre, 5–13, 73, 79–80, 93, 103–6,
133, 147
Geraldine, 50, 59–65. See also Fitzger-
ald, Elizabeth
Germanic, The, 52–55, 58, 76–78
Gestalt, 13, 117
Girard, René, 171n11
Goldberg, Jonathan, 21, 166n5,
169n22, 173n16, 181n7, 188n13
Golden Legend, The, 177n4
Goody, Jack, 167n8
Gower, John, 185n1
Greek, 65–66, 73, 151, 155, 157
Greenblatt, Stephen, 27, 46, 63, 80,
100, 103, 106, 112, 165n1, 166n5,
167nn7–8, 168n15, 171n7, 172n12,
175n16, 177n3, 179n10, 180n14,
182n9
Greene, Thomas, 166n5
Green Knight, 122. See Gascoigne,
George
Greville, Fulke (Lord Brooke), 120
Grey of Wilton, Lord, 128–29, 131–
32, 134
Gulliver, Lemuel, 81, 85
Guy, J.J., 178n6, 179n10

Hagiography, 18, 79, 81–84, 93, 98,
103–7, 177n4, 179n10, 181n8. See
also Martyr [-dom]
Halasz, Alexandra, 172n11, 175n16
Hall, Edward, 177n2
Hamlet, 77, 127, 136, 176n19
Harding, Davis P., 16, 169n20
Harpsfield, Nicholas, 104
Hedley, Jane, 184n8, 184n10, 184n14

Helen of Troy (in "Lucrece"), 147, 151, 157
Henry VII, 175n17
Henry VIII, 17, 27, 32, 37–38, 48–51, 54–55, 60, 63, 70, 82, 86, 90, 94, 100, 107, 109, 113, 175n17, 178n6, 182n12
Historicism, New, 2–3, 7, 9–10, 25, 37, 59, 128, 166n5, 167nn6–8, 168n9
Holland, Philemon, 185n1
Homer, 71, 126
Homosexuality, male, 65–66, 72–73, 156, 159–60, 162, 188n17
Homosocial. *See* Bond, male, homosocial
Horace, 9
Howard, Henry (Earl of Surrey), 60, 171n9; family of, 49, 59–61, 63–64. *See also* Surrey
—works: *Aeneid* translation, 52; "Dyvers thy death doo dyverslye bemone," 75–76; "From Tuscan cam my ladies worthi race," 59–63; "I never saw youe madam laye aparte," 62; "Love that doth raine and live within my thought," 58; "My Ratclif, when thy retchless youth offendes," 31; "Norfolk sprang thee, Lambeth holds thee dead," 64–66; "Thassyryans king, in peas with fowle desyre," 53–58; "The greate Macedon that out of Persy chased," 32, 63; "The soote season, that bud and blome furth bringes," 67–69; "So crewell prison, howe could betyde, alas," 70–74; "Wyat resteth here, that quicke coulde never rest," 31
Hulse, Clark, 169n21
Hundreth Sundrie Flowers, A (Gascoigne), 183n2
Hythlodaeus, Raphael (in *Utopia*), 87

Iago, 36
Identity, 28, 39, 42–46, 71, 79–80, 105, 124, 126–27, 142, 148, 150–54, 159. *See also* Nonidentity
Idyll [-ic], 42, 70, 73
Ignatius his Conclave, 181n7

Imitatio Christi, 134
Incest [-uousness], 95–100. *See also* Patriarchy
Irigaray, Luce, 169n23
Italy, 55. *See also* Petrarch [-an]

Jacobean, 21, 112, 120, 127, 140, 180n13
James I, 180n13
Jameson, Fredric, 168n14
Javitch, Daniel, 173n16
Jehova, 138–39. *See also* Representation, oedipal
John, Gospel according to, 172n14
Jocasta, 185n18
Jonson, Ben, 12; *Epigrammes*, 168n16; "Famous Voyage, The," 168n16; *Sejanus*, 176n16
Juvenal, 12

Kahn, Coppélia, 186n4
King Lear, 99, 180n13
Knight's Tale, The, 53, 71
Kristeller, Paul Oskar, 2, 181n2
Kristeva, Julia, 184n11
Kuhn, Thomas, 181n3
Kyd, Thomas, 13

Labé, Louise, 13
Langland, William, 68
Latin [-ity], 40–41, 52–53, 58, 65–68, 70, 73, 76–77, 88, 102, 173n16, 176n23, 185n1
Laura, 60–61. *See also* Petrarch [-an]
Lazarillo de Tormes, 179n11
Legend, Golden, The, 177n4
Lenin, Vladimir Ilych, 11
Lever, J. W., 175n12
Levine, Laura, 188n17
Lewis, Clive Staples, 13, 101, 120, 181n1
Liebestod, 52, 58, 76–77
Life and Death of Cardinal Wolsey, The, 101–18
Life of St. Cuthbert, The, 103–7
Life of Sir Thomas More, The, 79–100, 103–7, 112, 115, 176n2
Lives of the Noble Grecians and Romans, The, 104

Livy, 141, 143, 182n1; *Ad Urbe Con-dita*, 185n1
Loewenstein, Joseph, 182n1
"Lucrece," 4, 19–21, 48, 140–63, 186nn3–5, 187n10, 187n12, 188n16
Lucretia, legend of, 185n1
Lupton, Julia, 185n19
"Lycidas," 75
Lyly, John, 13
Lyric, 13, 74, 78, 121, 123, 125, 161; forms of, 4, 17, 39–40, 45, 51, 118

Machiavelli, Niccolo, 141, 175n17, 185n1; *Prince, The*, 179n11
Marius, Richard, 176n1, 177n2, 179n10
Marlowe, Christopher, 13
Marotti, Arthur, 22, 170n24, 171n4, 173n4
Martyr [-dom], 30–32, 82–84, 93, 113, 181n7. *See also* Hagiography
Marx, Karl, 6, 11, 91; *Capital*, 91; *Eighteenth Brumaire of Louis Bonaparte, The*, 11
Mason, H. A., 170n2
Matthew, Gospel according to, 172n14
Maus, Katherine Eisaman, 186n4
McCoy, Richard, 175n15
Mediation, 35, 140, 146, 172n11
Medieval, 106–8, 110
Merchant, Carolyn, 180n11
Meter, poetic, 23–26, 170n1. *See also* Tottel, Edward
Metamorphosis, 9, 12, 21, 43, 81
Michelet, Jules, 2, 6
Middle Ages, 101, 117
Midsummer Night's Dream, A, 125
Miller, Jacqueline, 13, 169n17
Milton, John, 125–26, 176n22, 182n8, 188n13; *Eikonoklastes*, 182n8; "Lyci-das," 75
Miscellany, Tottel's, 16, 23–26, 49–50, 61, 169n20, 171n5, 173n3
Misogyny, 19–20, 42–43
Montaigne, Michel de, 130, 133
Montrose, Louis Adrian, 148, 167n8, 173n4, 184n15, 187n9
Monty Python, 52, 174n6
More, Edward, 185n1
More, Thomas, 17, 48, 79–100, 101,

105, 110, 112, 114, 133, 176n1, 177n2, 178nn5–9, 179n10, 179n12, 181nn5–7, 182n11
Moriae, encomium, 79–100, 101
Morton, Cardinal, 80, 84. See also *Utopia*
Mourning, 69, 73–76, 166n2
Much Ado About Nothing, 187n12
Muir, Kenneth, 171n6
Mullaney, Steven, 167n8
"Mutabilitie," 177n4

Nachträglichkeit, 136
Narcissism, 9, 12, 28–29, 32, 69, 74–75, 77, 134, 135, 137, 145, 184n11. See also *Selbstsucht*
Nashe, Thomas, 48–51, 61, 174n6, 175n13; *Unfortunate Traveller, The*, 48–51, 61, 63, 175n13
Navarre, Marguerite of, 13
Neoclassicism, 52–53, 57, 62, 65, 71, 77–78, 141
Neoplatonism, 133, 165n4
Nero, 57
New Criticism, 15, 16, 24, 31, 33, 45, 47
Nietzsche, Friedrich, 6
Nonidentity, 42–44, 46, 151–52. See also Identity
Norfolk, Duke of, 87–88, 92
Novelty, 107, 115. See also Paradigm

Oedipal. See Representation, oedipal
Oedipus, 169n23
Oedipus complex, 139
Order, symbolic, 28, 119. See also Culture
Ovid, 141, 147, 160, 185n1

Painter, William, 185n1
Pan, 48, 67
Panofsky, Erwin, 2
Paradigm, 13, 48, 123, 181n3; Renais-sance, 101–18
Paradiso, 180n14, 182n8
Parliament of Fowls, The, 46, 67
Parr, Catherine, 14
Pastoral, 67–71, 74–75, 131, 184n15
Patriarchy, 13, 98–100, 155, 180n13
Patroclus, 156–60

Patronage, 128, 136, 159
Patterson, Annabel, 46, 171n7
Penitential Psalms, 32, 36, 45, 63, 182n8
Pericles, 99, 180n14
Petrarch [-an], 21, 23, 26–27, 29, 33–34, 50–58, 61–63, 65, 68, 72, 120–21, 126, 148–49, 151, 172n14, 174n9, 176n23, 183n4; *Ascent of Mont Ventoux, The*, 55, 174n9; "Italia mia, ben che'l parlar sia indarno," 55; "Una candida cerva sopra l'herba," 37–43
Petronius, 57
Phallomorphism, 4, 20, 121, 130
Philomel, figure of, 122, 160–62
Pleasure, principle of, 108–11. *See also* Theatricality
Plutarch, 104, 115
Poetics, 51–78, 123–27, 130, 165n4, 181n8
Posies, The (Gascoigne), 183n2
Postmodernism, 123–25
Poyntz, John, 46, 181n6
Praise of Folly, The, 133, 179n11. See also *Encomium moriae*
Primitive, The, 4, 8, 20, 44, 153, 155–56, 161
Prince, F. T., 186n5
Prince, The, 179n11
Prologue, General, 67
Prosopopoeia, 63
Prouty, Charles, 129, 185n16
Psalms, Penitential, 32, 36, 45, 63, 182n8
Pseudo-martyr, 181n7
Psychoanalysis, 139, 180n14, 185n19
Purgatorio, 182n8
Puttenham, George, 4, 38, 46, 119, 172n16
Python, Monty, 52, 174n6

Rape, writing of, 19, 140–65, 186n2, 186n4, 187n9
Rasmussen, Mark, 187n8
Rebholz, R. A., 170n2, 171n10, 172n14
Reification, 142–43, 146–47, 161, 186n4
Reinhard, Kenneth, 185n19
Renaissance, 15–16, 38, 44, 68, 79–81,

93, 96–100, 101–18, 147, 165n3, 166n5, 167nn6–8, 168n9, 168n11, 188n15; English, 4, 13, 15, 22, 38, 52, 80, 133; representation of, 1–22, 101–18
Repetition, 36, 39, 141–44
Reporter, The, 122, 184n7. *See* Gascoigne, George
Representation, 15, 18, 103, 142, 159, 163, 188n15; critical, 5, 7–22; cross, 150–63; hagiographic, 81–84, 101, 177n4; historical, 5–7, 9–13; oedipal, 99–100, 121–39, 175n19, 176n22, 185n19; romantic, 6–12, 165n5, 167nn6–8; satirical, 9–13, 15–22, 168n16; of difference, 140–63; of the Renaissance, 1–22, 101–18, 165n3, 165n5, 167nn6–8, 188n15
Res nulla, 187n7
Rich (Devereux), Penelope, 60. *See also* Stella
Rich, Richard, 93
Richardson, Samuel, 20, 143, 161, 186n3
Richmond, Earl of (Henry Fitzroy), 60, 70–71
Rollins, Hyder E., 169n20
Romance, 6–12, 42, 46, 50, 53, 165n5, 167nn6–8, 168n13. *See also* Representation
Rome, 40, 55, 111, 141, 176n23
Rondo, 26, 30, 33, 35, 37. *See also* Forms
Roper, Margaret, 81, 95–100, 179n10, 179n12
Roper, William, 18, 22, 79–100, 103–7, 112, 114–15, 176n2, 178n7, 179n11, 181n5; *Life of Sir Thomas More, The*, 79–100, 103–7, 112, 115, 176n2
Rose, Jacqueline, 185n18

Sacks, Peter, 172n11, 176n20
Sardanapalus, 54–57
Satire, 6–21, 42, 85, 89, 93, 133–34, 168n16, 174n6; criticism as, 9–13, 15–22
Saxo-Grammaticus, 77
Scarisbrick, J. J., 178n6
Scarry, Elaine, 11, 168n13
Schorsky, Karl, 168n11

Secretary, The, 124, 184n8. *See* Gascoigne, George
Sedgwick, Eve Kosofsky, 175n19
Sejanus, 173n16
Selbstmord, 52, 56, 74, 76–77
Selbstsucht, 78. *See also* Narcissism
Self-fashioning, 80, 103, 126
Seneca, 9, 57, 185n1
Shakespeare, William, 4, 13, 15, 19–20, 36, 65, 77, 117, 119–20, 124–25, 127, 136, 140–63, 180n14, 182n12, 183n4, 185n18, 186n3, 187n12
—works: *As You Like It*, 185n15; *Hamlet*, 77, 127, 136, 175n19; *King Lear*, 99, 180n13; "Lucrece," 4, 19–21, 48, 140–163, 186nn3–5, 187n10, 187n12, 188n16; *Midsummer Night's Dream, A*, 125; *Much Ado About Nothing*, 187n2; *Pericles*, 99, 180n14; *Tempest, The*, 99; *Troilus and Cressida*, 156–57; "Venus and Adonis," 150, 187n11
Shelton, Mary, 64–66, 71
Shepheardes Calender, The, 19, 48, 118, 126
Sidney, Mary, 14
Sidney, Philip, 19, 23, 60, 62, 70, 119–20, 175n15, 177n4; *Apology for Poetry, An*, 19, 177n4
Sinon (in "Lucrece"), 157–58
Skelton, John, 48
Socialization, 140, 161
Song of Solomon, 67
Sonnet, 50, 65, 67, 171n4, 173n2, 183n4; form(s) of, 39–45, 57–58, 68–69
Southampton, Earl of (Henry Wriothsley), 159
Spectacle, 101, 111–18, 131
Spectatorship, 97–98, 101, 114–18
Spenser, Edmund, 19, 48–49, 117, 127, 148, 177n4, 182n8, 183n3, 184n12; *Amoretti*, 120; *Faerie Queene, The*, 125, 177n4, 182n8; "Mutabilitie," 177n4; *Shepheardes Calender, The*, 19, 48, 118, 126
Sprezzatura, 33, 94
Stallybrass, Peter, 166n5
Stella, 60–62. *See also* Rich, Penelope
Stimson, Catherine, 187n9

Stoic [-ism], 9, 12, 35–36, 41, 43, 46–47, 56–58, 62, 65–66, 81, 87, 96, 105, 110, 134, 138, 158, 173n16, 177n4
Stone, Lawrence, 13
Stuart, 113
Subject, The, 27–28, 33, 36–38, 41, 77–78, 116, 128, 154, 161, 173n5, 188n15; construction of, 17–18, 39, 42–45, 51, 56, 126–27, 130, 134–35, 137–39, 166n5, 183n4, 184n11
Suicide, 35, 83, 88, 145; poetics of, 48–78
Supposes, 124
Supremacy, Act of, 90
Surrey, Earl of (Henry Howard), 18, 22, 24–25, 31, 33, 48–78, 118–19, 173n2, 173n5, 174n6, 174n8, 176n21; "style" of, 61, 63, 173n5
Surtz, Edward, 178n7
Swift, Jonathan, 168n16
Sylvester, Richard, 16, 54–55, 60, 64, 169n20, 170n3, 172n15, 174n7, 181n6, 184n13

Taboo, 100, 120
Tacitus, 12
Tartuffe, 106
Teleology, 52, 73
Tempest, The, 99
Tennenhouse, Leonard, 166n5
Theatricality, 80, 81, 86, 106, 112–14, 181n7, 182n12
Theocritus, 67, 69
Thompson, Patricia, 171n6
Tiberius, 172n16
Tillyard, E. M. W., 2, 167n7
Tincture(s), 148, 152
Tocqueville, Alexis de, 6
Tottel, Edward, 23–26, 33, 50–51, 52, 61; *Tottel's Miscellany*, 16, 23–26, 49–50, 61, 169n20, 171n5, 173n3
Toxophilus, 130–31, 185n17
Tradition, 12–13, 41, 67–68, 70, 105, 127; pastoral, 67–70
Translation, 9, 67–68
Troilus, figure of, 71
Troilus and Cressida, 156–57
Troilus and Criseyde, 53
Troy, 147, 156–59

Troy, Helen of (in "Lucrece"), 147, 151, 157
Tudor, 13, 16, 17, 50, 52, 61, 91, 113, 173n2; Mary, 60, 127
Turner, Victor, 167n8
Tuscany, 61–63
Twombley, R. B., 176n21
Two Early Tudor Lives, 16, 169n20, 176n2, 178n9
Unfortunate Traveller, The, 48–51, 61, 63, 175n13
Utopia, 87–88, 91, 94, 110, 133, 178n7, 179n11, 182n11

"Venus and Adonis," 150, 187n11
Verse, 121, 125
Vickers, Nancy, 187n9
Virgil [-ian], 9, 52, 58, 65, 67, 71, 77, 126; *Aeneid*, 52
Virgin Mary, 149
"Voyage, The Famous," 168n16

Waller, Marguerite, 172n14
Warner, William Beatty, 185n2, 186n4
White, Allon, 166n5
White, Hayden, 5–7, 10–11, 165n4, 168n10
Wilton, Lord Grey of, 128–29, 131–32, 134

Windsor, 60–61, 70, 73–74
Winters, Yvor, 118, 120–21, 182n1
Wisdom of the Ancients, The, 169n23
Witness, 85, 87, 89, 93–94, 97, 104, 114, 177n2. *See also* Martyr [-dom]
Wolsey, Cardinal (Thomas), 17, 86, 101–18, 175n13, 178n9, 181n5, 182n9
Wunderkind, 83–84
Wyatt, Thomas, 15–18, 21–22, 23–47, 50, 52, 57, 59, 62, 63–64, 75–76, 105–6, 118–19, 132, 134, 171nn6–7, 171nn10–11, 172nn13–15, 175n16, 176n20, 181n8; metrics of, 23–26
—works: "Goo burnyng sighes," 33–35; *Penitential Psalms*, 32, 36, 45, 63, 182n8; "Madame, withouten many wordes," 34; "My lute awake," 33, 39; "Myne owne John Poyntz," 45–46; "They fle from me," 47; "What vaileth trouth?" 26–33; "Who so list to hount," 37–45
Young Man (Shakespeare's sonnets), 120, 183n4

Zitner, S. P., 65, 173n2, 174n6, 175n13

Compositor: Wilsted & Taylor
Text: 10/13 Galliard
Display: Galliard